THE POWER OF THE PULPIT

THE POWER OF THE PULPIT

*Thoughts Addressed
to Christian Ministers
and Those who Hear Them*

GARDINER SPRING

SOLID GROUND CHRISTIAN BOOKS
BIRMINGHAM, ALABAMA USA

Solid Ground Christian Books
PO Box 660132
Vestavia Hills AL 35266
205-443-0311
sgcb@charter.net
solid-ground-books.com

The Power of the Pulpit
by Gardiner Spring (1785-1873)

First published in 1848
First Banner of Truth edition 1986
First Solid Ground edition September 2009

Cover design by Borgo Design, Tuscaloosa, AL

ISBN: 978-1-59925-220-9

DEDICATION

If his own days of active service were not so rapidly coming to a close, the writer would hesitate in again obtruding himself upon the notice of the religious community. No governing thought more frequently recurs to his own mind than that presented in the injunction, 'Whatsoever thy hand findeth to do, do it with thy might; for there is no work, nor knowledge, nor device in the grave whither thou goest.'

As the time is not far distant when he will be at a great remove from the sphere in which he now converses, he naturally thinks of those who are to come after him. And as the descending sun often quickens our pace, he confesses that he feels a desire to do something that shall give him a place in their thoughts, though it be but for a moment. He is not sure that the views he has expressed will meet with their approbation. He ardently hopes that time, whose instructions are clear and resistless, will show that, in the opinions to which he refers, he has judged correctly.

It is a wide, an enchanting field of labour, which opens upon the youthful ministry. Never was there such a work as that to which they are invited in the present age of the world. A growing conviction of the importance of the work itself, and a strong desire that those who come after him may better fulfil the ends of the sacred office than he has done, have encouraged him to suggest a few plain thoughts which he hopes may be profitable to his younger brethren. To them this work is respectfully dedicated, by their affectionate fellow-servant,

THE AUTHOR.

New York, April, 1848.

Contents

1	*The Pulpit has Power*	1
2	*The Same Subject Continued*	10
3	*The Same Subject Continued*	15
4	*The Same Subject Continued*	23
5	*The Same Subject Continued*	31
6	*The Truth of Which the Pulpit is the Vehicle*	36
7	*The Living Teacher*	49
8	*The Divine Authority of the Christian Ministry*	63
9	*The Pulpit Associated with the Power of God*	75
10	*The Great Object of Preaching*	84
11	*Ministerial Diligence*	94
12	*Every Thing Subservient to the Pulpit*	109
13	*The Preacher's Interest in His Immediate Subject*	126
14	*Ministers Must Be Men of Prayer*	137
15	*The Personal Piety of Ministers*	145
16	*The Example of Ministers*	155
17	*The Responsibility of Ministers*	167
18	*A Competent Ministry to be Procured*	174
19	*Ministry Compared with other Professions*	179
20	*The Fitting Education for the Christian Ministry*	196

21	*The Pecuniary Support of Ministers*	209
22	*Prayer for Ministers*	222
23	*The Consideration Due to the Christian Ministry*	228
24	*The Responsibility of Enjoying the Christian Ministry*	235

1: *The Fact Illustrated, that the Pulpit has Power*

It may not be deemed the most modest service in one who ministers at the altar, to select as the topic of somewhat discursive remark, *The Power of the Christian Pulpit*. 'Let another man praise thee, and not thine own mouth; a stranger, and not thine own lips.' The light of the pulpit ought so to shine before men as to need no other commendation, save its strong and steady radiance.

Yet it was no egotism in Paul, to 'magnify his office'. The work of the Christian Ministry is one which possesses strong peculiarities, and one which has strong claims. There is nothing that resembles it in the ordinary employments of men. While it has its full share of toil, it has solicitudes and discouragements, dependencies and disabilities, that are peculiarly its own. It has too, its successes, its expectations, its honours and its rewards. It knows its own bitterness, and 'a stranger does not intermeddle with its joy'.

For the purpose of presenting our subject in as practical a light as I am able, I propose to advert to *the fact itself that the pulpit has power*; to show what are the *constituent elements which invest it with this moral influence*; to point out *the duties of ministers themselves in order to make full proof of the power* with which it is invested; and to specify *the obligations which rest on the church of God to give it its due place and importance*. It is to the first of these thoughts that we shall devote the first five chapters – *the fact itself that the pulpit has power*.

Our first remark on this branch of the subject is that *the institution of such an order as religious teachers is deeply imbedded in the common principles and common wants of man as fallen by his iniquity*. Such is his intellectual and moral nature, that he imperatively demands religious teaching. The necessity is *perfectly absolute*. Teachers of religion are indispensable to the existence of religion in the world. No matter what the religion is; so long as *natural conscience* has a dwelling in the human bosom, there must be a class of men devoted to its services. So far as my information extends, there is no nation nor tribe, nor any age of the world, that ever has been utterly destitute of an order of men separated to sacred purposes. Paganism, in its more degraded as well as its more enlightened and polished forms, down to the 'Medicine man' of our own wilderness, has its shrines, its offerings, its sacrifices, and its priests. If man is not a religious, he is a superstitious being. In the most degenerate tribes the priests have been found even divided into different and distinct orders, and distinguished by their costume, as they have been simple soothsayers or astrologers or familiar with the arts of magic.

The Sacred Order constitutes one of the essential elements of the social state. Society can no more exist without it than without some form of civil government. Men *must* have some religious *ritual*; the form must exist where the reality is dead; and even where the reality itself is death, there must be a ritual to preserve the death-like reality. All religion is, to a certain extent, the religion of form; even that revealed from heaven is so far a religion of form, that its spirit is expressed in outward and instituted observances. Men will not consent to occupy a place in associated communities without the recognized dispensers of these religious rites. Conscience demands them for the living and the dead. Be it but necromancy, or some strange form of 'black art' conjuration, the mother demands them for her new-born child, and the child demands them at the obsequies of its parent. There is no stoicism, no sullen apathy, so strongly intrenched within its philosophic indifference, but that it is sometimes bathed in tears. Human wisdom never erects her temple so high as to be above the tempest. A voice that is oracular must speak to men in the day of their calamity, even though the oracle be unheeded in the elevation of their pride. A hand that is allied to what is unseen and unearthly is looked for to wipe away the tears from the face of sorrow, even though it be unsought amid the sunshine of joy.

This voice of nature is strong – in this respect is stronger than the 'strong man armed'. The infidel David Hume was no friend to the pulpit, yet has he left the lesson to the world, 'Look out for a people entirely void of religion; and if you find them at all, be assured they are but few degrees removed from the brutes'. Infidelity itself could not live without religion. Were every class and order of religious teachers now abolished, and every man of them exiled from the earth, not only, in some form or other, would the office be resuscitated and restored, but their most violent opposers would be clamorous for their restoration.

And what are these but indications that the institution of such a class of men as religious teachers has its foundations too deeply laid in the nature of man ever to be powerless? If it has power where its only aliment is the grossest darkness, and the most degrading superstition, it is no arrogance to say that power belongs to it where it is nurtured by God's truth. If it has power because man wills it, it is not too much to affirm that it has power because God wills it, and it rests upon his authority. If conscience demands it, and it is created by the wants of man, then in its best and truest form, is it no institution of mere arbitrary appointment, but one which abundantly indicates the wisdom and benevolence of its Divine Author.

But we pass from these regions of mere Theism and pagan darkness, instructive as they are. There is a *negative* influence which the pulpit exerts, which is not always appreciated. The importance of *suppressing the vicious habits of men* can be estimated only by the intrinsic turpitude of their vices, and the devastation and ruin which they spread over the world. It were no easy matter to calculate the vast sum of wretchedness suppressed, and misery prevented, by the influence of the Gospel. It is a thought of some interest, that the well-springs of overt and public iniquity are broken up just in the measure in which the pulpit has power over the minds of men. So absolutely is it at war with immorality and vice, that the vicious and immoral almost uniformly shun its instruction. Such persons are rarely found in the house of God. The atmosphere is one they cannot live in; and the honest, faithful preacher of the Gospel, to his honour be it spoken, one whose presence and influence they cannot abide. Plant a pulpit in the hot-bed of crime, and the atmosphere becomes gradually more pure; the fearful activity of wickedness is restrained, and low vices and black crime skulk away, and seek a shadow under some deadly Upas, rather than regale themselves beneath the Tree of Life. Men are not found worshipping a golden image, or a block of marble, or a crawling reptile, in lands where the Christian pulpit has a place. Those depraved passions and stupid and degraded vices, everywhere the attendants on the debasing systems of idolatry, prevail only in lands where this divine institution is not known, or where it just begins to be recognized. If the land in which we dwell is not as debased as ancient Egypt, or Phoenicia, or Babylon, or modern India, and if our sacred rites are not such as to shock every mind

[3]

that is touched with the least sense of decency and virtue, it is because the pulpit guards it by purer influences. Go to lands where there are no pulpits, or to those portions of the world where they are 'few and far between', and what do you hear, if not the most awful profanation of the name of the great God, even from the lips of lisping childhood and hoary age? and what do you see, if not the most mournful desecration of that Day of rest which the King of the universe claims for his own; which the God of life has given for the physical, intellectual, and moral benefit of man; and without which no bounds can be found that set a limit to the grossest ignorance and the grossest crimes? Who can tell the amount of wickedness which would be found in the various relations of human life, if the strong bonds of social organization were not interwoven with the uttered truths of God, and watched over and fortified by his ministers? Where would be the subordination of subjects to rulers, of children to their parents? and what would become of those ties of affection and delicacy which now bind so many thousand hearts, and which keep Christian lands from presenting the most dreadful scenes of anarchy and confusion, of contention and hatred? How many terrible convulsions has the warning voice of the pulpit suppressed or restrained? Men would be well-nigh fiends without it; spectacles of horror would be spread around them; 'their hand would be against every man, and every man's hand against them'; the sword would be bathed in blood, and their history would be written in 'mourning, lamentation, and woe'. And has the pulpit checked no licentiousness, imposed no restriction upon dissoluteness and profligacy of manners, prevented no libertinism, and kept no unhappy female, and no reckless man, from going down to the chambers of death? Has it set no bounds to idleness and prodigality, to iniquity, dishonesty, and fraud, to plunder and pillage? Has it not done more to keep men from this whole class of crimes than all the circumspection and vigilance of the civil law, and the strong arm of physical power? Has it made no liar tremulous, no slanderer silent, no revengeful man peaceable, no deceiver ashamed, no compact sacred, no oath binding, no tribunal of justice more pure? Has it done nothing to repress that unhallowed spirit of covetousness which would gratify its insatiable cravings by wrong-doing; which would corrupt magistrates and legislators, and enrich itself by trading in the souls of men? Has ambition never cowered before it?

and has it effected no diminution in the struggles and contests, the sufferings and sorrows, of mankind?

You may tell me that this prevention and diminution of crime and suffering are to be attributed to the influence of *Christianity*; but I would also have you tell me what the true influence of Christianity is without the pulpit. Bring the case home, by transplanting yourself beyond the reach of the pulpit, for the little remnant of your own short life. We cannot well conceive the evils that are diminished, or wholly prevented, by this humble instrumentality. Few know how much they are, in this respect, under obligations to the pulpit. They boast of other influences, but overlook this simple institution of heavenly wisdom. But for this single institution, what a world would this earth of ours have been! Blessed are the people that 'know the joyful sound'. Favoured is the man who bears even nothing more than the mark of the pulpit upon his conscience, exciting his fears, restraining his vices, and reaching forth its hand to keep him from the gulf of perdition before the time! If his heart is not the veriest sink of pollution, and his history the black record of the most loathsome vices and the foulest crimes, while he is thankful for other influences, let him lift his heart in gratitude to the 'Father of lights', that his kind and gracious Providence has determined his residence under the droppings of the sanctuary!

But we stop not with this negative influence of the pulpit; it exerts a *positive* influence which is still more important and not less observable. The world in which we dwell is ignorant of God, and must become acquainted with him; it is an irreligious world, and must become religious; it is an ungodly world, and must become godly – like God, consecrated to God, and rendering a sincere and habitual obedience to his will; it is a lost world, and must become sanctified and saved, through God's grace, and the redemptive work of his Son.

Our next thought therefore is, that the power of the pulpit is indicated by *those immediate and direct influences, which it exerts in producing and sustaining the interests of truth and godliness among men, and fitting them for a higher and nobler state of being.* We may not, at first view, be aware of the extent to which these results are to be attributed to the instrumentality of the pulpit. The sober fact is, that the *history* of true religion is substantially a history of its teachers. Its free course and peaceful progress, or its conflicts and low estate, are indicative of a corresponding career, and an alternate elevation and depression of those who minister in its sanctuaries. Its waxing and its waning, its trials and its triumphs, its errors and its truth, as well as the varied lights and shadows that fall upon its path, are but the varying phases of the pulpit, as clouds obscure it, or as it is darkened by an eclipse, or as the light of it breaks forth in noonday splendour. Its course has been far from uniform; while its legitimate and immediate object is the advancement of truth and holiness. This is its appropriate work; it is God's cause in which it is embarked; and its object and aim are a radical transformation of the characters of men, and the salvation of the soul.

God himself was the first religious teacher. Never was there such a theological school as that in Paradise, where the 'Father of lights' was the instructor, and our first parents the eager and docile listeners. Never have such intellectual endowments been since known among men; nor such a resemblance to the intelligence of the Deity; nor such rapid progress in knowledge and holiness, as during the period between their creation and their apostasy.

Among men, the first religious teacher was the first man. He once enjoyed unrestrained intercourse with his Maker; miraculous aid was imparted to him in his intellectual attainments; and though by his melancholy fall his understanding was darkened, and to human view he was ruined and lost, he was still rational and accountable. Intellect no longer maintained its supremacy; reason did indeed totter on her throne, and in her fall carried with her the marks of her subjection; yet was she reason still, though in chains of darkness. Our first father was the depository of the first promise; a promise which he could not fail assiduously to make known to his descendants; a promise which wrapt within its celestial covering the sum and substance of all future revelations. To what extent that great promise was understood in these earlier periods of the world, we are not informed; it is enough for us to know that it was the religious directory of the patriarchal age, the great beacon-light on the shores of this shipwrecked world; the torch of heaven, held forth by holy men, to light succeeding generations on their way to eternity.

As soon as men were sufficiently multiplied to form religious assemblies, there were *accredited religious teachers*. Such was

'Enoch, the seventh from Adam'; such was Noah, a 'preacher of righteousness'; and such were Abraham, Isaac, and Jacob, who received direct communications from heaven for the instruction of their fellow-men, and peculiar marks of God's favour, as his faithful servants.

Of the religious instruction and ritual of the nations that synchronized with the descendants of Abraham before the giving of the law, we have been able to learn little, save what may be deduced from the institution of sacrifices; and from the fact, that over that vast region of growing darkness there was at least one priest of the Most High God, so pre-eminent in dignity, that he gave his official blessing to Abraham 'as the less is blessed of the better'; and that he is distinguished as the prefiguration of our 'great High Priest, who is passed into the heavens'. If at the calling of Abraham, the world was 'given over to a reprobate mind', it seems hardly probable that there remained no traces whatever of the true religion. Jethro, Moses' father-in-law, was a priest of *Midian*, yet was he a worshipper of the true God, a 'light shining in a dark place'.

There was piety in the Patriarchal age; piety of a choice character, a piety that was not sustained by *written* communications from heaven. Men began early to associate, and to 'call upon the name of the Lord'. There were those who 'walked with God', like Enoch. There were men of faith like Abel, and Noah, and Joseph, and those fathers of the church – a 'cloud of witnesses', who 'though not having received the promises, saw them afar off'. They were not untaught and undisciplined men, but were schooled in the knowledge of God, and furnish, even to subsequent and more favoured generations, proofs of the power of religious teachers in a most unpromising age. 'God spake in time past to the fathers by the prophets.' Blind eyes were opened, deaf ears were unstopped, and vassals long enslaved by the prince of darkness were rescued and set free, as the first fruits of the early promise and the earnest of the harvest which this barren earth was to yield from this spiritual husbandry.

The office of the priesthood under the Jewish economy, formed no unimportant feature of that wonderful dispensation. It comprised no insignificant part of the nation itself, and received for their support one-tenth of the fruits of the land. It was a sacred office; and any encroachment upon it was punished with death.

The employment of the priests was not only that of serving at the altar and offering the gifts and sacrifices of the people – an employment in itself replete with instruction, and more especially that of the High Priest on the great day of Atonement – they conducted their devotions, and were their religious instructors. The *Prophets* constituted a distinct class of men, both in the wilderness, in Canaan, and during and after the captivity. We know who they were; and that they were distinguished for their piety, their faithfulness, and their power over the minds of kings and the people. Such was the power of both classes of these religious teachers, that during the entire history of the Jewish church, the interests of vital piety were mainly dependent on their instrumentality. With the exception of those godly princes whose names live on the page of sacred history, no class of men occupied so important a station or accomplished so much for the interests of vital piety.

The office of religious teachers among the Jews was a noble office. Without them, the Hebrew state had been an irreligious, ignorant, disjointed community. If men were converted to God; if, after seasons of deep declension, the interests of true religion were revived, and Zion, that had been long in mourning, put on her beautiful garments; and harps that had hung upon the willows again sung the Lord's song; their religious teachers were prominent in these seasons of refreshing, and their priests the first to blow the silver clarion of glad tidings. The nation was exalted or debased as their religious teachers were honoured or dishonoured, and as they exerted or failed to exert their appropriate influence. For fifteen hundred years they maintained this pre-eminence; and although their power was doubtless augmented by the exterior impressiveness and splendour of their economy, the right arm of their strength was their religious influence. So long as the nation was in its glory, its religious teachers were the glory and strength of the nation. Its darkest period, the four hundred years between Malachi and John the Baptist, was a period when the voice of their prophets was not heard. Yet even in this degenerate and afflicting period, there were not wanting God's consecrated priests among them, some of whom were like the salt that retained its savour, the lights and guardians of the church, and the adornment of their race. 'Salvation is of the Jews.' If there be piety in the world; if there be precious hopes and glorious prospects; if there be churches and Christian lands which live to honour God and bless his people; they are to be traced up to those schools of the prophets where Samuel and Elijah taught, and to those holy men who caught their falling mantle.

2: *The Same Subject Continued*

These rites and sacrifices are no more; 'there is no more any prophet'. The sacred fire is extinguished on their altars; the Shekinah has disappeared; and the glory is departed from the temple. The tribe of Levi cannot now be distinguished from the tribe of Judah or of Naphtali; every line of demarcation is obliterated in uncircumcised confusion; Judaism is merged in Christianity, and the Jewish priesthood in the Christian ministry.

The greatest of all Christian teachers was the Divine Founder of Christianity himself. There was an immeasurable distance between him and all who preceded, and all who came after him. None have equalled, or can equal him, in his perfect intelligence of the truth; in his firm conviction of its magnitude and importance; in simplicity and directness; in the pure and glowing affections with which he dispensed it; or in the authority with which he spake – the authority of truth, of goodness. There are no such powerful and sweet words in the records of earth – words bathed in the fountain of eternal love – as those which dropped like the rain, and distilled like the dew from his unearthly lips. 'The law was given by Moses, but grace and truth came by Jesus Christ.' Inspired men, and uninspired, in thousands, have preached the same *truths* which he preached; yet 'never man spake like this man'. It was indeed during *his humiliation* that he exercised the prophetic office; they were days of the 'hiding of his power'; the 'Spirit was not yet given, because Jesus was not yet glorified'; yet never before, nor since, did the Gospel exhibit so much of its native beauty and glory, as when uttered by the lips that tasted the wormwood and the gall.

The power of the pulpit during the apostolic age is ascertained mainly from that beautiful compend of ecclesiastical history which is contained in the *Acts of the Apostles*. They had some peculiar facilities for their work, and difficulties and discouragements that were peculiar. Everywhere they preached Jesus and the resurrec-

The Same Subject Continued

tion; in the temple, in the synagogues of the Jews, in the forum, in the market-place, in the school-room, in the streets, and in their own private lodgings; 'beginning at Jerusalem', and extending their labours throughout Asia Minor and parts of Europe. Imbued with the Spirit of their Master, nobly did these pioneers of the Christian faith 'do the work of evangelists, and make full proof of their ministry'. They put their divine armour to the test, and tried the excellency of its power. And what were its conquests? Here we read of *three thousand* subdued under a single sermon; soon after, and elsewhere, of *five thousand* more; and then of other thousands, till the kingdom of darkness shook 'from turret to foundation stone', and Satan seemed about to 'fall like lightning from heaven'. It were no easy matter to measure the influence they exerted; nor can it be measured by mortal man. Never were there such exemplifications of the power of the pulpit, as during the apostolic age. With no human helper, and no meretricious adornment, without wealth, standing alone as God's messenger to guilty men, the pulpit of that single age gave the new religion to the world, grounded it upon a firm basis, and established 'a kingdom which cannot be moved'. Wondrous scenes were they amid which these holy men stood; wondrous words which they spake; wondrous effects which they produced; and which we, at the distance of eighteen centuries, look back upon, when the 'rod of God's strength' first went forth out of Zion.

Even a brief historical sketch of the one hundred and fifty years after the ascension of our Divine Lord is forbidden us in these observations. It was the beginning, rich in promise, of that great moral transformation, which was destined to make the wilderness like Eden, and the desert as the garden of God. The emblems of power might be exhausted in the triumphs of the first Christian pulpit. The great deceiver of the nations received a check in his usurpation, never to be forgotten. 'He that sat on the pale horse, whose name was Death, and Hell followed with him', was arrested in the very frenzy of his course. A magnetic light was thrown forth in its concentrated power upon the nations; and that mighty crowd that were treading their way so quietly to the pit, fell to the earth and exclaimed, 'Lord, what wilt thou have us to do?' A new world sprang into being at the voice which preached a crucified Saviour, and told of redemption through the blood of Calvary.

Pulpits there have been since, and still are, which speak for God and his Christ. More especially from the fifteenth century to the present hour has their influence been directly felt in the conversion and sanctification of men. The remarkable revival of pure and undefiled religion, at the beginning and during the progress of the great Protestant Reformation, is an event which speaks volumes in favour of a truly Christian ministry. Among the millions of Christendom, and amid all the ignorance and unblushing profligacy of the church of Rome, some few there were who could read the Scriptures; who did read them; whose bosoms responded to their soul-transforming and transporting truths; and who could not disobey the command, 'Come out of her, my people, lest ye be partakers of her plagues!' They dared not throw aside their commission as preachers of the Gospel, because the more thorough their inquiries, the more thorough and solemn was their conviction, that never till then had they known what the true Gospel was. They did preach it. They were mighty in the Scriptures; and terrible was the struggle: but they were valiant men, and God was with them. It was a new era in the history of preaching; men of that age had never heard any thing like this kind of preaching before. It was not the indulgences of the Augustinian friar that they preached; it was not the crucifix; it was the cross of Christ contending with sin in every form, and lifted up in earnest. It was no longer the age of forms and homilies, but of scriptural exposition and instructive discourses; and the results were glorious to God, and honourable to his chosen servants. The pulpit sent forth its rays in every direction, and 'men started as from the slumbers of a dream'. Its object was not so much to make them anti-Romanists, as Christians; men born of God; and they were abundantly honoured in so doing. Christianity was once more recognized in her native loveliness, coming forth from the smothering vapour and mists of ages, in her heavenly radiance. It was the *re*-emancipation of the world. It was the Sun of righteousness bursting forth from almost total eclipse.

There were deep and melancholy declensions in the pulpit after the Reformation. In England it vacillated from Protestantism to Popery, and from Popery back again to Protestantism. The reign of Elizabeth was illustrious for men distinguished in the sanctuary, as well as men distinguished in the cabinet and the forum; yet with all its advances, it was a dark reign. Under James there was a false theology, which, for the most part, was far from magnifying the grace of God in the Gospel of his Son: and which prepared the way for that laxity both in faith and in morals which mark with such indelible infamy the reign of the second Charles. A few there were, like Tillotson and Barrow, in the Established Church, but they were cold and savoured little of evangelical doctrine; more there were among the Dissenters, like Watts and Doddridge, who breathed the spirit of a purer and more fervid Christianity; but it was not until that sacred band sent forth from the University of Oxford, arose, consisting of such men as Whitefield, Wesley, Ingham, and Hervey, patronized by the rank and piety and resources of that most devoted and remarkable of all Christian women, *Selina*, the *Countess of Huntingdon*, that the pulpit once more entered upon its appropriate work of winning souls to the Divine Redeemer.* Treading closely in their steps, we find Fletcher and Haime, Romaine and Venn, Berridge and Hill, Toplady and Grimshaw, De Courcy and Madan, Howel Harris and Shirley, Cadogan and Winter, Waugh, Bogue, and Simeon, and others not a few, who, notwithstanding the variety of their views, had an unction from the Holy One, and gave an impulse to the pulpit which it had not felt since the days of the Reformation. These were great days for Britain. Then it was that dukes and duchesses bowed before the cross; and such men as Chesterfield and Bolingbroke, Mr. Pitt and Lord North, the Duke of Grafton and Mr. Fox, and Garrick and Shuter, and the flower of the aristocracy, writhed under the burning rays of 'the Tabernacle'. Of all men since the days of the Apostles, *George Whitefield* is the man who gave the pulpit its true power. John Newton says of him,

---

*The dissenting ministers of England ever have been a noble class of men. During a discussion in Parliament, some time, if I mistake not, between the years 1772 and 1780, upon the Bill favourable to religious liberty, the celebrated Dr. Drummond, the Archbishop of York, attacked the Dissenters with great virulence, stigmatizing them as men of 'close ambition'. In reply to this attack, the elder Pitt, the Earl of Chatham, made the following remarks: 'This is judging uncharitably, and whoever brings here a charge without proof, defames. The dissenting ministers are represented as men of close ambition. They are so, my lords; and their ambition is to keep close to the college of fishermen, not of cardinals; and to the doctrine of inspired apostles, not to the decrees of interested and aspiring bishops. *They* contend for a scriptural creed and a scriptural worship; *we* have a Calvinistic creed, a Popish liturgy, and an Arminian clergy. The Reformation has laid open the Scriptures to all; let not the bishops shut them again. Laws in support of ecclesiastical power are pleaded, which it would shock humanity to execute. It is said that religious sects have done great mischief when they were not kept under restraint; but history offers no proof that sects have ever been mischievous when they were not oppressed and persecuted by the ruling church.'

'He was the original of popular preaching, and all our popular ministers are only his copies.' By popular preaching, he means, preaching most effectively addressed to the popular mind. He relates the remarkable fact, that 'at the time of Mr. Whitefield's greatest persecution, when obliged to preach in the streets, he received, in *one week*, not fewer than a *thousand letters* from persons distressed in their consciences by the energy of his preaching'.

The two most remarkable revivals of true religion since the days of the Apostles, were probably those which took place at the Protestant Reformation, in the fifteenth and sixteenth centuries, and under Whitefield and his coadjutors and followers in the eighteenth. It would be too much, perhaps, to say, that the results of the pulpit at these particular periods have not been duly appreciated. But they were days of power. Human instrumentality was most truly abundantly honoured. God himself was there. It was the Spirit of God poured from on high. It was a cloud of heavenly mercy, which, with the exception of Spain, refreshed the nations of Europe. Nor did it stop in its course, but sailed across the ocean, watered the fields of this New World, and as it melted away, left the bow of promise spanning the whole heavens. Millions and millions have been born of the Spirit, since Wickliffe, Huss, Jerome, and Luther, and Whitefield first lifted up their voices to the infatuated nations. Germany, Holland, France, Switzerland, the United Kingdom of Great Britain, and these American States, together with those distant lands in the remoter eastern hemisphere, and those islands of the sea which have come under the influence of Gospel truth, all stand forth before the world as illustrations of its power. Its trophies are in almost every land; its song of triumph is echoed from pole to pole.

3: *The Same Subject Continued*

Intimately allied to the thought on which we have just been dwelling, we remark, in the next place, that every system of religious teaching, and almost every pulpit in Christian lands, has some strong peculiarities. *Different ages of the world, and different lands, and different departments of the Christian church, are a sort of transcript of the pulpits that have instructed them, and bear their peculiarities to the present hour.* It would be curious, but it would be no difficult matter, to trace this resemblance minutely, and mark those strong peculiarities by which some communities are distinguished, and note the striking conformity between them and their religious teachers. The gross idolatry of the patriarchal ages, from the worship they paid to the heavenly bodies to the debasing homage they offered to the elements of nature, to senseless images and brutes, was changed from time to time through the influence of their priests. The crimes which drew down the wrath of heaven upon the nations, were perpetrated at their altars. The Jew is a Jew still, and a Jew everywhere, because his religious teachers are the same. The hybrid character of the colony planted by the king of Babylon in Samaria, to supply the place of the ten tribes whom he had carried into captivity, may be attributed to the mingled influence of the pagan and the Jewish priesthoods. The Epicurean, the Stoic, and the Platonic philosophy formed a community like themselves. All the prominent features of the different branches of the entire Mahometan world find their exact counterpart in the teaching of the Arabian impostor. The character of the Chinese remains less changed than that of any other portion of the human race; and it is because, amid all the corruptions which have been ingrafted upon their religious system during so many successive ages, and amid all the varieties of their priesthood, it is a variety which is scarcely distinguishable.

These remarks are not less true in their application to the different classes of men calling themselves Christians. As a general fact, the Romanist is everywhere a *fac-simile* of the priesthood. The great feature of his religion is, that he knows nothing of personal responsibility. He reads not, he thinks not, he eats not, without the special permission of his priest; while, at his bidding, he kneels reverently before the altar, and then, as in our own times, and in wretched Ireland, he marks his solitary victim, or enters on the holy work of pillage, plunder, and blood. Proud and haughty England, with all her excellences, is just the image of her arrogant Prelacy. Scotland too, what is she, what has she been, if not the reflection of her noble ministry? And young England, in her new and Puritan garb on the rocks of Plymouth, what was she but the counterpart of the spirit and character of the Lollards – the foe of the hierarchy and the friend of God? And in her degeneracy, what has she done but tread in the footsteps of her religious teachers, deny the Lord that bought her, and in the excess of her liberality, give the right hand of fellowship to the beast and the false prophet?

Not only does the pulpit stamp its impress on the passing times, but it leaves its mark for a long time to come. It does its work so thoroughly, that it requires more than one generation to obliterate the impression. Many generations will pass away before Germany can obliterate the influence of Luther; Holland, of Van Mastricht; Switzerland, of Calvin; Scotland, of John Knox; England, of Howe; or this New World, of Jonathan Edwards.

We see these things for ourselves; we have examples of them before our eyes. We have but to overlook the land and inspect the people who have been under the same religious instruction for some ten, twenty, or forty years, and, with the exception of those large cities, where the population is ever changing, we know the people when we know their minister. Almost every observing man can fix his thoughts upon more than one community which has been distinguished for commendable peculiarities. They retain them at home, and those who remove from them carry the savour of them wherever the providence of God determines their residence abroad. It would be no difficult task to name the pulpit that stamped this character upon them, almost with the precision of the image to the seal. There it stands; it cannot be mistaken! The image is perfect. It is the venerable preacher, long since sleeping with his fathers, reappearing, and living among men, in the strong lineaments of those who have come after him.

The Same Subject Continued

Advert now to these influences in a new aspect. They have been exerted, very often *under great embarrassment, and in the face of the fiercest and most malignant opposition.*

There is great force in that mechanical machinery which contends successfully with the wild elements; which not only walks like 'a thing of life' over the tranquil lake, but which buffets the infuriated winds and waves, and holds in mysterious subordination the raging storm. Never were greater nor more desperate efforts made, than to destroy the Christian ministry. In almost every age of the world, from the time that 'he that was after the flesh persecuted him that was after the Spirit', these appointed guardians of God's truth have encountered hostilities directed against no other class of men. Sometimes this hostility has assumed ensnaring forms, with the view of rendering their work ineffectual; sometimes the form of obloquy and slander; sometimes it has resorted to blood. It stoned and slew the Prophets; the lone and defenceless precursor of the great Messiah it beheaded in prison; his Apostles it consigned to the stake and the scaffold, and their adorable Master to the cross.

Bitter are the conflicts which the pulpit has encountered. The waters have been troubled and lashed to fury by the 'Prince of the power of the air'; yet has its voice been heard in the midst of, and above the fierce elements. Though, for the most part, the first, the least pitied, and the most signal victims of this malignity, its ministers have held fast the testimony of Jesus. It is a fact of deep interest, that from the death of its Divine Founder, the history of the pulpit may be traced, not in the martyrdom only, but in the successes and triumphs of its martyred preachers.

The first three centuries, immediately after the death of the last of the Apostles, form a remarkable era in the history of the pulpit. The corruption of subsequent ages had not yet so changed its character, but that it still bore the prominent features of Christianity. We have found no means of ascertaining to what extent its ministers were multiplied at this early period; but from the multitude of the Jewish priests that were obedient to the faith, and from the number and flourishing condition of the churches that were organized during the ministry of the Apostles, and soon after, we have no reason to think they were few. There were such men as *Simeon* of Jerusalem, *Ignatius* of Antioch, *Justin Martyr*, *Polycarp*, *Irenæus*, *Clemens*, *Cyprian*, and others, through whom multitudes, especially of the middle and lower orders of society, were brought to the knowledge of the truth. Ecclesiastical historians unite in the testimony that the Christians of this period furnish rare specimens of the true faith and the true charity. Nor were these triumphs limited to the lower classes; high-born, and highly-nurtured men and women, and illustrious families there were, whose zeal, liberality, brotherly love, and heavenliness of spirit and deportment, as well as their fortitude in suffering, evinced the victorious strength of those truths that were 'to the Jews a stumbling block, and to the Greeks foolishness'.

During the latter part of this period, there were dissensions; there was even schism; but there was self-denying, persevering piety – piety that rose superior to the favour and frowns of the world. There was less of its favours than its frowns; for the most part, it was a period of storms; while amid the severity of the storm, the ministers of God, instead of seeking a refuge from its fury, buried themselves in its angry waters, and rather than prove recreant to their trust, chose to be dragged from the pulpit to the scaffold.

Of the latter part of this age of terrific persecution it is difficult to speak. It has no need of painting and poetry to add to it one sombre hue, or one lyric strain. The sober facts are, that the utter extermination of Christianity was the favourite object of the Pagan world. The public assemblies of the people of God were forbidden; their prayers and their praises, and the voices of their beloved teachers were heard in the fastnesses of the mountains, and in dens and caves of the earth. Christianity was stigmatized as the plague of the nations, and the procuring cause of all their calamity; it was slandered as the disloyal religion, and the enemy of princes, and the blood of its ministers flooded the land. Human ingenuity was tasked to augment their sufferings, and to render the most revolting scenes of cruelty the amusement of the people. The pulpit was covered with the pall of death, and the 'witnesses prophesied in sackcloth'.

But 'why did the heathen rage, and the people imagine a vain thing?' Jew and Gentile, princes and people, polytheism and philosophy, stood forth as God's selected testimony that these martyred men triumphed in Christ, and made manifest the savour of his name in every place. Christ triumphed in the triumph of his Gospel, and his ministers triumphed in him. The few who were left in that terrible age, uniting their living testimony with the 'poor dumb mouths' of the dead, carried the truth to the high places of the earth, made disciples of persecutors and converts of kings, and turned the temples of Paganism into churches for the worship of the living God.

We need not descend to later times. It was, in some memorable periods of the world, substantially the same tale of suffering and of conquest, with this difference only, that the former were the cruel deeds of *Paganism*, the latter, the more cruel deeds of a power baptized with the *Christian name*! Yes, the Christian name – I blush to say it – the Christian name! Oh Christianity! Christianity! what deeds of darkness and of blood have not been imputed to thy pure and lovely nature, and perpetrated under the cover of thy holy cross! That sweet emblem of peace and of thee has been upon their bosoms when they have shed the blood of *thy saints*! So insatiate was blood-thirsty Rome, that the rising generation grew up only to take the place of their slaughtered fathers, and the children at school spake familiarly of being educated for the scaffold. Yet, strange to say, the same historian who tells us these things, tells also, that while the Protestant prisoners were so numerous that it was impossible to put them all to death, it was the complaint of the Catholics that the heretics were increasing every day; 'so mightily grew the word of God and prevailed'. The pulpit weathered the storm.

If we speak of our own times, we can only say, 'the offence of the cross has not ceased'. God has chained the arm of persecution in this land, but he has not sealed the lips of obloquy. Nor is it 'as though some strange thing had happened to us', that men there are who are never more eloquent than when speaking and writing against God's ministers. If we were to give a word of counsel to these men, we would tell them that it is the devil's work they are doing, and we would caution them against spitting out their venom so freely at the foot of God's altars. One thing comforts us. Such men are not wont to contend with shadows. The pulpit may glory in having such enemies, for it shows its worth and importance. It must have power, else would it never have excited so much concern and suspicion, and provoked such ribaldry and rage. That it has a being in such a world as this, is proof that it has power which even such a world cannot overcome.

There is still *another view*. If you derange the main shaft of a steam-engine, or the mainspring of a watch, you disturb the whole machinery, and it stops. And what does this indicate, but that the shaft of the engine and the spring of the watch have a place that is essential to the complicated machinery; or if they are but partially deranged, and still act, they act irregularly, and perhaps furiously. And this shows again that they have power.

In the moral machinery of this world, that great engine, the pulpit, has not unfrequently been thus deranged. It has been entangled with other and distinct parts of this moral mechanism; and the consequence has been just what might have been expected from an agency so effective; its movements have been erratic, wild, furious, and destructive. Now we affirm, *that this very derangement and abuse of the pulpit is evidence of its power.* We acknowledge that it has often been perverted to unworthy ends; but what if it be so? What if, in some lands, the church has become so entangled with the State, that the pulpit has lost its spiritual character, and been thrust out of its place? Was it powerless? Was it the weakness of the pulpit seeking to support itself by alliance with the State; or was it the weakness of the State seeking to sustain itself by alliance with the pulpit? There is but one answer to these inquiries; and that is, the moral has ever been demanded to guard and augment the civil power. The only instances with which I am familiar, in which the pulpit has sought alliance with the State, have been those in which the church has first been weakened by the 'powers that be'. Constantine and Theodosius made the pulpit dependent on the civil power; but they destroyed its spiritual character, in which all its native energy consists. When Pepin laid the foundation of the temporal power of the Roman Pontiffs, he ruined the pulpits of the Church of Rome.

There is such a thing as a degenerate and corrupted priesthood. At the close of that period of bitter persecution, to which we have already referred, the time was drawing near when the pulpit entered upon that career of spiritual domination, which was not less its own dishonour than the infamy and curse of the church. During what are called the 'middle ages', comprising a period of a thousand years, from the fall of Rome by the Goths in the fifth century, to the fall of Constantinople in the fifteenth before the Turks, little can be said of the true power of the pulpit. They were 'dark ages'. Ministers of religion there were, but they were not *teachers*. Ignorance could not, in those days, be more emphatically

The Same Subject Continued

stigmatized, than to say of any man, that he is 'ignorant as a priest'. Altars there were, and dumb images, and senseless relics, and unmeaning rites and ceremonies. Priests there were, with splendid robes, and shaven and mitred head. There were retired confessionals, and penance, and indulgences, and ridiculous controversies. But places of religious worship, pulpits devoted to the teaching of the people, religious services in the vernacular tongue, were like fountains sparsely scattered in the Arabian desert. One thing seems, indeed, to have been authoritatively taught, and it was the sum and substance of the teaching. Boldly and without shame was the dogma enforced, that *ignorance is the mother of devotion*; and it sank into the minds of the people. It was easily believed and digested; for it was an easy religion. 'Like priest, like people.' The people 'loved to have it so'. Priests and people were true to their principles. They had no need of pulpits; for a long period, there was not such a thing known as for a pope, a cardinal, or even a bishop, to preach.

I would not be misunderstood. There were some few truly Christian pulpits in the Dark Ages. Augustine and Lactantius of the Latin, and Chrysostom and Basil of the Greek church, furnish examples of rich, eloquent, and effective preaching. Men there were of illumined intellect and sanctified heart, like Athanasius, Ambrose, Gregory Nazianzen, and *Claude* of Turin; but they were like solitary lights travelling across this night of deep and protracted darkness. And it is because they were so few, and these few not a little tinged with the Platonic philosophy, and so embarrassed by the restrictions of a spiritual despotism, and some, even of these, led away by the same grasping ambition, that the pulpit had so little power as the depository of Christian instruction, and so much as the engine of a secular policy.

The pulpits that were not Christian, too, had power; and it was tremendous power, wandering as they did so far from their legitimate sphere as to exhaust their energies for evil. Peter the Hermit was a simple ecclesiastic; yet did he rouse the whole of Christendom to arms. The Spanish Inquisition too, was the offspring of the priesthood. Nor is there any thing that detracts from the power of the anti-Christian pulpit, in these and subsequent times, but the simple fact, that it is so much easier to do wrong than it is to do right – to effect evil than to effect good – to give an impulse to the downward current of men's passions, than to resist and control it. It is a very small capacity which is necessary for mischief; yet was that capacity exerted to the utmost. The barbarous Attila, that 'scourge of God', did not more certainly spread terror and desolation over Europe, than the Romish hierarchy diffused far and wide an influence destructive to true religion.

When the enemies of religion tell us to look at the Dark Ages for exemplifications of the power of the pulpit, it is just where we wish to look, because they furnish the strongest proofs of the gross perversion of that moral influence in which the Christian pulpit glories. It was an age far more replete with danger to the true ministers of Christ than were the most stringent proscriptions of the Roman Emperors, and the sorrow and mourning of the ten memorable persecutions that preceded it. The pulpit fell before it, and, to show its power, every thing holy was buried in its fall.

What is the pulpit without the preacher? A block of wood, or a slab of marble. And what is the preacher, without the word of truth? Just a block of wood, or a slab of marble. Extinguish the *light* of the pulpit, and it no longer deserves the name. The pulpit of the Dark Ages is the merest caricature of the Christian pulpit. The house of God was metamorphosed into the synagogue of Satan, and its ministry was the ministry of death. It was but the emissary of the Man of Sin, promulgating new doctrines of iniquity and blasphemy in the name of God the Holy.

Just change that thousand years into the nineteenth century. Light up that dark night with but a thousand suns as bright as Isaac Barrow and William Bates, Stephen Charnock, Jeremy Taylor, and John Owen, and where would have been the Dark Ages? Had there been a few men like the Apostle Paul, to have raised their voices amid all that worldliness and pride; nay, had there been one pulpit within every thousand square miles, that spake with a voice like Luther, the clouds had been dispersed, and that dark night had never overshadowed the earth.

4: *The Same Subject Continued*

But there is a thought different from any of those to which our attention has been thus far directed. In aiming at the great and single object the pulpit has in view, it gains *other things*; which it does not so directly aim at, but which *belong to it as its natural allies, which are incidental to it, and follow in its train of influences and blessings*.

The mere fact that it has a ready and almost constant access to the minds of the people, is itself an index of its power. 'To the poor the Gospel is preached.' The pulpit is a popular and democratic institution, fitted to protect the rights of all classes of men, and to diffuse a universal spirit of industry, virtue, kindness, and peace. In the organization of human society, it is the only official bond between the aristocracy and democracy of the Christian world. Its sphere of influence lies first and chiefly with the middle and lower classes; nor is there one of the institutions which are designed to make them better and more useful men, but may be traced to the pulpit as its founder. I am ashamed that, in one respect, the corrupt Church of Rome reads an affecting lesson to Protestants; and it is in their solicitude to bring the poor to the house of God. There are no churches for the rich in Papal lands; this is an expedient of Protestantism, and a modern refinement upon that Christianity which teaches that 'the *poor* ye have *always* WITH *you*'. 'The rich and the poor *meet together*: the Lord is the Maker of them all.' So it ought to be, and so it will be, in every prosperous church. These *select* churches ought all to have died with lukewarm Laodicea. In other spheres we look for distinctions among men; Christianity looks for them; but not in the church of God. The pulpit is the great spiritual leveller, because it is the expositor of a common Christianity, a Christianity that is 'no respecter of persons', a Christianity that swallows up all that is adventitious in the mortal, in his immortality. This is one department where it performs its appropriate functions. The difference in the social institutions in Pagan and Christian lands, in the attachments, virtues, characters, and thousand agencies in domestic and public life, cannot be accounted for without its influence.

It has also truths and obligations, and a benevolence, and a morality addressed to the higher classes. Its voice has been often heard on subjects of high public interest. Its influence has been felt in scenes which 'tried men's souls', and amid revolutions which have alternately jeoparded and advanced the well-being of the world. But whether they have been for good or for evil; whether they have been religious, or civil, or of a mixed character; the influence of the pulpit has been felt in them all. That great event in the history of the world, the American Revolution, never would have been achieved without the influence of the pulpit. Political society 'moved on the axis of religion'. The religious movement gave its character to the social movement. Men who knew there was a 'church without a bishop', knew also there could be a 'State without a King'. Had the pulpits of New England and the Presbyterian Church occupied the same position on this question which was occupied by so many of the pulpits which I could name, we should have been colonies still.

Nor does this event stand alone as exemplifying the power of the pulpit in affairs not purely religious. The religion of a nation is not only one of the elements of its existence, but the varied modifications of that religion affect every part of it and give it its character. We are at some loss for a selection of facts to illustrate this remark, because they crowd upon us from every quarter. Take the following as examples. Few measures have exerted a greater influence upon national character, than the adoption of the *Thirty-nine Articles*, and the *Book of Common Prayer*, of the Church of England – the *Solemn League and Covenant*, of the Church and people of Scotland – the *Augsburg Confession* – the *League of the Protestant Princes of Smalkalde* – the *Westminster Confession of Faith* – the *Articles of the Synod of Dort* – and the *Cambridge and Saybrook Platform*. Yet were all these either the subject matter of legislative provision and enactment, or ratified in assemblies in which the princes of the empire were present. The influence of the pulpit was felt in them all. There is a young republic which has sprung into being in our times, on the shores of Africa; and on its deep foundations are the names of Hopkins, Mills, Finley, and Ashmun – names not soon forgotten in the history of the American pulpit.

The Same Subject Continued

There is one department where this incidental influence of the pulpit ever has been acknowledged; I mean that of *learning and science*. In the Hebrew state, its religious teachers were the chief depositaries of its literature. Men like Moses and Samuel, Ezra and Nehemiah, Isaiah and Daniel, as well as the Scribes and Pharisees, and Rabbins of later times, could not long dwell among an uncouth and ignorant people. The standard writers upon Jewish antiquities lead us to conclude that the cities of the Levites were seats of learning, and that the schools of the Prophets were not unlike the schools of Grecian philosophy, where the young men associated with their teachers, and were qualified to be the teachers of the nation. The Jewish priests are declared to have been set apart to their office, that they 'might *teach* the children of Israel all the statutes which the Lord had spoken unto them by the hand of Moses'. They must have been men of no inconsiderable learning in order to have performed this service. If it is a fair supposition that the Jewish priesthood understood their own religious laws, as well as they were understood by Witsius, Warburton, Graves, and Michaelis, they must have exerted no humble influence on the literature of this people.

There are strong sympathies, and a most natural alliance, between religion and learning, Christianity and every department of human science. In the brightest periods of the church and of literature, this alliance has been seen and felt. It cannot be otherwise than that a class of men, to whom is committed the religious instruction of the people, should exert an influence upon their literature, if it were only in liberating the mind from bondage, imparting an impression of personal responsibility, and stimulating to intellectual effort. Every competent teacher of a Sabbath school knows that the alliance of which we are speaking is the most natural thing in the world. Were the Bible made a text-book in our common schools, our academies and colleges, as this Book of God ought to be in every one of them, there is no department which, from the varied learning it requires, it would be so difficult to supply with an accomplished professor; nor is there one in which so much general information of every kind might be communicated. The mere *facts* recorded in the sacred writings require extensive research in almost every department of human knowledge. Chronology, history, the natural sciences, the science of law and government, and political economy, to say nothing of the laws of language, are important auxiliaries to just and enlarged views of the divine oracles.

Nowhere is there a finer field for such researches than in the five books of Moses, the greater Prophets, and the Acts of the Apostles. The book of Genesis alone is the source of all knowledge. It is a mountain where lofty cedars, the cedars of God, strike their roots deep; in whose recesses there is golden ore; on whose surface there is a wilderness of native flowers and fruit; through whose ravines run mighty rivers, and where ancient nations dwelt that were many and strong. Men of learning have traversed it; imagination has culled its purest flowers; curious research has traced out its time-worn channels; and patient and discriminating toil has dug about its roots; and they are all found fresh and pure, and the soil inexhaustible.

It is no presumption to say that human learning is under obligations to the pulpit. To say nothing of the present age, what a host of names has it furnished, in days past, that are inscribed on the temple of learning and science, throughout the Continent of Europe and the British Islands! It were a chasm to be felt, were the pulpit no longer to have a place in the University of the literary world.

These and other incidental influences of the pulpit are so obvious, that it is a fact which deserves to be noticed, that *historians* have found it impracticable to separate the profane from the sacred. Robertson, Hume, Gibbon, Sully, could not give an impartial account of the civil without presenting the ecclesiastical. Oral traditions, historical poems, laws, archives of state, monuments, coins, medals, books of heraldry and sepulchral stones, are not more important sources of history than the pulpit. That were a lame history of France, in which the names of Petavius, Beza, Lorraine, Bossuet, and Pascal had no place. And what would be the history of Germany, where the reader did not find the portraits of Luther, Melanchthon, and Bucer? Who that desired to do justice to his theme would write the history of England, and suppress the deeds of Wickliffe, Ridley, Latimer, Cranmer, Jewel, Leighton, and Baxter? Or what scholar would give to the world a history of Scotland, and keep out of sight such men as Patrick Hamilton, Wishart, Knox, Henderson, Gillespie, and Rutherford? Or who would risk his reputation as the historian of New England without recurring to the name of Robertson, and the

The Same Subject Continued

pulpits of Hooker, Davenport, Cotton, and Mather? Or where shall we look for any valuable historical sketch of the Middle States, without being introduced to the 'Log College', and to such men as Tennent, Blair, Burr, Dickenson, and Davies?

We may not pursue this prolific thought. It would be a pleasant service to us to enter into some specifications, and direct the attention of the reader, with more minuteness, to several portions of the Christian world, where the pulpit has exerted this incidental influence. We may perhaps be allowed to direct his attention to the little state of New Jersey, and to the states of New England. Look at New Jersey. What a beautiful commonwealth spreads itself between the bay of New York and The Delaware bay and river! Christian seminaries of learning, a Christian bench and bar, a Christian legislature, a Christian pulpit – what an adornment to the land! My own preferences for New England, as one of her native sons, may be supposed to disqualify me to speak impartially of that fair land; but I will use the language of one who has never been accused of any such partialities.[*] 'Two centuries have elapsed', says this well known and able writer, 'since the first persecuted settlers of New England set their feet on these shores, to rear a church in all the liberty wherewith Christ has made us free. The population of that section of country has increased from a few individuals to eighteen hundred thousand, and there is now one minister to every thousand souls; a proportion greater than in some of the oldest countries of Europe; and there is doubtless *no equal population upon earth* to whom the Gospel is administered with greater purity and fidelity.' What would New England have been without her pulpit? With it, what is she, and where is not her influence felt? not simply in her own civil organizations, but in those of other states of this Union. There is no part of Christendom that has not acknowledged these incidental influences of the pulpit, in forming its habits and character, in elevating and purifying its institutions, in stimulating and extending its literature, in modifying its usages and laws, and in giving more or less of peculiarity to the measures and policy of its government. It necessarily gives a direction to the current of human thought; men of talent, in every department of human life, feel its influence. It

---

[*]Introductory lecture delivered in the Theological Seminary at Princeton, N.J., Nov. 1818, by Charles Hodge, D.D.

has been felt everywhere, in the councils of warriors in the field, and of statesmen in the Senate-house. Kings on their thrones have listened to its voice, and the populace has been moved by it. Men of all religious persuasions, and of no religious persuasion, believers and infidels, feel its influence; all orders and combinations are, to a greater or less extent, subjected to its power. In past ages of the world, few moral causes did more in moulding the habits of human thought than the various forms of the scholastic philosophy; but its powerful influence waned, and eventually was eclipsed by the Christian pulpit. Other influences there are which act upon the public mind; the press acts upon it; seminaries of learning act upon it; legislation acts upon it; courts of law act upon it; the theatre and the opera act upon it; the fine arts act upon it; and the exchange acts upon it; and all with prodigious power. Some of these are the immediate and direct antagonists of the pulpit; and its business is to oppose and neutralize them. Some of them are directly auxiliary to it, and some of them indirectly. As such, we honour them. But if we draw a line around any other department of human influence, and compare it with the pulpit, we must do the greater honour to this divine institution. It has no physical force to boast of; it is its moral power which is its glory. Its conflict is not the conflict of rushing bayonets, but of truth with error; nor are its victories those where men are trodden down and trampled on, but where they are lifted up. It has power above the field of battle, above the Forum, above the Senate-house. Yes, it has power above them all. Compare them. Inspect them. And then say which has the more important influence upon national character. Inspect them impartially; and whose sway is the widest, and which occupies the largest space? Who has accomplished most for this land, its warriors and its statesmen, or the ministers of the Gospel? Who most for England, Edmund Burke[*] and William Pitt, or George

---

[*]There is a fact in regard to Edmund Burke which ought to be remembered. In the years 1771 and 1772, during the reign of George III, an association was formed by some of the Clergy of the Established Church, and a few of the laity, for the purpose of substituting a declaration of assent to the sufficiency of the Holy Scriptures for the required subscription to the thirty-nine articles. From the place of their meeting, it was called the 'Feathers Tavern Association'. When the petition was presented to the House of Commons, by Sir William Meredith, the brother-in-law of the unhappy Lord Ferrers, the vote stood in favour of it seventy-one, and against it two hundred and seventeen.

The Same Subject Continued

Whitefield and Robert Hall? Who for Scotland most, Robert Bruce and William Wallace, or John Knox and Thomas Chalmers? Mark this comparison between the most influential of secular men and the more humble minister of Christ, and it is no difficult matter to see on which side the advantage lies. Look at them through the whole of their course, from the beginning to its close, and let their own lips utter the decision. There was an humble minister of Christ cradled in our native hills, who occupied but twenty short years in preaching the Gospel of his Divine Master, who, as his term of service was about to close, said, 'Oh, if ministers only saw the inconceivable glory that is before them, and the preciousness of Christ, they would not be able to refrain from going about, leaping and clapping their hands for joy, and exclaiming, *I am a minister of Christ! I am a minister of Christ!*' Another distinguished individual there was, the contemporary of the one just spoken of, and in political life, the most distinguished of his age – the sagacious counsellor of kings, and the companion and supporter of their thrones – high in office during successive revolutions which overturned the government of his country, and changed the face of Europe; and more respected, and more feared than any diplomatist of his age – a man who was the origin and conductor of more and the most important negotiations, than any

---

The part which that distinguished statesman and ornament of the British Senate, Edmund Burke, acted on this occasion, is worthy of all praise. In the prospect of this discussion, he wrote to the Countess of Huntingdon, as follows:

'MADAM – I am sensible your kindness and partiality to me will induce you to put the most favourable construction on my seeming neglect of the communication which your ladyship did me the honour to address to me. Permit me to assure you that disregard and inattention to the contents of your letter, and the wishes of your ladyship, had not the smallest share in it. I honour and respect the great activity you have evinced on this occasion, and shall make it my study to merit the good opinion you entertain of me, which is so flattering to my feelings.

'It is with shame I find myself so late in answering a letter which gave me such sincere pleasure. I am happy in coinciding with your ladyship in attachment for the Established Church. I wish to see her walls raised on the foundation laid in the volume of divine truth, that she may crush the conspiracy of atheism, and those principles which will not leave to religion even a toleration. My sentiments in regard to the petition of the Clergy, praying to be relieved from subscription to the thirty-nine articles, are in opposition to the opinions of nearly all my own party. There is every probability of its being thrown out; and you may rely on my determined opposition to it in every stage.

'I have the honour to be, madam, with the highest esteem and regard,
'Your ladyship's most faithful and obedient humble servant,

'EDMUND BURKE.'

[29]

statesman who has lived – sometimes a staunch republican, and sometimes a *jus divinum* monarchist; oppressed with honours, and loaded with almost immeasured wealth, who left on his table the day previous to his death, the following lines: 'Behold eighty-three years passed away! What cares! what agitations! what anxieties! what ill-will! what sad complications! And all without other result, except great fatigue of body and mind, a profound sentiment of discouragement of the future, and disgust of the past!' Which was the more important to the world, the pulpit of Portland, or the cabinet of the Bourbons? Who would not rather have been Edward Payson than Prince Talleyrand!

5: *The Same Subject Continued*

I add a single thought more. It may present a vivid impression of the power of the pulpit, to *suppose it actually abolished throughout the world*. What if the dream of some modern reformers could be realized, and the expressed wishes of a well-known class of men among us were gratified; and every minister in God's Zion were silenced, and exiled, and every sanctuary in Christendom razed to its foundation! Can any one doubt, if this reckless experiment were fully made, that the moral, the social, the civil condition of the world would be melancholy to the last degree? What an immensity of wickedness would be found to exist among men! What 'mighty labour of human depravity!' and what a stupendous amount of crimes!

Nor is this altogether hypothesis; for we have several classes of facts to go upon in our illustration of this idea. Take, for example, several instances in the history of Papal kingdoms, where they have been placed under *interdict* by the reigning Pope. When, in the thirteenth century, King John of England had incurred the displeasure of Pope Innocent III, and his kingdom was laid under interdict; when Otho, the Emperor of Germany, was for a similar cause, put under interdict by the same Pope; the result was calamitous beyond the endurance of the people. So it was, when Philip the Fair, of France, became involved in a quarrel with his Holiness, and was laid under interdict by Pope Boniface IX; and when in the fourteenth century, Pope Clement V dispatched a nuncio to Venice, and on the rejection of his demands, excommunicated the Doge, and put his dominions under interdict. The immediate effect of this sentence, as you well know, was, that every church in these kingdoms was closed, every priest forbidden to exercise his office, and all religious services of every kind indefinitely suspended. The Sabbath bell was unhung: the voice of prayer and praise was heard only in retirement; the living teacher spoke not; baptism was denied to the newly born, religious consolation to the dying, and Christian burial to the dead. The clergy avoided the land groaning under the malediction of the Pope; the people were excited against their own princes, because they were so slow to become reconciled to Rome. Conspiracy after conspiracy sprang up till the ruling powers were constrained to submission to the Papal authority, through the fear of open insurrection. In some of these instances, the distress of the people is described as verging on madness; it was the madness of despair, because their religious privileges were denied them. Have them they would, even at the expense of revolt and massacre.

Let us suppose such a state of things realized among Protestants, and that the countries of England or Scotland, or the United States, were placed under the ban of some governmental *interdict*, and their ministers banished, and their churches closed. The time was when this supposition was in part realized, even in Protestant England, and by the barbarous Act of Uniformity, in the year 1662, under the reign of the treacherous Charles II. And as the fatal day of St. Bartholomew approached, when the non-conformist ministers were to relinquish their pulpits, or sign articles which they could not in conscience subscribe to, *two thousand* pulpits were put under interdict, and two thousand of God's faithful servants were virtually driven into exile. Prelacy triumphed for a while, as her elder sister had done before her: and such men as Calamy and Baxter, Manton, Bates, and Mead, instead of resisting unto blood, wept in silence. It was a dark day in England. There was great mourning. The land mourned 'every family apart; the family of the house of David apart, and their wives apart; the family of the house of Nathan apart, and their wives apart; and the family of the *house of Levi* apart, and their wives apart! *All* the families that remained, every family apart, and their wives apart'.

There was another scene of this same kind, though of more terrific aspect. During the reign of Louis XIV of France, the spirit of persecution against Protestants, and especially Protestant ministers, was extended to such unrelenting severity, that on the revocation of the Edict of Nantes, the Protestant pulpit was annihilated, and its ministers slain and mutilated, with every species of barbarity. It was the jubilee of Rome; but it was the funeral-day of the people of God. No, it was not their funeral-day, for so many of them died without burial, that the inhabitants of some cities were obliged to remove from them to an atmosphere less corrupted by the bodies of the slain. Those who could escape this scene of horror fled; they fled to other lands. *Two hundred thousand* of them fled; and not a few of the descendants of these noble men are here among ourselves, where the sword of persecution does not smite them, and where they perish not by 'a famine of the word of the Lord'.

There is a still more affecting exemplification of the truth we are illustrating, and one that is fresh in the memory of some who are living. The writer of these pages remembers it well, when in the days of his childhood, the church bell of his native parish tolled for the downfall of Christianity in France. By one sweeping and atheistic law, the French people decided that there was no God. Her pulpits were silenced, Papal and Protestant. God's day of holy rest was annihilated, and the Decade instituted in its room. And what was the consequence? Instructive, beyond exaggeration, instructive, to a degree which language is too poor to express. Subsequent events tell what it was. The guillotine proclaims it. The murderous band stationed at the prison doors proclaims it. A voice from one vast slaughterhouse of men proclaims it. France herself infatuated as she was, could not endure the destitution. Infidelity could not endure it. Atheism staggered and fell under the weight of its own wickedness. Every thing human tottered, because every thing perished that was divine. Infidelity, atheism, and France, were obliged to fall back upon institutions which they had scorned, seek the law at the lips of God's ministers, and in buildings which they had so shamelessly desecrated and profaned.

But let us return to the fiction of our hypothesis. What if the pulpits of this land were put under Papal interdict? What if some cruel and tyrannical 'Act of Uniformity' were to exile even two thousand of her ministers? What if Papacy should procure a revocation of the charter that gives liberty of conscience, and speech, and preaching? or Atheism should pass a resolution that there is no God, and should close our churches, and bid us all speak no more in his name? Tell me, ye who rail so eloquently at God's ministers, have you any expedient to bridge the chasm? What fountains of life have *you* to open in the desert, and what trees of righteousness to plant in the parched wilderness? Drain it of these waters, if you will; burn it over, if you will; and then bear in mind that on *you* rests the responsibility of reclaiming it. Piety sickens at such a view; humanity weeps over it. Such a land were a defiled inheritance, 'given to salt, and that cannot be healed'. Let infidelity ever become so rife among us, and so rampant as to disrobe our ministry, and close our churches; and whatever else might be the result, proof would not be wanting that *moral power* had been withdrawn from the land. Let her pulpits be closed for a quarter of a century, and the result cannot be doubtful. More practical evil would flow from such a destitution, than from all other causes put together. Law would vanish with religion. No corrupt propensity would be kept under restraint; there would be no corrective, and no limit but selfishness to the depravity of the human heart. The virtuous would be driven to despair, and the vicious to the darkness and crimes of paganism. It would be a Pagan land, dark and dreary as though the Sun of righteousness had never risen upon it. Owls would dwell there, and satyrs would dance there; and around such a dreadful cavern of iniquity, the dragons of the pit would linger and dwell as in their own habitation. And the curse of God would be upon it, as it was upon Sodom; and he would extirpate the inhabitants of it as he did the nations of Canaan. His judgments would go forth against it, and as though seven thunders uttered their voices, it would be said in heaven, 'WOE, WOE, WOE TO THE LAND THAT IS NOT THE LAND OF SABBATHS, AND CHURCHES, AND MINISTERS!'

We may not extend these illustrations. The pulpit speaks for itself. There it stands, nor is it possible to escape its influence. Men must not only go out of the sanctuary, but exile themselves from Christian lands, if they would avoid its influence. Many are the springs of thought which it sets in motion, not only in the bosoms of those who seek its instructions, but of those who never come within hearing of the preacher's voice. The mightiest are no more exempt from it than the meanest, the most hostile than the most friendly. Everywhere its power is felt; it acts on them for eternity.

Yes, it acts on them for eternity! The years are short and few. Soon will it be known whether it has been to them a savour of death unto death, or a savour of life unto life; whether the seed it scatters has found no congenial soil, and has become petrified to adamant, or whether it has taken root and struck deep, because it is nourished by the waters of the sanctuary.

Different, widely different, will be the reflections of these two different classes of persons as they look back upon the pulpit –the one from the bright, the other from the dark abodes of the eternal world.

That pulpit, with what emotions of bitterness will it be remembered by the millions of the lost! 'That sanctuary and that man of God', will many a reprobate in the prison of despair exclaim, 'forewarned me of this dreadful immortality, but I heeded not the admonition. That sacred desk told me of redemption through the blood of Jesus; but I scorned the message, and trod that blood of the covenant under my feet. I might have been happy on the same gracious and condescending terms with those I now see at God's right hand; but I would not come to Christ that I might have life! And now I am lost – lost – lost! O how dreadful this eternal hell! *That pulpit*, O that pulpit! how it aggravates my woes! Why did it speak to me at all, if only thus to add fuel to these flames!'

On the other hand, there will be those, and 'a great multitude, which no man can number', who will remember the influence of the pulpit with grateful and adoring praise to Him, who 'through the foolishness of preaching saves them that believe'. *That house of God*, how many will remember it in heaven! 'That pulpit, which looked upon me when I was a child, which taught me when I was ignorant, and reclaimed me when I was a wanderer; which reminded me of my wickedness, and told me all things that ever I did; which spake to me of my immortality, and made me tremble and made me weep; never can it be blotted from memory. *That pulpit*, which told me of a Saviour's love, and how he bled, and died, and waited to long-suffering, that I might accept his saving mercy; which comforted me when I was cast down, and cheered me in my fatigue; which dissipated my delusions, and helped me to escape the snare of the fowler; which dispensed to me the bread of life when I was hungry, and when I was thirsty gave me the waters of salvation; which brought its messages of peace to my bed of languishing, soothed my aching head, and when I was dying, told me not to let my heart be troubled': – *that pulpit*, may millions now in glory say, 'warned me of yonder fiery prison, and directed me to these mansions in my Father's house!'

6: *The Truth of Which the Pulpit is the Vehicle*

We have thus far simply illustrated the *fact itself*, that the pulpit has power.

From its divine origin, and from the benevolent ends it was designed to accomplish, it would be natural to conclude that the elements of its influence possess a fitness to their end, and that, in some respects, they are above every thing that is human. Our object is now to inquire,

WHAT ARE THE CONSTITUENT ELEMENTS OF THE POWER WITH WHICH IT IS THUS INVESTED?

While the pulpit possesses all that belongs to the province of moral suasion in its ordinary and best forms, it has peculiarities which the ordinary forms of moral suasion do not possess. There are principles, some of which, at least, account for the power it exerts, beyond that which is exerted by any other means of intellectual conviction, or any other moral influences that are known among men.

The first of these is *the truth itself, of which it is the vehicle*.

The God of heaven is the God of Truth; truth is infinitely dear to his pure and holy mind. He is its great assertor and guardian; nor will he be respected, loved and obeyed, and this earth filled with his glory until it is flooded with his truth, as the waters cover the sea. The Scriptures instruct us that truth is the great instrumentality by which his purposes of mercy are accomplished, the wisely selected means by which he operates, a means well adapted to the end; nay, the necessary and indispensable means, because truth alone presents the only objects of all that variety of right thoughts and holy affections and emotions which constitute true religion. The pulpit has no other instrumentality. It has accomplished its vocation when it has fully, clearly, and with a right spirit, exhibited the claims of truth. The factitious and artificial arrangements which have been so extensively relied on, are altogether foreign to its aims. Truth is that to which there is a response in the understanding and conscience; which convinces even where it does not persuade, and confounds where it does not control; and which, where it controls, becomes 'the wisdom of God, and the power of God unto salvation.'

There are other truths which have a different vehicle; they are truths which intellect honours, and to which an enlightened moral virtue does reverence; truth which, while it has its own appropriate sphere of influence, is an important auxiliary to the truth proclaimed from the pulpit.

There is no conflict between the truth of God's Word and any other truth in the universe; rather is there a delightful harmony between this and all other truth. They form one beautifully compacted system, and all unite in proclaiming the perfection and glory of their great Author. The Author of nature is the Author of a supernatural revelation; he is the same Being, and governs the world with the same unerring wisdom, in both these great departments. But while they thus confirm, illustrate, and adorn each other, they have not the same place, nor are they revealed for the same immediate purposes. The pulpit has objects of its own; it has a higher and more sacred vocation than natural science or mere human learning. It is emphatically *the truth of God's written word* which it utters, and which he has revealed for the salvation of men.

There is no error in truth; light is not more opposed to darkness, sweet to bitter, good to evil, than truth is opposed to error. Error has power, but it is to make men wicked and miserable. The empire of the great Adversary is founded in error; its first great principle was the first lie; and from that hour to the present, it has been extended and sustained by a succession of flagitious and impudent falsehoods. The human mind is naturally under the direction of error. It is one of the evils to which sin has subjected the descendants of the first transgressor, that they 'go astray from the womb, speaking lies'. Error is a sort of magnet, which attracts to it all wickedness; and such and so strong are the sympathies between them, that all the practical tendencies of the apostate mind invariably fall in with some form of error, in principle. Pulpits there are which are the teachers of error, and which make it their business to cast contempt upon all the great and distinguishing truths of the Gospel. But they are not Christian pulpits; and by how much they have power, by so much do they derive it from the depraved and corrupt hearts of men, and from the Prince of error whom they serve. It is his cause in which they are employed.

THE POWER OF THE PULPIT

There are Christian pulpits too which have an immingling of error with truth; but just in the measure in which this confusion exists, is the power of truth neutralized. Good is often done by such a ministry; but it is not because there is any amalgamation between truth and error, for they are different in their origin, their nature, and their effects. The chaff is often severed from the wheat, even where they are both sown broad-cast. Where the mind and conscience are awake to the obligations of the Gospel, they are sometimes quick to discern the difference, and to cast the chaff away. It is not the error which such a defective ministry preaches that gives it power, but the little truth that is winnowed from the mass, by that Spirit 'whose fan is in his hand'.

There must not unfrequently be controversy in the pulpit; the pulpit is the place where men who are 'set for the defence of the Gospel' must 'contend earnestly for the faith once delivered to the saints'. But in doing this, in doing it boldly and freely, and humbly too, there is something more to be done than refute error, and prostrate the adversaries of truth. Very little is accomplished merely by driving the enemy from his refuges of lies; he must be intrenched within the citadel of truth, and induced to flee to the strong-hold as a prisoner of hope. The sword that cuts him in pieces is not always the sword of the Spirit. The enemies of the Church of Rome found vigorous and formidable opponents in the pens of infidels; but this was nothing more than error contending with error. It was of comparatively little consequence which banner was victorious, for the conqueror was himself to be conquered.

There were two men greatly distinguished in the history of modern Europe, whose influence upon their fellow-men is felt to the present hour. Both began their career young; both possessed superior powers of mind, and great moral courage; both were highly educated men, one in the severe Universities of Germany, the other in the more refined University of Paris; and both well trained for the part they acted. Both were thrown upon the world in a period of great moral darkness; a period during which Europe had been long oppressed by the odious claims, the corrupt aristocracy, and the debasing institutions of the Papal Church, inwoven and inlaid in every department of human society, from the courts of princes, to the humblest domestic relations. Both also had the same immediate object – the emancipation of the human mind from the bondage of Rome. They were intensely exciting scenes into the midst of which these two remarkable men were introduced; for within the memory of the present and past generation, no events have taken place of greater importance than the great Protestant Reformation, and the memorable Revolution in France.

But Luther and Voltaire were very different men. The one was impelled by that atheistical and ruthless fanaticism which was the precursor of the 'reign of terror;' the other by a firm belief and ardent love of the truth of God. Luther was actuated by the boldest, the most steady, the noblest and most unselfish motives and passions ever known to fallen humanity since the days of Paul. Voltaire too, was actuated by motives which were bold, active, persevering, but the most reckless and vile. Under equally strong impulses, with the same sanguine expectations of success rousing, invigorating all their powers of body and mind, each pursued his own chosen and different way. And the difference was just this. Luther, anticipating momentous results from the controversy, controlled by the goodness, not simply of his proximate, but his ultimate object, and deeply sensible that it was much easier to pull down than to build up, and much more difficult to implant right principles than to eradicate wrong ones, took great pains to build up before he began to pull down. Voltaire, reckless of the future, deaf to every cool and benevolent consideration, dead to every consideration but one, did nothing but pull down.

Luther took the truth of God for his guide, and having first firmly established a few radical principles of Christianity against all the confederate counsels of princes, legates, and synods, held them forth, and gave them to Rome, against the time of need when her own rotten bulwarks and proud towers should fall. And having thus laid his foundation, and indicated it to Europe, he levelled blow after blow against Rome, and tore up her decayed battlements, leaving her the Word of God to stand upon.

Voltaire saw the absurdities, and felt the evils of the Church of Rome, as well as Luther, and was resolved on some radical transformation, if not reform. But the change he aimed at was without truth, without religion, without God. 'An evil spirit troubled him'; he had not the foresight, or if he had the foresight, he had not the moral principle, to perceive that, in destroying the religion of Rome, and giving France nothing in its stead, the result would be the most inhuman violence and barbarity. He defamed the Bible, trod it under his feet, and then spat upon and besmeared it. He professed to enlighten the minds of men, but threw over them the pall of darkness and death; he professed to be the people's friend, but was their malignant enemy. He shut his ears against plain and conclusive argument, yet made his appeal to reason, dark, proud reason; he deified her, and the nation, by solemn legislative enactments, resolved that she was God! Paris, like the city of Ephesus of old, was filled with confusion, 'some crying one thing, some another', till at length the populace, impersonating the goddess of reason, rushed to Notre Dame, with a vile prostitute on their shoulders, set her in the midst of God's temple, and all called out for the space of two hours, *'There is no God but reason, and death is an eternal sleep!'*

Voltaire gained his object. The mind of France was liberated from Rome; he had knocked off its fetters; it was free. No man ever accomplished his object more effectually. So did Luther accomplish his object; he accomplished it manfully; he revolutionized Germany, and other countries of Europe, and left the human mind free. The deeds of these two men are done; the scenes are past; and we, at this distance of time, can look at them. The fruit has had time to grow and become ripe; and what is it? Look at the effects of that controversy conducted by Luther, in Germany, Britain, Switzerland, Prussia, and even France itself; on the iron-bound coast and granite hills of New England; in the Hollanders and Huguenots of New Jersey and the Southern States, and the fermenting, swelling mass, of every name and kind, that are spreading between the Alleghany and the Rocky Mountains.

We can see also the effects of that disastrous revolution effected by Voltaire; some of us remember it, and the deep knell that sounded it to Europe and the world still sounds in our ears. Romanism was destroyed in France, but there was nothing left, save selfish, violent, cruel passion, rioting in cruelty. The lion was unchained, and the hands that unchained him were the victims of his fury. A fire was kindled that nothing could put out; it wasted itself, and the land was burnt over. Every thing was destroyed; religion, morality, the marriage bond, kings, law, order, priests and altars, even liberty itself – every thing was involved in the universal ruin. Voltaire 'made a desert, and called it peace'. It was a desert truly, such a moral wilderness, created in a Christian land, as the world had never seen before, nor since; it was carnage, it was the reform of infidelity. It records a lesson which all subsequent ages will read – that men may be mighty controversialists, and move mighty minds, and mighty nations; but if they do nothing more than triumph over their prostrate foe, they accomplish nothing for the honour of God or the best interests of their fellow men.

If there must be errors in the world, it is that 'the *truth* may be made manifest'. Error is the cloud that envelops the truth; it is of no service that the cloud be dissipated, unless truth be made to shine with the greater brilliancy. The pulpit had better have nothing to do with error, unless it be exposed and refuted with so masterly a hand, that, like a thin leaf of dull metal, placed under precious stones to make them appear the more transparent, it is made the 'foil of truth'. It is pure truth which it inculcates, unless it goes out of its province; it is truth positive, and not simply errors refuted. There is no saving power but in God's truth.

The pulpit also has a conflict with ignorance. No absolutely vacant mind can be a holy mind; even if it has no errors, and is simply denuded of every religious truth, it cannot be holy. If we expect fruit, we must plant the tree that is to bear it; it will not grow unless it is planted, any more than after it is planted it will grow among thorns. Whatever agency the pulpit exerts, it exerts through *light* – light poured upon the understanding, illuminating the conscience, and penetrating and perforating the gloomy prison of the heart. The prince of darkness holds his empire over all the faculties of the soul; and nothing disturbs it so certainly as truth. He would fain amuse men with fables, perplex them with sophistry, bind them by tradition, hold them in bondage by the decrees of Popes and Councils, and present his claims before his awe-stricken hearers, surrounded in clouds and darkness.

Truth disclaims all such appeals to human ignorance and superstition; her object is to instruct and convince. Men never were made Christians in any other way than on conviction. Nor does the Christian pulpit desire to make them Christians in any other way. It has no oracular decisions, save when it utters the oracles of God. Whatever deference may be solicited for its instructions, no other is claimed for them than that which is the result of sober and enlightened thought, and which is called for by a sense of responsibility to God alone. It is for *'lack of knowledge'* that the people are destroyed; it is 'through the *ignorance* that is in them, because of the blindness of their heart'; it is because 'they do *not know*, and will not consider'; because they 'are a generation which *know not* the Lord'; because 'they hated *knowledge*'; because they count not 'all things but loss for the *knowledge* of Christ'; because they come not 'to the *knowledge* of the truth', and are ever 'a people of *no understanding*'. There is ineffable splendour in God's truth; and where these bright rays have no access to the soul, the light of it is put out, and it is 'reserved to the blackness of darkness for ever'. The truth proclaimed from the pulpit has wondrous efficacy in dissipating these dense and heavy mists of ignorance. They are 'manifestations of the sovereign intelligence', and have 'a glow of divinity' about them, before which this intellectual darkness, and these thick vapours, are exhaled and dispelled. Erect a pulpit in the dark wilderness, where the man of God shall stand, thoroughly furnished for his work; and though it stand alone, its light shall be seen from afar, and the benighted and lost traveller shall hail it with joy. Multiply such pulpits, scatter them in clusters, and the desert would become like the Goshen of Israel, amid the thick darkness of Egypt.

The truth of which the pulpit is the vehicle, has also a contest with something more than error and ignorance. At the threshold of its career, there is the insensate stupidity and the deeply imbedded hostility of the human mind. Indifferent to its claims as long as it can be, it resists them when it can no longer maintain its indifference. Truth has an energy to disturb and wake up this almost imperturbable indifference. Single-handed and alone, it cannot subdue this hostility. But it can check it; it can show its deformity and ugliness; it can throw around it those bonds of obligation, which nothing can relax, and bind by convictions which it is impossible to struggle with without a contest that is sometimes painful, even to despair. For this it has a fitness in its subject matter, and in the excellence, the force, the grandeur of its themes. They are lofty and subduing themes; themes which the preacher cannot approach without a feeling of solemnity, nor without some consciousness at least, that they bear him away from the narrow limits of earth, and the circumscribed sphere of time.

Nor are they 'smooth things', but 'right things', which are never smooth. There is not one of them, rightly understood, that is fitted to please and gratify a mind that is enmity against God. They are weighty and solemn truths, 'hard sayings', and never agreeable to the corrupted taste of men. They do not fall in with their natural love of error; they destroy their good opinion of themselves; they oppose their worldly projects, and render them unhappy. They are universally obnoxious, except to pious and humble men. To all others it is a hardship to hear them, and a greater hardship to be under obligations to believe and love them. Give the pulpit a hearing, and it has truths to utter which will arouse men to fear and trembling. It has so many painful and unwelcome things to say, that the preacher must often brace his nerves to meet fierce opposition, and clothe himself with superhuman meekness and humility. It has nothing to do with suppressing, or modifying the truth of God, for the sake of pleasing men. The trust is too awful, the experiment too hazardous, either to blunt the edge of the sword, or throw away any part of the divine armour. When, with the simplicity of dependence on God, these weapons are faithfully and skilfully used, they constitute the parts of that heavenly panoply which find the most ready access to the conscience. They are aimed at the heart. They are designed to search and try the characters of men, and they make fearful discriminations between 'him that serveth God and him that serveth him not'. They 'take forth the precious from the vile', and say to the righteous, that 'It shall be well with him', and 'Woe unto the wicked, it shall be ill with him'.

The Scriptures do not presume on an unresisted course for the truth of God. They foresee vigorous opposition; but their language to every religious teacher is, 'Be not dismayed at their faces'; – 'speak all that I command thee to speak, diminish not a word'; – 'speak all my words, whether they will hear, or whether they will forbear'. This the Apostles did. They did not, as many do, 'corrupt the word of God'; their exhortation 'was not of deceit, nor of uncleanness, nor of guile'; they 'spake as of the oracles of God', and as men who 'feared not them which could kill the body, but rather him who is able to destroy both soul and body in hell'. They went forth as 'sheep in the midst of wolves', assured that it was 'enough for the disciple to be as his Master, and the servant as his Lord'; all of them 'brethren and companions in tribulation, in the kingdom and patience of Jesus Christ'.

A faithful preacher of the Gospel scarcely fails to produce uneasiness and dissatisfaction in the minds of the thoughtless. Even the most thoughtless not infrequently have painful and distressing views of the truth, because they are sensible of the obligations which it enforces, and the everlasting consequences which it draws after it. The time is past when they care nothing about it; and if they contest and abuse it, if they cavil, and complain, and resist, if they do all in their power to throw off its obligations, it is but augmented proof of its power; the more they struggle against it, the faster does it bind them in its chains.

Nor is this all which the truth accomplishes. 'The law of the Lord is perfect, converting the soul; the testimonies of the Lord are sure, making wise the simple.' God leads some in gentler ways, and by milder methods than others; yet are the struggles of the carnal mind ordinarily the death-struggles, the throes of expiring nature, when grace introduces the new-born soul into the kingdom of God. Truth is the instrumentality in its conversion. 'Of his own will begat he us *with the word of truth.*' Being born again, 'not of corruptible seed, but of incorruptible, by the *word of God*'. 'I have begotten you, *through the Gospel.*' Since religion consists in 'receiving the truth in the love of it', it cannot be received in love unless it be present to the thoughts, unless its obligations are perceived and felt by the conscience, unless its beauty and loveliness be recognized and acquiesced in by the gratified affections. There is no better definition of spiritual and practical Christianity, than that it is *the counterpart of truth* in the heart and in the life. It is the fruit of God's Spirit operating by his truth, and producing in the once alienated heart that delightful reconciliation to its nature and claims which constitutes the life of God in the soul of man. It is the image of the heavenly, where, but just now, there was nothing but the image of the earthly. It is the loveliest exhibition of the power of truth, when men 'gladly receive the word', the 'ingrafted word, which is able to save the soul'; when the darkened understanding is illuminated, and the truth is thus understood and received. The Gospel comes, then, 'not in word only, but also in power, and in the Holy Ghost, and in much assurance'. It comes with peace and joy. It binds up the heart, it comforts the mourner, it sets the captive free. It solaces the soul with divine love; it shows it the path of life; it begets it to a 'living hope of an inheritance, incorruptible, undefiled, and which fadeth not away'.

Nor does the truth leave its work unfinished. The whole progress of sanctification, in all its parts and varieties, and in all the varieties of character in which it is effected, is not only consulted, but

The Truth of Which the Pulpit is the Vehicle

promoted by God's truth. *'Sanctify* them through thy truth.' Truth is the aliment of every gracious principle, and every gracious exercise. The Christian lives upon it; he grows in grace, as he grows in knowledge. It is a 'feast of fat things' to the soul, of 'wines on the lees; of fat things full of marrow, of wines on the lees well refined'. Thus fed and nourished, instead of pining away, and dragging out a pale and sickly existence, it 'flourishes like the palm-tree, and grows like the cedar in Lebanon'; advances in holiness and is comforted in hope, till it 'reaches the stature of the perfect man in Christ Jesus'.

In estimating the power of the pulpit, therefore, we give the first place to the truth of which it is the vehicle. Depraved as men are, they are controlled by moral causes, rather than by those that are physical; and nowhere are these moral causes so concentrated, nowhere have they so ready access to the human mind, and from no other source do they flow out in so many thousand channels, sometimes in streamlets that cherish the solitary and drooping plant, and sometimes in rivers that overflow the plain, as from this mountain of the Lord's house.

But *what is truth*? Let a thinking man, after a day of wearied and anxious toil, throw himself upon his pillow, and ask this question; and he may indulge in almost endless reverie. He will look up to the heavens, and as he watches the stars, and sees the moon walking in her brightness, he will almost involuntarily exclaim, *There* is truth. He reads lessons there which he can understand. He will look over the earth, scan its mountains and valleys, and measure its streams; he will survey the blue ocean, where, at the presence of God, the 'deep utters his voice, and lifts up his hands on high'; and he will say, *There* too is truth, thrilling truth, uttered by the voice of him who 'laid the beams of his chambers upon the mighty waters, and walks upon the wings of the wind'. He will inspect the dominion of an all-governing Providence, and there he will see in legible and dark characters the notices which the righteous Arbiter has imprinted of himself. He will think of the rise and fall of empires, of earthquakes, pestilence, famine, war, and death – relentless death. And he will say, *that* is truth – terrible truth! It were no marvel, if his heart should sicken at such a view. His mind is enveloped in a shroud; it is wrapt in a pall of darkness. Truth here is denuded of her loveliness; it is gloomy, horrible truth. Yet is it *truth* – indisputable truth! There is no scepticism here. Men cannot dispute about such truths as these. They see them; they know them; they feel them. And this is just where the Bible places man, untaught and unillumined by brighter lights than these. He is in darkness. These truths are terrible, because they have the reality, the permanence, the majesty of truth; it is this which gives them all their force. They are truths so obvious that men do not oppose them. The deist and the infidel believe them. They constitute the basis of their religion; dark as they are, they are truths they cling to, and defend, though at the expense of undermining another and more complete superstructure.

Amid such reflections, it were no marvel if the thought should occur to the wakeful mind of the inquirer, that there must be another manifestation of the truth, in order to relieve the mind – to relieve the *world* from this dreadful pressure. Then perhaps he will think of the Lord God walking in the garden in the cool of the day, and of that early and impregnated promise; and he will feel the burden lightened, and will exclaim with joy, *That* too is truth. Then he will think of Moses receiving the law from God in the mount, amid the thunderings, and the lightnings, and the voice of words; and then another law, both combined in one, through which this newly manifested truth receives the sanction and the seal of that everlasting covenant, which is ordered in all things, and sure. Here in this early age of the world, that truth began its course, which glimmered in types and shadows and sacrifices, all pointing to the Lamb of God. He finds these prefigurations perpetuated from age to age, illustrated by predictions, of which Christ is the object; fortified by promises of which Christ is the fulfilment; all and every one of them recognizing Christ as the medium of access to the injured Deity, the channel of all his grace and mercy, having himself obtained them, merited them, and, through the efficacy of his obedience unto death, become the dispenser of them to fallen man. Here his restive mind finds repose. He has found *the truth* – the 'truth as it is in Jesus.' Life and immortality are brought to light in the Gospel; and he presses to his bosom that wondrous system of truth which is the light and the life of men.

Yet, strange to say, though this is the only truth which sheds light on the path of man, it is that which must needs be enforced by all the power of argument and persuasion. Obscure truths interest men. Nature's light, which tells them of the grave, and reason's flickering lamp, they will follow, even though it goes out at the tomb, and conducts them to a dark eternity. It is not with darkness, death, and despair that they have any contest. 'They have *loved* darkness'. It is light that they quarrel with – with life, with hope, with immortality, and eternal glory.

Yet is this the truth which gives the pulpit all its power. Its facts, its doctrines, its duties, its scrutiny, its rebukes, its invitations, its threatenings, its promises, its consolations, its motives, its worship, its ordinances, and more than all, its ATONING SAVIOUR, himself the beginning and the end, the first and the last – this is the truth which constitutes the power of the pulpit. 'I have determined to know nothing among you', says the great Apostle of the Gentiles, 'save *Jesus Christ, and him crucified*'. The pulpit is powerless where the cross of Christ is not magnified. Christ must be the theme, the scope, the life, the soul of the pulpit. It may have the subtleties of philosophy, the attainments of accomplished literature, and the enticing words which man's 'wisdom teacheth'; but it has no powerful attraction of God's truth, where Christ is wanting. The preacher may not hope to see the strong cords of earth broken, the fetters of gold dissolved, or any of the fascinations of sin disturbed by which the spell-bound mind is held in bondage, until he throws around it the stronger attractions of redeeming love. There is wondrous power in the pulpit where the cross is lifted up, and where, instead of attracting men to himself, the minister of God would fain attract them to his and their Saviour. What savours not of the cross of Christ, belongs not to the work of a Christian minister. A sinner, saved by grace, who is a preacher of glad tidings to his fellow-men, will keep as near the cross as he can. He may sometimes make a larger circuit around it than at other times because it unfolds 'the depth of the riches both of the wisdom and the knowledge of God'; but his favourite themes are drawn from it, and the arrows he makes the most use of are dipped in its blood. 'Christ is my armoury', says that lovely preacher, McCheyne, 'I go to him for the whole armour of God – the armour of *light*. My sword and my buckler, my sling and my stone are all laid up in Jesus'. In no other way can the dark, depraved, obdurate mind be brought under the enlightening, convincing, converting, sustaining, purifying influence of God's truth.

Such truth has power. It is 'mighty through God'. It is truth in all its forms, offices, and urgency. It is truth demonstrated, illustrated, embellished, and enforced. It is rousing, convincing, transforming truth. It is truth pleading with the obdurate, encouraging the discouraged and desponding, comforting sorrow, and giving exultation and triumph to hope. It is truth rebuking, truth weeping, truth rejoicing. It is truth in full-robed loveliness and glory, shining on the darkness of time, and discovering the strong and steady light of eternity, lifting the veil from the habitations of the second death – travelling on towards glory, honour, immortality and eternal life.

Such truth has power, and it is the power the pulpit aims at. It asks not any other triumphs, it seeks the glory of no other empire. It craves the privilege of carrying the light of heaven to this dark and dungeon earth, and of lighting up the beacon of hope in this world of despair. Give it this, and all other influences combined do not accomplish a tithe of that which is accomplished by this simple instrumentality. Other influences are as widely different from this as the words of men from the words of God, and as the powers of earth from the powers of heaven. There is nothing like it in this low world.

Beautiful, unutterably beautiful, are these achievements of truth. What wonders has it wrought? Greater are its victories than were ever won on the field of battle; its laurels greener than ever Cæsar wore. God hath given his truth a tongue; it may be the tongue of the learned, or the tongue of artless, but effective expostulation; but it is expostulation which every heart feels that is not like a rock of granite. Nay, adamant as it is, God's truth is the 'fire and the hammer that breaketh the rock in pieces'. It is the 'rod of *God's strength*' which he sent out of Zion. It is the 'sword of the Spirit' which the Mighty Conqueror girds on when he rides forth to his most brilliant victories; it is the inscription on his banner, when he returns from the field of triumph.

7: *The Living Teacher*

While the truth of which the pulpit is the vehicle, is in the order of time and nature, the first great element of its power, it is not truth presented in every form. Among the constituent elements of its usefulness must undoubtedly be reckoned the fact, that the *selected method by which it communicates God's truth is the living teacher.*

The earliest communications to men were not made by written documents, nor by the press. Our first parents were not, as some have supposed, the rude children of nature, nor were they untaught. It was the paternal *voice* of God that fell with such impressiveness upon their listening and obedient ear, before their apostasy. It was also through this channel that the subtle Deceiver conveyed his poison; the snare was laid by whispering his word of promise to the *ear*.

For the first twenty-five hundred years after the creation, all the revelations from heaven, with the few exceptions of supernatural dreams, visions, and reveries, were conveyed, either from the lips of God himself, or from angelic, or human voices. Very often the angels of God were sent from heaven to hold converse with worms; and face to face, to utter to men the messages of divine instruction, rebuke, and mercy. During the long period between Adam and Moses, these divine communications were made in no other way. We have no authentic proof of the introduction of alphabetical writing prior to the giving of the Law on Mount Sinai, or even prior to the date of the Pentateuch. To make a permanent revelation of God's will to men, it was necessary that it should be in *writing*; so that it might remain as the exhaustless depository, and unchanging standard of truth, unmingled with the fictions of men, uncorrupted by fable, and independent of the uncertainties of tradition. But the instructions that were designed for *immediate effect* were communicated in a way better fitted to arrest the attention, and less liable to perversion and abuse.

We find so many representations of this sort in the Scriptures, that it is almost superfluous to refer to them. 'God *spake* to Jacob at Bethel.' 'God *spake* all these words, saying, I am the Lord.' 'The Lord our God *spake* unto us in Horeb.' He *spake* to Abraham; he *spake* in the bush to Moses; he *spake* to the Prophets, and through them he spake to his people. I do not know that we find the phraseology anywhere in the Scriptures, that he *wrote* to his ancient people, that all Israel might *read*; but we do find the phraseology, that he *spake* to them, and commanded others to *speak* to them, 'so that all Israel might *hear*'.

When Moses expressed his reluctance to appear before Pharaoh, it was because he was conscious that he 'was slow of speech and of a slow tongue'. He had every other qualification and attainment which Egyptian and divine learning could give; but he had not the faculty of uttering in an impressive manner what he knew. When God directed him to associate Aaron in this embassy, the reason he gave for this arrangement was the qualifications of Aaron as a public speaker – 'for I know that *he* can SPEAK WELL'. It would seem, that in the judgment of Infinite Wisdom, truth must be *spoken*, and *well spoken*, in order to have its proper effect.

That they might make a deeper impression still, not unfrequently these divine communications were reduced to rhythm, and *sung*; as in the Song of Moses at the Red Sea, and the Song of Deborah, and the Psalms of David. The truths contained in these divine songs were not only spoken *to* the people; the people were required to utter and *rehearse* them in *sacred song*; that they might understand and remember them; peradventure, the sweet sounds that conveyed them to their ears, might find a lingering echo in their hearts. Sacred music is the highest style of sacred eloquence. 'Singing and making melody in our hearts unto the Lord'; to 'sing with the spirit and with the *understanding* also', is one of the most effective measures of making a deep and permanent impression of divine truth upon the mind. Some of the most successful preachers of the Gospel have made abundant use of this method of religious instruction; and in more than one printed narrative of revivals of religion in this land, this method of teaching has been specified as one of the honoured means of grace and salvation. And who has not read of it in the usages of those noble and slandered men, the Scottish Covenanters, and the Puritans of England, in the days of Cromwell? Not a few

Christians will be found who are in the habit of adding this method of instruction to their private devotions, and who have found in it no ordinary means of spiritual advancement.

The sacred writers concede high pre-eminence to the *tongue* of man; it is his glory and his disgrace; the best member of his frame, when devoted to purposes that are good; when devoted to evil purposes, it is the worst. It blesses and it blasphemes; it diffuses a healthy and heavenly influence, or it is like a firebrand, scorching and burning as though it were ignited at the flames that never shall be quenched. 'By thy *words* thou shalt be justified', says the Saviour, 'and by thy *words* thou shalt be condemned'. 'If any man offend not in *word*', says James, 'the same is a perfect man'. The tongue exerts the great controlling influence in the world. It turns about, and governs the mass of minds on which it acts, just as the horse obeys the bit, or the ship the helm. There is a peculiarity in the sins of the tongue which the Bible stigmatizes above all other sins. There are instances in which men may lawfully deceive by their silence, or by actions which they mean should be misconstrued. To *act* such a deception, is a different thing from *uttering* it; the action *may* be right and just, the uttered falsehood nothing can justify. The tendency of the principle that falsehood is justifiable, would be ruinous; the mere act *utters* nothing; it is dubious in its import, and *may* be as innocent as a man's taking a different path from that which he seemed to take, for the purpose of avoiding his pursuer. The enormity of the unpardonable sin consists in the fact that it is an *uttered* sin. It may exist in the heart, or it may be uttered in the retirement of the closet, and may be repented of and forgiven; but if uttered in the ears of men, it has aggravations which put the perpetrator beyond repentance, and therefore beyond pardon. And the reason for the discrimination is, the all-controlling influence of the tongue.

These remarks may not be hastily deemed a digression from our main object; they are designed to show that the best way of addressing divine truth to the mind is not so much through the *eye* as through the *ear*. It is not by lofty domes, nor gorgeous priestly apparel, nor splendid paintings, and sculptured images; these mislead the mind, and form rather the religion of the imagination than the religion of the understanding and the heart. There is no small amount of such religion in the world. We would not wage indiscriminate warfare with the religion of the imagination; it is the province of true religion to elevate and sanctify all the faculties of the soul; but we need not be taught that the religion in which the imagination predominates is a very imperfect religion, nor that the religion of which the imagination constitutes the sum and substance is spurious and false. It displaces the religion of the heart; it is sentimentalism, and not piety: it originates in false principles; it expends itself in outward parade and solemnity; it exhausts itself in forms. It is the religion of art and architecture, of walls and altars; of silver shrines and golden gods; of unmeaning ceremonies and phantasms, which distract thought, and unfit the mind for the worship of him who is a Spirit, and must be worshipped in spirit and in truth.

The Church of Rome places her great reliance upon this sort of teaching, and her religion is in keeping with her policy. The great desire of her worshippers is to be pleased; and the secret of her success is that she pleases them. Instructive and humbling truths are things she little thinks of; she speaks to the eye, she fascinates the senses, and if there be some truths inwoven in her system, they are neutralized by the manner in which they are presented, and evaporate with the fragrance of her incense. Unhappily, there is a strong tendency in the age in which we live, to this sort of religion, even in some Protestant churches. Preaching the truth of God is a very small matter with them; beyond the circle of Apostolical Succession, and the participation of divine ordinances at the hands of their own priesthood, as the indispensable condition of salvation, there are few subjects on which they are well informed. Some among them indeed there are, not 'of the straitest sect', who are faithful preachers of Christ and him crucified; who at the same time, on these controverted topics know more than they preach, and have not the persecutors's excuse, 'I did it ignorantly and in unbelief'.

We have adverted to the teachings of the Old Testament on the subjects of oral, religious instruction; let us briefly advert to the teaching of the New. Timothy was exhorted by Paul, 'to give attendance to *reading*'; but it was that he might become an able *preacher*. There are passages in the New Testament which speak of the importance of *reading* God's truth. The Saviour *read* the Scriptures in the Synagogue of Nazareth; he demanded of the inquiring Lawyer, 'What is written in the Law; how *readest* thou?' Paul's epistles were written to be read; he charges the Thessalonians, that his epistle to them 'be *read* by all the holy brethren'; and he gives the like charge to the Colossians, that his epistle to them be *read* in the church of the Laodiceans'; and that the Colossians 'likewise read the epistle from Laodicea'. The revelation which the angel made to John is prefaced by the declaration, 'Blessed is he that *readeth* and understandeth the words of this prophecy'. Yet does the whole scope of their instructions show, that it is not so much through the printed page, as a *preached* Gospel, that men are converted to God. 'As ye go, *preach*.' 'Go, *preach* my Gospel.' God hath sent me to *preach* the Gospel. 'To me, who am less than the least of all saints, is this grace given, that I should *preach* the unsearchable riches of Christ.' It is the great law of God's kingdom, that 'it pleased God by the foolishness of PREACHING to save them that believe'. There it stands too, inscribed on the foundations of Zion. 'So then faith cometh by *hearing*' – not by seeing, nor by reading, but by *hearing*. 'He that hath ears to *hear*, let him hear what the Spirit saith to the churches.' The parable of the Sower teaches this same fact; and hence, at the close of that parable, the Saviour deduces from it this great practical inference, 'Take heed, therefore, how ye *hear*!' Paul declares to Timothy, that God 'hath in due time manifested his word through *preaching*'. The instrumentality in the salvation of men which they emphasize, is 'the *hearing* of faith'.

The fact is too obvious from observation and experience, that 'the Spirit of God maketh the reading, but especially the *preaching* of the word an effectual means of convincing and converting sinners, and of building them in holiness and comfort, through faith unto salvation'. Robert Hall, that wise observer of the operations of God's grace, in a 'Circular Letter on Hearing the Word', addressed to the ministers and churches of the Northamptonshire Association, among other excellent remarks, makes the observation, that 'there is every reason to suppose that the far greater part of those who have been truly sanctified and enlightened, will ascribe the change they have experienced, to the *hearing of faith*'. 'Religion', says Dr. Dwight, 'has been so co-extensive with preaching, that where preaching has not been, there has, with scarcely a solitary exception, been no religion: and wherever preaching has existed for any length of time, religion has almost invariably existed also.'

God's institutions are wise. 'With him is wisdom and strength; he hath counsel and understanding.' Nothing is more obvious than the wisdom of this divine arrangement; upon all the principles of our common nature, it is the best fitted for effect. Among its peculiar advantages, the following are worthy of consideration.

It reaches *the greatest numbers in the shortest time*. The Gospel is a message to the race; to millions it would be a dead letter, if it were not a *preached* Gospel. Constituted as men are, more minds are reached from the pulpit than in any other way. Men would not read it, if it were simply a printed Gospel, because it treats of subjects in which they feel little concern, and to which they are naturally hostile; and because the mass of men have not time for profitable reading. They will read a newspaper, because it tells them what they wish to know; but they will not read a religious discourse. But they will hear it; and they do hear a multitude of such discourses, which, if carried to their doors, and laid upon their tables, they would never read. Hundreds, and sometimes thousands, are virtually reading the same book, when thus listening to the instructions of a single living preacher. It is not often that so many persons read so good a book as they thus hear read, or spoken from the pulpit. Nor is it often that the same amount of instruction is communicated to them all in any other way; and never within the same compass of time, and with the same intellectual effort on the part of the instructed.

Such instructions, too, are more apt *to be understood* by the mass of mankind, than the same instructions when merely spread before the eye. The mass of men are not thinking men; such are their intellectual habits, that had they ever so much time, they are not reading men; their minds are not subjected to the patient discipline which renders reading pleasant and profitable. We honour the press; we know its vast importance to the world; but the men who profit from the religious press are not the mass of mankind, nor even the mass of those who hear the most instructive preaching. They are the reading and thinking men who profit by it; and the mass of mankind are profited only as the former class of men become their teachers. There is no reason to believe that one in ten of the excellent *religious tracts* that are so widely distributed, are ever read; though we may not doubt the wisdom, the Christian duty of distributing them; for if one in ten be read and understood, the seed so widely scattered cannot fail to yield a joyous harvest. There is more reason to doubt the wisdom of this distribution in heathen lands, and especially at so heavy an expenditure of funds as has been reported by the American Tract Society for several years last past. The same amount of funds expended in sending the *living ministry* – funds, and a ministry so earnestly demanded – would, I am persuaded, accomplish more extensively and more effectively the great objects of that noble institution.

It affords me not a little pleasure, since the writing the preceding paragraphs, and before these pages go to the press, to have ascertained from the indefatigable Secretary of the American Board of Commissioners for Foreign Missions, that this subject is now the matter of wakeful discussion by their Prudential Committee. It gives me the opportunity of adding thoughts, confirming my own impressions, which, in the original draught of the present chapter, I knew not were entertained by others.

In the 'Missionary Herald' for March, (1848), is a very interesting communication from the Rev. Mr. Pohlman, missionary at Amoy, in China, on the subject of which we are speaking. The vast population of China has generally been supposed to be a more *reading* people than that of any other Pagan land; and on this account quite as accessible to the efforts of the press, as to the instructions of the living teacher. On this subject Mr. Pohlman says, 'I rejoice that the Committee have laid down as a starting point, that the grand object for which the Board should sustain missions in China is the *oral* publication of the Gospel to the Chinese people.' The writer proceeds to substantiate this view, by several distinct considerations, clearly conceived, and ably illustrated, prefacing his illustrations with the important remark, that his 'statements and conclusions are the results of several years' labour at Amoy'. His positions are, that 'the number of intelligent readers, compared with the whole population, is very small'; that 'the mass of superstitions and traditions afloat among the people is a peculiarity calling for faithful preachers of the Gospel'; that 'the language of China is addressed more to the ear than to the eye'; that 'the inability of the Chinese fully to understand our books, presents a loud call for teachers to guide them'; that 'the social character of the people invites the labours of oral instructors'; that 'in the progress of civilization in China, a foundation is laid for the preacher'; that 'public preaching is not a novel thing to the Chinese'; and that 'the desire of many of the people to hear foreigners is another loud call for preaching missionaries'.

In confirmation of these thoughts, in a recent work professing to furnish a 'Survey of the Chinese Empire', entitled 'The Middle

Kingdom', by S. W. Williams it is stated, that notwithstanding the extensive distribution of the Scriptures, and of other religious books and tracts, by Liang Afah and Gutzlatf, and subsequently by Messrs. Medhurst, Stevens and Lay, and Messrs. Dickenson and Wolfe, scattering as they did fifty thousand volumes on the coast, and double that number about Canton and Macao, 'so far as is known not an instance has occurred of a Chinese coming to a Missionary to have any passage explained, nor any person converted who has attributed his interest in religion to the unassisted reading of these books'. These are all forcible considerations; and we will venture to ask, not only if they are not conclusive in regard to China, but in regard to every other heathen land?

I confess a smile passed over my countenance, when I read the communications just referred to, and I said within myself, These beloved men have been reading their Bibles. The truth is, human nature is the same thing all over the world. *All* language is addressed more to 'the ear than to the eye'. This is the meaning and definition of language. It is thought uttered by the tongue. It is *the* teaching of the world; if men are slow to believe and act upon this obvious truth, they will most certainly be taught by experience. It requires an intellect in no small degree cultivated, to read any work, beyond the simplest narrative, to advantage. One reason why works of a purely narrative character are read by so large a portion of readers, in preference to more grave and spirited discussions is, that the latter demand too much intellectual effort.

We are not so foolish and arrogant as to claim all the intelligence in the world for the ministers of the Gospel; while it is our firm conviction, that the great benefit which the *religious* press confers on the great masses of men, is by first instructing their religious teachers. Nor is it too much to say, that those among them who become profited readers of religious books, become so because they are first taught by the pulpit. There is very little religious reading where the mind is not awakened to it and prepared for it, by the instructions of the sanctuary.

Reading does men no good any farther than they *understand* it. It is recorded in the Old Testament, that the religious leaders of Israel 'read in the Book of the Law of God, *distinctly*, and *gave the sense*, and caused the people to *understand* the reading'. '*Understandest* thou what thou readest?' said Philip to the Eunuch of

Ethiopia. '*How can I*', replied he, 'unless some man should guide me?' Then Philip opened his mouth, 'and began at the same Scripture, and *preached* unto him Jesus'. Our blessed Lord, after having delivered in succession several of his most interesting and instructive parables, *explained* them to his disciples. It is delightful to mark his care and condescension in this particular, and this remarkable characteristic of his instructions. He took them aside by themselves, and when they were alone, not only made his explanations full and explicit, but after he had done so, asked them, *Do you understand*? They were solemn truths he had been uttering, and he desired that they should be understood. 'Jesus saith unto them, *Have ye understood* all these things?' They say unto him, '*Yea, Lord.*' Favoured disciples! blessed Teacher! This is the preacher's business. His trumpet may not give an uncertain sound; it must be distinct and determinate. If he is intelligent, he will be intelligible; if he is faithful, he not only may but must be understood.

We are persuaded also that the method of instructing men by a preached Gospel is the most *economical* arrangement. This is no unimportant consideration, however trifling the remark may seem. No such amount of religious instruction can be imparted with the same certainty, at so little cost. A rural pastor of a congregation consisting of a thousand souls, furnishes, at a moderate estimate, including the exercises of the Sabbath and the week, one hundred and fifty-six discourses a year; including other exercises, five hundred and sixty-eight. He virtually distributes a thousand tracts every sermon he preaches, and every prayer he offers. This is an aggregate of forty-six thousand and eight hundred tracts a year. And if his salary be a thousand dollars, at the average expense of one dollar a year, each individual is supplied with this number of tracts. Can human ingenuity devise a more economical arrangement for furnishing the world with religious instruction?

But what is of greater importance, the instructions of the living teacher are beyond measure *more impressive and affecting* than any other method of instruction. Men are the creatures, not of thought only, but of feeling; they have susceptibilities to emotion; they are susceptibilities which seek to be gratified, and which ought to be turned to good account. Nature demands the presence, the sympathy, the eye, the voice, the action, the expressive countenance of the living teacher. Thought, and shades and emphasis of thought, are thus expressed which must otherwise be concealed. It is thus that the parent influences his child, the teacher his pupil, and the men of the world one another. Men are interested in what the speaker says, by observing *how* he says it. His vividness of voice and gesture often tells even more than his words. They note his sincerity and earnestness; they observe the emotions by which his own bosom is agitated; and even though unconvinced, and unwon, they are not unmoved. The most powerful appeals ever made to the reason, the conscience, the interest, or the passions of men, are not made from the press, but from the warm heart and glowing lips of the living speaker. The Areopagus of Athens, the Senate House of Rome, the British Parliament, the French Chambers, the halls of the American Congress, and the Bar, furnish abundant tribute to the power of the living speaker over all other methods of instruction and influence. Mighty events have been suspended on the uttered words of men.

That terrible scene, the French Revolution, a page in history never to be blotted out, was produced more by the impassioned and inflammatory harangues of Mirabeau, Danton, Marat, and Robespierre, than even by the ferocious mob of Paris. 'Frenchmen', said Marat, borne on the shoulders of the rabble through the Rue St. Honore, 'there is a conspiracy on foot to murder the patriots of Paris. The troops of the provinces are coming, by order of the king, to put man, woman, and child, to the sword. The fête at Marseilles is given to the vanguard of the army, to pledge them to this terrible purpose. The governors of the provinces are all in this league of blood. The bakers of Paris have received an order from Versailles to put poison in all their loaves within the next twenty-four hours. Frenchmen, do you love your wives and children? Will you suffer them to die in agonies before your eyes? Wait, and you will have nothing to do but dig their graves. Advance, and you will have nothing to do but drive the tyrant, with his horde of priests and nobles, into the Seine. Pause, and you are massacred; arm, and you are invincible.' The livid villain was 'answered by shouts of vengeance'. Burning words like these formed the cascade, the torrent, that set in motion tht mighty revolutionary engine; they were the fires in those Jacobinical clubs that made the steam for that furious machinery.

So it has been elsewhere. Pym, Hampden, and Vane, in the

stormy days of the Commonwealth of England, gave impulse to the sword of Cromwell, Fairfax, and Ireton. And what was it that has given a single man, in our own times, such wondrous ascendancy over Ireland, that the populace moved at his bidding, but his power to 'agitate and agitate', by being thus brought into direct and personal communication with his countrymen in their public assemblies? It were a great oversight in us to overlook that noble exemplification of the power of oral above all other methods of influencing the minds of men which has just been furnished by an accomplished modern orator. Paris was all on fire; the mob had already the taste of blood, and was ripe for every form and degree of lawless vengeance. Nor was it until after six long hours of bold and impassioned appeal, that their infuriate madness could be arrested. But Leviathan was tamed; there was a charm in the eloquence of Lamartine that laid the angry populace at his feet.

This is a pre-eminence that may be occupied by good men, and in a good cause. It is occupied by the pulpit: mind is here brought into contact with mind, face with face, heart with heart. Whatever there is of riches, greatness and force in the truth of God, and whatever of power in human language, and of moving sympathy in the living preacher, urging that truth with all the clearness, and ardour, and enthusiasm he is enabled to bring to his great vocation, here have the best opportunity of forming the characters of men.

There is no more impressive illustration of the power of the living teacher, than that which results from a comparison of the printed and uttered discourses of the most powerful preachers. When you *read* the discourses of Whitefield, you can scarcely be persuaded that he was the prince of preachers; and that the author of those printed pages was the man who collected 20,000 hearers on the open field at Leeds; who fascinated all ranks of society; who held Hume in profound admiration; and who brought the infidel Chesterfield to his feet, with outstretched arms, to rescue the wanderer from the fold of God, whom the preacher represented in the act of falling over the precipice. You read his sermons, but the *preacher* is not there. That glance of his piercing eye that hushed thousands to silence in the open field, is not there. That voice, at a single intonation of which a whole audience has been known to burst into tears, is not there. That instant communication between the living speaker and his hearers, which creates so powerful a sympathy, is not there.

Some of the best discourses of the late Dr. Mason, the distinguished preacher of our own city, have been given to the world; but rich as they are in matter, and forcible in style, and though they exhibit not a few of the peculiarities of their great author, they make a feeble impression upon the mind of the *reader*, compared with that made upon the minds of those who listened to them from the pulpit. That celebrated and beautiful discourse entitled, 'The Value of the Gospel', from the text, 'To the poor the Gospel is preached', was preached in the city of New Haven, in the year 1808, in the presence of one of the largest, most intellectual, and Christian audiences ever assembled in this land. The sun had just risen, when torrents of *men* were seen pouring to the house of God. There were ministers of the Gospel, both the aged and the young. Learned Professors, reflecting Judges of the law, and Lawyers in their pride, were there. There were Senators and men of learning, from every part of the land. There sat the venerable Dwight, and the not less venerable Backus, melted into a *flood* of tears. That vast auditory, which seemed at first only to listen with interest, and then gaze with admiration, with few exceptions covered their faces and wept. Yet when you read the discourse, the charm is gone. There was a dignity, a majesty, and withal an attractive tenderness where the preacher stood, which are not found in the printed page. That memorable discourse of the late Dr. Dwight, entitled 'Life a Race,' as well as that so effectively pronounced, in more than one of our pulpits, by the late Dr. Griffin, on the 'Knowledge of God,' will both be long remembered as an honour to the American ministry; but who that *heard* them does not dwell rather on the memory of the past, and turn from the dead volume to the living preacher?

It depends on the *reader* whether the thoughts in the printed page have emphasis; in uttered discourses it depends on the speaker. An intimate friend of the late John Fletcher, remarks in a letter to Mr. Gilpin, that 'he would rather have *heard* one sermon from Mr. Fletcher, than *read* a volume of his works'. His words are clothed with power as we *read* them; but just conceive such a man as Fletcher uttering, as he did, such burning, melting thoughts as the following: 'See, pardon for lost sinners is written with pointed steel, and streaming blood. His open arms invite, draw, welcome

The Living Teacher

the returning prodigal. Fly then, miserable sinner, if thy flesh is not brass, and thou canst not dwell with everlasting burnings, fly for shelter to the bloody cross of Jesus!' Such emotions have no counterpart in types and paper.

We have already remarked that the Christian ministry enjoys the *opportunity* of exerting this influence beyond any other class of public speakers. They enjoy it on the Lord's Day, and more usually once at least during the week. More than one hundred and fifty times a year, they ordinarily come before the great congregation, with the messages of God's eternal truth. The privilege is theirs *without interruption*, no man forbidding them, and none contradicting, or opposing them. The entire field of discussion and expostulation and appeal is, by law and courtesy, their own. Wonderful power is this over the minds of men! Give it to the demagogue, and what more would he ask? The late Aaron Burr, at the close of the last religious service of the American troops, as they were just about embarking for Quebec, under Arnold, said to the chaplain of the detachment, a man of no mean powers, 'Sir, you gentlemen of the black cloth have greater opportunities of influencing the minds of men, than the gentlemen of any other profession.' Nor was the remark extravagant. Multiply the missionaries of evil as the Christian pulpits are multiplied, and what more would the Spirit of Evil desire?

Nor is this all. The Christian ministry addresses men under all those *adventitious circumstances* that are fitted to give them influence. It is the Day of God and his sanctuary that convokes them, and those who hear them; the day when men rest from the care and toil of earth; the house of prayer, none other than the gate of heaven, which they go to knock at. Multitudes are there, and unearthly influences are around them. The God of heaven and the King of the universe is there, and it is from his oracles that they hear and learn the way of life. They are his altars on which the sacrifice is offered, and it is consecrated by the voice of prayer and praise. There may be no pomp and magnificence in the worship; there may be no massive architecture, no decorated walls and altars, no deep-toned organ and enchanting choir, no ceremony to strike the senses and exalt the imagination, and nothing more than the simplest worship offered to Him who 'dwelleth not in temples made with hands'. But there is impressive and imposing solemnity. There is the worship of the heart offered to One who is himself 'a Spirit, and must be worshipped in spirit and in truth'.

Nor may the thought be depreciated, that the scene is one, where everything which the preacher utters is enforced by all the sympathies of social life; sympathies that are never purer, and never more hallowed and delightful, than in the house of God. They are the families of God's people that are there assembled, adorned in the beauties of holiness, attracted to the sanctuary by all that is affectionate in the love of parents to their children, and all that is beautiful in the honour paid by children to their parents.

And where, if not amid such scenes, and listening to such truths, can the mind of man ever hope to exert an influence over other minds? Ought not such a ministry to be clothed with power? What cause has such a hearing as that of the Christian pulpit?

8: *The Divine Authority of the Christian Ministry*

The truth of God has power, be it uttered by whom it may. It possesses the authority *of truth*; and ought, even though uttered by the meanest lips, to control the understanding, the conscience, the heart, and the life.

But there is superadded to the power of truth, as thus uttered, a circumstance of some importance, which constitutes one of the elements of that influence which is exerted by the Christian pulpit. *The truth it communicates is uttered in God's name, and by God's authority.*

There is a sense in which *every man* is authorized to utter the truth of God, and to urge home its obligations on the consciences of his fellows. There is no law of nature, of rectitude, or of God, that locks his lips in silence. The mere fact that he is acquainted with truths that are essential to the salvation of his fellow-men, with which they are unacquainted, lays him under obligations to make them known, and to impress and enforce them. Truth herself authorizes him to utter them; she says to every one of her disciples, imbued with her principles, and filled with her spirit, 'Go and proclaim them; make them known to those who are shrouded in darkness; make them understood by the ignorant, and felt by the thoughtless, and do whatever in you lies to reclaim and save those who are wandering in the perverse and crooked ways of sin and death. Be blameless and harmless, the sons of God without rebuke, in the midst of a crooked and perverse nation, among whom ye shine as lights in the world; *holding forth the word of life.*'

Truth is personified in the Scriptures as everywhere announcing her own claims; she does this by the lips and lives of her disciples. 'Doth not wisdom cry, and understanding put forth her voice? She standeth in the top of high places, by the way in the places of the paths. She crieth at the gates, at the entry of the city, at the coming in at the doors. Unto you, O men, I call, and my voice is to the sons of men!' The last message of the Saviour's love ever given to this lost world, is contained in those precious words, 'And the Spirit and the *Bride* say, Come; and let *him that heareth* say, Come; and whosoever will, let him take the water of life freely!' The gracious invitation should sound forth from every tongue, and through every land.

The church of God ought everywhere to invite men to Jesus; the voice of all her members ought everywhere to unite with the voice of his Spirit, in presenting the invitations of his mercy to a lost world. The personal obligations of every believer, to assist in spreading the truth, can hardly be called in question. The field is large, and there is abundant room for the combined efforts of all the friends of the Redeemer in this blessed work. 'Come and hear, all ye that fear God', says the Psalmist, 'and I will tell what the Lord hath done for my soul.'

The agency of judicious and private Christians has ever been appreciated during those seasons when God, in a remarkable manner, has poured out his Spirit; it is required, it is absolutely necessary. Ministers cannot perform all the work; a multitude of minds must be moving in concert with theirs, and a multitude of hands employed. No man may refuse to speak a word for Christ, because he is not an ordained minister of the Gospel; nor fold up his talent in a napkin, and bury it in the earth because it is but *one* talent. 'The manifestation of the Spirit is given to *every man* to profit withal.' He may not have the gift of prophecy, and be called to the sacred ministry; but if there be given to him 'the word of wisdom' and the 'word of knowledge', it is that he may be *profitable* to others and employ the gift for the salvation of men.

But while these are truths that ought neither to be forgotten nor abused, it is equally true, that no private Christian is authorized to utter the truths of the Gospel *in God's name, and as his commissioned ambassador*. He may, and ought to speak for God, in his private capacity; but not as a minister of the Gospel. When two nations are at war, the private citizens of both, who are resident in the land of the enemy, may, in their *private capacity*, urge the claims of their own land; while as *commissioned ambassadors*, they have no authority, and in that capacity have no claim to be heard. This world is at war with God: every friend of God in this revolted empire of his dominion, is bound to act the part of a friend, and in his capacity as a private citizen of the divine kingdom, to urge men to cease from their rebellion, and become reconciled to their injured and offended Lord; but he has no instructions to do this as God's special ambassador.

The legitimate occupants of the pulpit claim this as their prerogative; they are appointed by God himself to this responsible service. God has invested them with this high office; and they have ever claimed and exercised it in every age of the world. When Moses and Aaron appeared in the presence of Pharaoh, they carried with them the credentials that they were commissioned by him, and spake by his authority, and in his name. When Samuel, one of the most eminent of the Jewish prophets, appeared before Saul and the people of Israel, it was a question of great moment that it should be known and confessed that he was God's special messenger. Hence we have this record concerning him: 'And Samuel grew, and the Lord was with him, and did let none of his words fall to the ground; and all Israel, from Dan to Beersheba, *knew* that Samuel was *established* to be a prophet of the Lord'. When Nathan appeared in the presence of David, when Elijah went before Ahab, when later Prophets presented themselves before the kings and people of Israel and Judah, it was not without the evidence of their divine appointment.

False prophets there were, of whom it is written, that 'they ran, but God did not send them'; they were dishonoured in the eyes of the people; God poured contempt upon them, and 'cast dung upon their faces'. From the calling of Enoch to the present hour, with one exception, there never has been a period during which divinely commissioned teachers of religion were not found among men. The exception is that sombre age of four hundred years, between Malachi, the last of the Jewish prophets, and John the Baptist. Priests there were; authorized and commissioned prophets there were none. Sacred writings there were; but the voice of the living prophet, sent by the God of Israel to his apostate people in their calamity, was silent. The last sentence from heaven which that degenerate people listened to, was the memorable declaration of the last of their prophets, 'Behold I will send you Elijah the prophet before the coming of the great and dreadful day of the Lord; and he shall turn the heart of the fathers to the children, and the heart of the children to their fathers, lest I come and smite the earth with a curse'.

John the Baptist and the seventy, received their commission from a divine source. When the Saviour sent forth the twelve

Apostles, they went by his special appointment, and in his name; they had his promise that he would be with them, as well as the additional evidence of their commission which was furnished by their possession of miraculous powers.

In perfect accordance with this brief statement is the general language of the Scriptures in relation to the authority by which these divinely commissioned teachers were invested. 'Thou shalt hear the word at my mouth, and warn them *from me.*' I warn them by you: it is as though I spake to them, when you speak in my name. 'Go, preach the preaching that *I bid thee.*' 'As my Father hath sent me, *even so send I you.*' 'We are *ambassadors* for Christ, as though *God* did beseech you *by us*, we pray you, in *Christ's stead*, be ye reconciled to God.'

The Christian ministry, in every age of the world since the ascension of its great Founder, possesses, virtually, the same commission. The institution and the perpetuity of this order of men is, of all others, the most important arrangement for the enlargement and perpetuity of the Christian church, and the salvation of men. By them the public worship of God is to be conducted, the ordinances of the Gospel dispensed, and the faith and order of God's house are to be preserved. It is not a *moral*, but a *positive* institution, growing out of the moral wants of our race; and its authority depends entirely upon the will of its great Founder.

After our triumphant Lord had risen from the dead, he came and spake to his disciples, saying, 'All power is given unto me in heaven and in earth. Go ye therefore and teach all nations, baptizing them in the name of the Father, and of the Son, and of the Holy Ghost: teaching them to observe all things whatsoever I have commanded you: and lo, I am with you alway, even unto the end of the world.' And then he added his own solemn and emphatic *Amen*. The office originates with him, who, after his resurrection, was invested with the mediatorial crown, and formally appointed to be 'Head over all things to the church'. This commission was originally given to the eleven Apostles upon a mountain in Galilee, where the Saviour had made an appointment for this special interview; nor is there any evidence that it was given to any others. The service for which it was designed was to make disciples of the Christian faith, to baptize them and to instruct them in all the doctrines, precepts, and institutions of the Gospel. The duration for which it was to continue is 'to the end of the world'. It must be so from the nature of the case, and in order to accomplish its object, which was, 'for the perfecting of the saints, for the work of the ministry, and for the edifying of the body of Christ'. This object could not be accomplished if the commission expired with the lives of the Apostles. The promise appended to the commission, also, was to have effect till the consummation of time; for if the ministry be not continued, there are no objects of the promise; it is a dead letter, and has not been fulfilled. The commission, therefore, is perpetual; the legitimate ministry of every age act under its authority, and have a right to the promise. Their appointment is not, indeed, by an audible voice from heaven; nor is it conferred by miraculous powers. But though the commission is but a recorded one, and the age of miracles is past, yet is the Christian ministry as truly of divine appointment as was that of the Seventy, or the eleven Apostles.

It is no part of our design, in these pages to discuss the vexed question of Apostolical, or Ministerial succession. Whether the Christian ministry receives its authority immediately from Jesus Christ himself, or in an unbroken series from their predecessors in office; whether a formal induction to it by the laying on of the hands of bishops, or presbyters, or the church, be essential to the office itself; or whether the external rite of transfer be a matter of order or of substance. These are questions on which there are, and will be different opinions. We dare not affirm that an uninterrupted line of succession is indispensable to the Christian ministry. The burden of proof lies upon those who affirm that it *is* indispensable. It is a heavy burden, perhaps too weighty for them or their fathers to bear; nor do we know that they have ever made out, that in no possible case can the Christian ministry be perpetuated in any other way. We are not converts to this doctrine, we confess; and for ourselves, as Presbyterians, we are not disturbed by it, if it is true. We scarcely know how this question is viewed by the 'straitest sect' of Prelatists. Sometimes, it seems to us they look upon it as one of the great problems of transcendental metaphysics; and then again it would appear that they regard it as one of those questions which are too plain to need discussion, and that exclusive prelacy belongs to that class of universal truths which it is impossible to consider as doubtful. The conviction of its truth is connate and instinctive; all that is necessary is to have boldness enough to own it. The grounds of the belief, it would seem, are of little consequence; the belief itself is the result of what a comparatively modern writer on Logic calls 'the unreasoning faculty'. To us it appears that the ministers of the Gospel are all of one order; that a division of their powers is inconsistent with the commission under which they hold their office; and that their powers are one and the same. We honour the office as one derived from heaven; nor are we prepared to regard those 'as polluted and put from the priesthood', who, while they hold to the doctrine of ministerial succession, are so utterly unable to produce the proof that the commission under which they themselves individually preach the Gospel is any thing better than a nullity. We are no exclusionists; we believe that the water of life retains its healing virtue, by whatever consecrated channel it is communicated. Exclusiveness has its pretensions, mutual forbearance its claims.

It is sufficient to our present purpose to assume, that the Christian ministry is a distinct order of men; and that every man who possesses the necessary qualifications, and is approved and set apart to the office by the expressed judgment of *the church*, acting either in her own capacity, or by her official representatives, be those representatives a presbytery, or an ecclesiastical council, or a single bishop, is a divinely commissioned minister of Christ.

Every denomination of Christians regards its *own ministry* as divinely commissioned. It looks upon them, and they look upon themselves, as 'called of God as was Aaron,' and sent in the name, and by the authority of the great Head of the church, to proclaim the truths, and enforce the obligations of the Gospel. This is the fact we here dwell upon; because it is one which cannot be affirmed of any other class of men. No public teachers in the world, save those who serve the church carry this divine commission.

Enthusiasts and fanatics there may be, who place themselves upon this eminence. Men of the 'fifth monarchy' did so in England, as also do some mad zealots in our own day. So have false prophets, and false apostles, and false christs in times that are gone by. Satan himself assumes the form of an angel of light. But the church is in little danger from such deceivers; they do not commend themselves to the consciences of men. Public teachers there are too, of great worth, who neither have nor claim any such authority. The statesman, the jurist, the popular lecturer, however important the truths they deliver, teach not in the name and by the authority of the Living God. Nor does every teacher of true religion. The parent does not, however wise, faithful, affectionate, and successful his instructions to his children. He has his warrant; it is divine; but it is simply and purely patriarchal. It is a different commission from that of the Christian ministry; it is not so extensive, but is limited to his own household, and does not include many duties that belong appropriately to the ministers of Christ. It is a commission of vast importance so far as it extends, nor has the Christian ministry any more important auxiliary than the religious influence of pious parents, and the religious instruction which they are authorized and required to give *officially* to their children. Yet the commission under which they act is not the ministerial commission. Nor does the ruling elder teach in God's name, and by God's authority. He is not a *teaching*, but a ruling elder. He rules in God's name, and by his authority; when he 'labours in word and doctrine', it is rather a service which is incidental to his office, an appendage to it, rather than an official act. He may often perform this service; there are exigencies in which it is necessary that he should conduct the religious exercises of the congregation; but it is a matter of fitness and propriety, rather than strictly a duty that belongs to his office. Nor does it belong to the deacons to be public religious teachers; they have an expressed commission from God for another and a different service. The doctrine of the Episcopal church on this subject is not the doctrine of the New Testament. No deacon, *as such*, has a right to preach and baptize; the moment this right is conferred upon him, he ceases to be a deacon, and becomes a teaching presbyter. It is not by virtue of his office as a preacher that he attends to the ministration of the poor; nor by virtue of the deacon's office that he gives himself to prayer and the ministry of the word. The same thing may be said with equal, if not greater emphasis, of every other class of men. The mere tract distributer is not a minister of the Gospel: he does not speak in the name, and by the authority of Christ. Nor does any private Christian, male or female, however laborious their teaching and their prayers, and however great the service they may render to the cause of Christ.

The ministers of the Gospel are the appointed ambassadors of the Head and King of the church; he sends them on their great and responsible errand, and they possess authority to publish his Gospel in his name, which belongs exclusively to themselves. It is not an authority which they usurp, nor an office which they themselves have sought, but one which has been imposed upon them. The responsibilities of it are of no enviable kind; they must give an account of their stewardship, and such an one as no other men must render. Nor are the disabilities and dependencies of the office to be envied. No honest, right-minded man was ever invested with it without much fear and trembling; nor is there one among them all who would ever have consented to this investiture but for the constraints of conscience. They have been *thrust* forth into the harvest. The office is upon them, nor may they disclaim either the responsibilities or the commission, without being recreant to their trust.

Now this is one of the strong peculiarities of the pulpit, and places it upon high vantage ground. Its legitimate occupants are divinely commissioned men. Inspired men they are not, but sinning and fallible, like their fellows; yet do they utter his truth, not on their own responsibility, but God's; not in their own names, but his; not for themselves, but for him; not as men merely, but as accredited ministers of their divine Lord who sent them. Their messages are not wise counsels merely, nor are they merely seasonable rebukes and encouragements, which men may regard at their option: they come clothed with obligations that are authoritative, and authority infinitely above that of those who utter them. Though they themselves are but men, sinning men, worms of the dust, they speak in God's name, and what God himself would utter were he in their place. It is not simply the authority of *truth* with which they speak; for then every man who utters truth would be invested with this authority: it is the authority of truth uttered by those whom God has raised up, and qualified, and sealed by solemn sacrament, and sent forth, and specially authorized to utter the things that are commanded them of him. This is one of the elements of power which belongs to the pulpit, and which gives it a prevalent and permanent superiority over every other method of religious instruction. Arrogant as this claim may be in the views of some, despised as it may be by others, and abused as it has been, is, and will be, by an ambitious and tyrannical priesthood – this pre-eminence God has given it.

God's arrangements are all wise. His wisdom, whether regarded absolutely and in itself, or relatively to us, challenges our highest homage. Its arrangements in the particular we are contemplating are enlightened and benevolent. It seems to be lowering the great subject, to say that it was an expression of the wisest policy to clothe his ministers with this authority; but I know not better how to express my admiration of this arrangement. Its legitimate influence upon the mind of the *preacher* must, in every view, be potent for good, and not for evil. Well may it humble him in the dust, to reflect that he stands before men as 'the legate of the skies'. He must be a most weak, as well as a most wicked man, whose heart is lifted up by such a thought as this. In every view, it is a most solemn thought, and in some views a most depressing one; and in contemplating it, it were no marvel if the preacher should exclaim, 'Who is sufficient for these things?' We may all well tremble at the thought of standing in God's name, and by his appointment proclaiming the truths of the everlasting Gospel. There is responsibility in uttering it, be the lips whose they may. How great the responsibility when uttered in God's name! O, how often does this thought rush upon the preacher's mind, as he treads his way to the house of God! How it awes him into reverence, moves him to fidelity and earnestness, and gives solemnity and tenderness even to his severest admonitions! How is it fitted to quench his thirst for fame, to call to mind that he speaks in His name who was despised and rejected of men – who was spit upon, scourged, and crucified! What has such a man to do with being a 'fashionable preacher', or with aiming to gratify the gay world? It is the Master who sent him whose approbation he seeks; the only testimonial that can satisfy him as a man of God, and a Christian minister, is from the lips of his divine Lord, 'Well done, good and faithful servant!'

There is one particular in which this thought has a most appropriate and powerful influence. Few personal qualities are more indispensable to a minister of the Gospel than a high degree of moral courage. His mind must be familiar with great things and preserve itself undaunted amidst opposition and danger. The fear 'of man bringeth a snare' and should find no place in the pulpit. And whence the victory over a pusillanimous mind, which embarrasses so many preachers, if not from the thought that they are God's servants? Moses trembled not before the haughty despot of Egypt, because he was the messenger of Israel's God. Elijah quailed not in the presence of the bloody Ahab, because God sent him. 'Fear not, Paul, thou must be brought before kings'; and he did not fear, because he stood before them in the name and by the authority of him who is the 'Prince of the kings of the earth', and the Lord of the universe. See him at Athens, at Jerusalem, at Caesarea, when philosophers cowered before him, and the proud Roman trembled: 'Whether it be right to hearken unto *you*, more than unto *God*, judge ye' – this was the bold appeal of God's commissioned servants in other days. No matter what the difficulty, or danger, that lies in his course, there is that in the bosom of every intrepid teacher of God's truth, that, whether he wake or sleep, is reiterating the thought, *God sends me, and I must go; God speaks by me, and I must speak.*

What but thoughts and sentiments like these, sustained John Huss and Jerome of Prague, in the presence of the perfidious Sigismund; and John Knox, in the presence of the almost adored Queen of Scotland? When entreated not to present himself at the Diet about to convene in the imperial city of Worms, in Germany, '*I must go*', says Luther, 'were there as many devils in Worms as there are tiles on the houses.' 'Nil desperandum, Christo duce'; – it is the order of his Master, and he had nothing to be afraid of. That distinguished American preacher, Samuel Davies, then the President of the College of New Jersey, when on a visit to England, in behalf of the College, was invited to preach before George III. His youthful queen was sitting by his side; and so enchanted were they by the preacher's eloquence, that the king expressed his admiration in no measured terms, and so audibly and rudely as to draw the attention of the audience, and interrupt the service. The preacher made a sudden and solemn pause in his discourse, looked around upon the audience, and fixing his piercing eye upon England's noisy monarch, said, 'When the lion roars, the beasts of the forest tremble; when Jehovah speaks, let the kings of the earth keep silence before him!' He was God's messenger; he feared not man, who is a worm. It is not God's ministers who tremble amid such scenes.

Shall I speak of the influence of this thought upon the *hearers*? Who has not felt it? The Apostle, writing to the Thessalonians, says 'For this cause also thank we God without ceasing, because, when ye received the word of God which ye heard of us, ye received it not as the word of men, but as it is in truth, the word of God.' Men would hear very differently if they were satisfied that ministers had no authority to preach. They need the thought that they are listening to instructions uttered by higher than any human authority, in order to give weight and emphasis to those instructions. When Cornelius and his fellow-worshippers were assembled in the presence of Peter, he addressed this apostle in the memorable and beautiful words, 'Now, therefore, are we all here present before God, *to hear all things that are commanded thee of God.*' The thought that God's messenger was coming to address them, brought them together: no one was absent; 'we are *all* here'. It made them sensible in whose *presence* they were; 'we are all here present *before God*'. It disposed them to *hear*; no matter what the message, or how unwelcome, they would hear it *all*; – 'all *things that are commanded thee of God*'. And it was because God had *commanded* him to speak in his name.

The thought is one which may well fill the hearers with awe, as well as their ministers. 'He that heareth *you*', saith the Saviour, 'heareth *me*, and he that despiseth *you*, despiseth me.' It is not ministers whom men honour, or dishonour, when they honour or dishonour their message; they dishonour him who sent them. They come to a guilty world, with their letters patent, their instructions signed and sealed from the Court of Heaven; and woe to the people or the man that accounts their message a little matter! Nothing can relieve them from the obligation of receiving them, and the truth which they utter. It was of one of his ancient ministers that God said, 'I will put my words in his mouth, and he shall speak all that I command him. And it shall come to pass, that whosoever will *not hearken* to my words, which he shall speak in *my name*, I WILL REQUIRE IT OF HIM.' When the Lord first commissioned the twelve disciples, he told them, 'Whosoever shall *not* receive you, nor hear your words, when ye depart out of that house or city, shake off the dust of your feet. Verily I say unto you, it shall be more tolerable for the land of Sodom and Gomorrah, in the day of judgment, than for that city.' It is a solemn truth, but one which the Bible utters, that the eternal happiness of men is suspended upon their receiving the Gospel thus preached in Christ's name. There is no one thing they are more bound to do than this. They may quarrel with God's ministers, and quarrel they may with God's truth, but this does not relax the bond. They may think little of the ministerial office; but this does not relieve them. Nothing is little which is of God's appointment. There is a reality in the ministerial commission; and though we claim for it no magical influence, and none of the authority of the civil power, yet is it one of those elements of influence and of strong moral power with which God himself has invested the ambassadors of his truth and grace. It stands upon a sure foundation, and the gates of hell shall not prevail against it. It cannot be a weak and insignificant agency. There is power in the pulpit, when girt round by such a rock as this.

9: *The Pulpit Associated with the Power of God*

The more immediate result to be secured by the instructions of the pulpit, is the reception of the truth it inculcates. The alienated mind and heart of man must be made to fall in with the truth of God, else is the word preached no better than seed cast upon the barren rock.

There is one fact in relation to the pulpit, which is of more importance than any one which we have hitherto suggested. It is that *the pulpit is associated with the mighty power of God in the conviction and conversion of men*. Let this fact be determined, and the pulpit is just as powerful as Omnipotence itself.

The different views which have been taken of the doctrine of divine influence are altogether dependent on the views which different persons have taken of the revealed doctrine of human depravity. The scriptural views of this latter doctrine, we conceive to be very plain. Man is far off from God by nature; he is very far gone from original righteousness. It is a fearful charge, but no less true than fearful, that 'the carnal mind is *enmity* against God'. 'That which is born of the flesh is flesh'; and this carnal mind, this whole nature of fallen man is corrupt; there is nothing either in his understanding, conscience, or affections that leads him to sincere and cordial subjection to the truth of God. He is not an ignorant man merely, he is a wicked man; he is not a mistaken and inadvertent rebel, he is a deliberate and obdurate one; he is not merely dead to holiness, but active to sin. He loves not the character of God; he cannot abide his government and law; his heart is desperately wicked, and he is restrained from the greatest excesses in wickedness only by those outward circumstances and those inward fears that are found in the preventing providence and grace of the Most High.

Nothing can subdue such a spirit but Omnipotent power. Every man in this fallen world is sure to fall out with the truth of God, unless there be superadded to the presentation of the truth itself, the omnipotent power of the Holy Spirit, causing him to receive it in love. The sacred Scriptures are full of this truth. It is taught by all those instructions in the Old Testament, which speak of 'circumcising the heart to love the Lord'; of 'creating a clean heart, and renewing a right spirit'; of 'taking away the heart of stone, and giving a heart of flesh'; of 'putting the fear of God in the heart, and writing his law upon it'; and of 'making his people willing in the day of his power'. And what is the import of those instructions in the New Testament, which speak of 'being born, not of blood, nor of the will of the flesh, nor of the will of man, but of God'; of 'God working in them to will and to do of his good pleasure'; of no man being able 'to come to Christ, except the Father draw him'; of the Spirit 'convincing of sin, of righteousness, and of judgment'; of his 'taking the things that are Christ's and showing them to men'; of his 'opening the heart to attend to the thing spoken'; his 'turning men from darkness to light, and from the power of Satan unto God'; his 'commanding the light to shine out of darkness, and shining in the heart to give the light of the knowledge of God's glory in the face of Jesus Christ'; of his rescuing 'from the power of darkness, and translating into the kingdom of God's dear Son'; and of his quickening those who are dead in trespasses and sins'? There can be no doubt as to the import of such declarations as these.

Nor can there be any doubt that the Word of God teaches with equal explicitness, that while his Spirit is the cause, his truth is the instrument of this great moral transformation. It is the truth which affects us, but it is the Spirit of God which causes us to receive the truth. God does not operate less really, or less effectually, because he operates instrumentally. He is the cause, the omnipotent cause, whether he condescends to make use of the most brilliant, or the meanest preacher. The pulpit is the great instrumentality in this work of mercy, but it is no more. 'Paul may plant, and Apollos may water, but it is God that giveth the increase.'

The dependence of men on the efficient power of the Holy Spirit is one of the great peculiarities of the Christian faith. And, like all its great peculiarities, it is as precious as it is peculiar. To none is it more precious than the pulpit; it is not its auxiliary, but its life-giving power. When we preach that the foundation of the spiritual edifice is laid deep, and its corner-stone cemented with the blood of the Lamb, we fix our hopes on the Spirit of God as the Almighty

The Pulpit Associated with the Power of God

Architect who is to rear and beautify the living temple. We cut the sinews of the Christian ministry when we depreciate the work of the Holy Spirit. Better, so far as the spiritual interests of men are concerned, demolish our sanctuaries than exclude from them this heavenly Guest.

We feel our dependence upon God for meaner things than the conversion of the soul. 'Except the Lord build the house, they labour in vain that build it.' The meanest seed does not vegetate without his power; the lily grows and is arrayed in all its gorgeous beauty by his unseen, but omnipotent hand. The achievements of science, the triumphs of liberty, the wealth and powers of man, are all his gift. Why his presence and power should be excluded from other scenes, and why men should be eager to throw it into retirement in that greatest of all his works, the perfected redemption of the human soul, it is difficult to tell. There is a point where every other work of God terminates and dies; this is onward, for ever onward, and because it is God's work.

No created thing is greater than the power of the human mind; it is power which Omnipotence only can control. The arguments of the pulpit may convince it; the eloquence of the pulpit may move it; but neither argument nor persuasion can effect the great moral transformation which it needs. It cannot break one chain of its fearful vassalage. It can scarcely arrest the ravages of the malady which curses it, much less reach the sources of the disease and cure the plague within. There is not even any great display of human instrumentality in the work. They are the weak contending with the strong; the instrument is like the saw and the hammer, effective only by extraneous power. The 'strong man armed' is to be overcome, and is vanquished only by One who is 'stronger than he'. Human instrumentality is never so effective in this work as when it is most conscious of its own weakness and keeps itself most out of sight. It is the secret agency of God that accomplishes it; and no flesh may glory in his presence. 'It is not of him that willeth, nor of him that runneth, but of God that showeth mercy.' His power shines and triumphs. It is an influence from above, designed to prostrate the creature in the dust, and give everlasting glory to him who died. 'He shall glorify me; for he shall take of mine, and show it unto you.' If there is any thing in which man is nothing, and God is all, it is in the great work of quickening those who are dead in trespasses and sins.

Nothing is more plain than that this is God's method of saving the souls of men. To lose sight of it is either to sink in dejection, or be puffed with pride and fall into the snare of the devil. 'He giveth grace to the humble; the proud he knoweth afar off.'

We have not been without fears for the pulpit within a few years past, because, in some quarters of the land, there is so much loose teaching on the subject of which we are speaking. One teaches that the Spirit of God does as much for one man as another; another affirms, that the holiness which is caused by Omnipotent power cannot be holiness because it is thus caused; and a third more boldly declares with Pelagius, that 'for us to be men is of God, but that for us to be righteous is of ourselves'. We look upon all such teaching as a death-blow to the power of the pulpit. If it ended in mere theory, and were a question which concerns different systems of intellectual philosophy only, we would not open our lips. But these are matters which strike at the highest interests of holiness. It is not a little to be wondered at that men are not afraid thus to tamper with a truth on which all the success of the Christian ministry depends, lest they should grieve the Spirit from the churches, and be left to mourn over their own folly, though too late to repair the evil they have done. If there be any hope for the anxious heart of a minister of the Gospel, this dependence on the power of the Holy Spirit is the rock on which he rests. And never is that dependence more deeply felt than when the Spirit is most freely imparted.

The work of Christ in the matter of the sinner's justification is not more important than the work of his Spirit in his conversion and progressive fitness for heaven. I would no sooner take the crown from the head of God the Sanctifier than from the head of God the Redeemer. I would prove the true and proper divinity of the Sanctifier, just as I would the true and proper divinity of the Redeemer – by his *works*. A creature might as well commission the sun to rise, and appoint the place of his going down, as assume the prerogative of God's mighty Spirit in the work of man's salvation. Nor would I guard this prerogative the less cautiously, because it is recorded of this ever-blessed Spirit, that he 'shall not speak of himself'; he has left his *great work* in our world to *speak for him*, to be the asserter of his divine glories. I would guard it the more cautiously, too, because he has but just entered on his wonder-working career, and because his divine glory has been left so long in abeyance, and seen only in dim retirement compared with the bright splendour with which he will hereafter be encircled. The time is coming when this third Person in the adorable Trinity will more illustriously clothe himself with Deity, and his Godhead will shine forth in all the wonders of his power, and when the evidence of it will be carried home to the soul. As the church and the world behold more and more of his omnipotent influence, and as the mountains flow down at his presence, no longer will it be questioned that he is the gracious God, and that the fruits of his grace are proofs of his omnipotence.

We read in the Scriptures of 'the love of the Spirit'. We should be cautious lest we show ourselves ungrateful. One of the most affecting views of the thought we are attempting to illustrate is the wide, the infinite contrast it presents between the rigid and severe obduracy of the human heart and the unutterable love of the Heavenly Comforter. Where truth enlightens, convinces, urges, and is repelled, his work is eminently one of love and mercy. He bows the heavens, and comes down; yea, he dwells with men. Such love is more than human. It is not found on earth. It does not belong to men. Its dwelling is in heaven. Heaven is the residence of infinite love – love that stoops to dwell with men on the earth and to light up their hopes; love that smiles and throws such rich charms over this desponding world. 'Upon the land of my people shall come up thorns and briers; yea, upon all the houses of joy in the joyous city. The palaces shall be forsaken; the multitude of the city shall be left; the forts and towers shall be for dens for ever; a joy of wild asses, a pasture of flocks, *until the Spirit be poured from on high.*'

It may be thought, by some, that these remarks are not called for. We differ from those who form such conclusions, and think them in keeping with our theme. None need to feel them so deeply as the ministers of Christ. No matter how learned or simple the instructions of the pulpit may be; no matter how rich and varied, or how well adapted and spiritual; did it speak with the tongue of Paul, or of angels, it would be powerless without the superadded power of God. Depression and discouragement would everywhere attend it, could not the ministry, and the people, on their behalf, take hold of God's everlasting strength. I see not how any man could consent to occupy it, who calls in question this delightfully animating truth. Cast down, discouraged, depressed even to despair may those of us be who minister to the people of the Lord, if we despair not of help from creatures, and betake not ourselves to higher resources than an arm of flesh.

When the Prophet Ezekiel was set down in the valley of bones, 'very many and very dry', the God of Israel said to him, 'Son of man, can these *bones* live?' What answer could he give? 'O Lord God, *thou* knowest!'. There was no other answer. When God's ministers are sent to prophesy to men dead in sin, *they* do not know the results of their message. There is nothing in ministers themselves, nothing in the mere truth they utter, nothing in the present character of those they address, that furnishes a favourable solution of this great problem. God only knows, because he only sees the end from the beginning, and he only is able to quicken those who are dead in trespasses and sins. There is but this one source of light and hope: 'Prophesy unto the *wind*, prophesy, son of man, and say unto the wind, Thus saith the *Lord God*, Come from the four winds, O breath, and breathe upon these slain that they may live!' Now the death-like scene is altered; it is no longer the silent and motionless valley. There is a noise and a shaking; bone comes to his bone, flesh and sinews come up upon them; that field of death is transformed to an exceeding great multitude of living men, the strong pulsations of the warm heart are there, and there are the voices of praise.

So it is with every preacher of the Gospel, so far as it regards his perfect and absolute dependence upon the Spirit of God for the success of his ministrations. The treasures of truth are committed to him, 'earthen vessel' as he is, that 'the excellency of the power may be of God, and not of him'. Never, till the excellency of God's power is revealed, is the power of the pulpit known. Nor may we hope that God's mighty arm will be revealed, until this truth is known and felt. One reason why God's Spirit is so often withheld is that this great truth is lost sight of; or, if not lost sight of, is coldly recognized, and does but form a feature of that languid and dead orthodoxy, which, while it may govern the views, has very little to do with the heart. This is not the place which such a truth deserves; it must be thought of, and prized, and leaned upon, and prove itself the most delightful of all incitements to effort. Just as the sinner, in the last stages of conviction, is driven from every other refuge to the power and sovereignty of that immeasurable grace which he has so long quarrelled with, must the ministers of the Gospel, as well as those to whom they minister, after they have laboured in vain, and spent their strength for nought and in vain, lift their eyes beyond the everlasting hills, and say – 'My soul, wait thou ONLY upon God, for my expectation is from him!'

They would not so often labour in vain, were those happy seasons of more frequent recurrence when this truth is truly felt. Jehoshaphat was strong, even before the combined forces of Ammon, and Moab, and Mount Seir, when he 'stood in the house of the Lord before the new court, and said, O our God, wilt *thou* not judge them? for *we* have *no might* against this great company that cometh against us; neither *know we what to do*; but our eyes *are upon thee!*' The strength of the pulpit is in its own conscious weakness, and in God's almighty power. Ministers always feel strong when they have this reliance. 'Never', said Samuel Pearce, 'have I been more deeply taught my own nothingness; and never hath the power of God more evidently rested upon me.' And thousands of the living ministry, and tens of thousands among the dead, have responded to this delightful truth.

There is power in the pulpit when it is thus allied to the power of God. We can do everything through him, without whom we can do nothing. The pulpit asks but this; in this it is diligent in labour, resolute in trial, buoyant with hope, and strong in weakness. Study and research are no longer abortive, because the power of the Highest overshadows the retirement of the preacher. Sabbaths are no longer powerless, because the Lord of the Sabbath gives testimony to the word of his grace. The patient and untiring man of God no longer faints under difficulty and discouragement, nor sinks under a sense of his own responsibility and infirmities, because he staggers not at the promise, 'As the rain cometh down, and the snow from heaven, and returneth not thither, but watereth the earth, that it may give seed to the sower and bread to the eater; so shall my word be, that goeth forth out of my mouth; it shall not return void, but accomplish that which I please, and prosper in the thing whereto I send it.' Light dawns upon the preacher's path then. 'He goes out with joy, and is led forth with peace. The mountains and the hills break forth before him into singing, and all the trees of the field clap their hands.' The fir comes up instead of the thorn, and the myrtle in the place of the brier.

Such days there have been, and such days there will be, whenever the arm of the Eternal King is made bare, and Jesus, being by the right hand of God exalted, and having received of the Father the promise of the Holy Ghost, sheds forth his influence upon the sons of men. Ministers will then have more honourable thoughts of God, and the promise will be fulfilled – 'Them that honour me, I will honour.' The lofty shall be bowed down, and the lowly shall be lifted up, and the Lord alone exalted in that day. 'When the Lord doth build up Zion, he shall appear in his glory.' He that dwells between the cherubim shall shine forth in the glory of his holiness, in the glory of his justice, in the glory of his mercy, in the glory of his faithfulness, in the glory of all his great and glorious designs, and in nothing more than in the glory of his power. The Father shall be exalted, the Son shall be exalted, and the Spirit, little known hitherto among men, shall claim his honours by his mighty deeds. There are no scenes more beautiful this side the heavenly city, than these; scenes amid which the angels of God may well delight to linger, and from which they retire only to bear the tidings that the dead live, and the lost are found.

Such is the power of the pulpit, and such are the constituent elements of that power. They are the *truth* of which it is the vehicle; truth from the *living teacher*; truth uttered in *the name and by the authority of God*; truth *accompanied with his mighty power*. This is the great agency by which our lost race, in augmented numbers, is to be subdued to the faith of the Gospel. Other agencies there are, and will be; but they are all associated with a preached Gospel. They derive their influence from it, and to this selected instrumentality of heavenly wisdom is to be attributed their very being. By these four great elements of power, the pulpit is destined to govern the world, to the full extent to which it will be governed by the truth and grace that are revealed from heaven. Its influence will run parallel with the religious and moral advancement of the race. The gloomy speculations of infidelity will give way before it, and give place to a faith that generates immortal hopes. The mutual animosities of men will be lost in the tranquillity of their social joys, and lawless anarchy and iron-hearted depotism will be superseded by that rapid and general progress of human society that is based on good and wholesome laws, wisely administered by men who fear God and hate evil. Senates will yet listen to the voice of God's messengers and kings will respect their message. It will yet make kings nursing fathers, and queens nursing mothers to God's church. It will yet vanquish and annihilate armies, and beat their swords into ploughshares, and their spears into pruninghooks, so that the nations shall learn war no more. As the Lord liveth, and his only begotten Son sits on the right hand of the Majesty in the heavens, it shall yet pursue its conquests over ignorance, idolatry, error, and every species of immorality and crime, till the 'skies drop down from above, and the earth opens and brings forth salvation'; till there shall be 'new heavens and a new earth', because the Lord God 'clothes his priests with salvation', and creates 'Jerusalem a rejoicing, and her people a joy'. 'Not by might, nor by power': man is a little thing, God is all. The pulpit is nothing, save when these elements of an unearthly influence gather around it. Heaven is the seat of power. The controversy is sharp and bitter; yet the One 'that hath the key of David, and openeth and no man shutteth, and shutteth and no man openeth, will break in pieces the gates of brass, and cut the bars of iron asunder'. His Spirit shall disarm the strong man, dislodge the enemy from his fortresses, gather his honours on the field of a bloodless conquest, and find his reward in the purity and blessedness of a redeemed and regenerated world.

10: *The Great Object of Preaching*

The *third* general object we have in view in illustrating the power of the pulpit, relates to the duty of ministers themselves. The inquiry is certainly an appropriate one, *What course of conduct is incumbent on ministers themselves, in order to make full proof of the power with which the pulpit is invested?*

The constituent elements of this power are more than human, yet are they intrusted to men. It is no infringement upon the divine prerogative to affirm that the preacher himself has an agency in carrying the designs of the pulpit into effect. If he is a mere blower of the Gospel trumpet, he ought to know how to blow it; his own heart must be in sweet accordance with the glad tidings which he utters, and his fingers trained to sweep the strings of the sacred lyre. It is a mighty trust which is committed to him. He has something *to do* in the work which the pulpit accomplishes; he himself is employed in giving direction to this great moral machinery. He is not a mere automaton, set up in the sanctuary for show; a something for men to look at, and then go away and talk about, as they would about the acts, and scenes, and persons, of a dramatic exhibition. It is not enough that he go through the labour of preparing two or three discourses a week; and then, when the Sabbath bell calls him, repair to the house of God, and with all sobriety and decency deliver them to the people of his charge, in the name and by the authority of his divine Master. His work is not done then; it may be it is not truly begun. Nor may he, if this is all that he does, soothe his conscience with the thought that though his pulpit be powerless, and his hearers are not saved, 'he has delivered his own soul'. The Gospel ought not to lose its energy in his hands; rather ought his ministrations to be such, and so fortified and adorned, as to develop and express that energy, to the glory of God, and the salvation of men.

A broad field here opens upon us, did we purpose to traverse it. Our course is a limited one, and must exclude many topics, for the purpose of dwelling on the few. No man of evangelical views

The Great Object of Preaching

hesitates to affirm that those who occupy the pulpit should be men of respectable talents, and 'apt to teach'; nor that they should be able and thoroughly educated men, fitted by their intellectual furniture for the exigencies of the church and the world; nor that they should be orthodox men, and fearless advocates of God's truth. These qualifications cannot be too thoroughly urged, and insisted on: where they are wanting, the pulpit is shorn of its strength.

This is not all that the pulpit demands. It must have something more than this, or it can never exert its appropriate influence. Just before Paul was about to be led forth from his prison at Rome to the scaffold, among other paternal and divinely-inspired counsels, he uttered many of deep interest to the ministry of reconciliation. He himself had struggled hard, and was just about to finish his course. He had contended honourably and lawfully, and was in daily expectation of his crown. 'I am now', says he, 'ready to be offered, and the time of my departure is at hand.' Timothy was young; he had just put on the armour; and it was a most seasonable and every way fitting injunction for such an one as 'Paul the aged' to say to him, 'Do the work of an evangelist; *make full proof* of thy ministry.' These general remarks, though we cannot enforce them as we desire to do, deserve at least the following illustrations.

The first thought which suggests itself on this branch of our subject is the *importance of a single eye to the great object of preaching the Gospel.*

In this world men are educated for eternity; a process is here going on which is destined to exert an influence, when earth and time shall have passed away. This is but the dawn of intelligence. The movement of the human intellect, but for an occasional untoward and anomalous influence, is perpetually onward. There are instances in which its approach to the confines of the eternal world has given an unwonted impetus to its powers, and imparted not only the consciousness that God made it to live, and think, and act for ever, but some strong anticipations of its progressive career. It does not brighten in its course, to sink like the setting sun, dazzling with its splendour, and gilding the scenery only as long as it is seen; it sets to rise on other spheres, where millions follow it with their admiring gaze. Time is but the outer court of the temple where this thinking existence remains only to be ushered into the sanctuary of God, and to stand in the presence of the ineffable glory. From the sun in the firmament, to the humblest flower that blushes on its stalk, an influence goes out to train it up for eternity. Sympathies and solicitudes are exhausted upon it, that find no such fitting objects in the universe; nor may it ever be forgotten, that under one of these influences, it is making its way to the splendours of the throne, or to the outer darkness. Yet can it not go from this world of ignorance and sin, into the presence of the Holy One, except by a miracle of his mercy. He makes it the pupil of his providence and truth, giving it line upon line, precept upon precept, and commissioning unnumbered agencies in the natural and moral world, to 'show to it the path of life'.

Of all the agencies he thus employs, the most important is the Gospel of his grace; the most effective dispensation of that Gospel is the preached word – the living ministry of his Son. All the goodness, and all the high-born hopes in this fallen world, are to be attributed to the revelation of God in the person of Jesus Christ, and to a cordial reception of him as there revealed. If we advert to the teaching of the Apostles, we find that their first object was to make men Christians; and then their great solicitude was that they should become well-informed, stable, and useful Christians, who should shine as lights in the world. Not only must truth find its way to the conscience and heart, and men be elevated from a state of sin to a state of grace, but there must be the habitual presence and power of godliness, like the rising light which shineth more and more unto the perfect day. Hallowed desires must be awakened, renewed, and invigorated; there must be a clear, and still more clear perception of divine things, and that assurance of them which is enriched by heavenly consolations, and which is the great impulse to spiritual attainment. There must be an abiding awe of God, chastened by filial confidence; by joy in him and from him; and by that fellowship of man with his Maker, by which God dwells in us, and we in him. There must be a sensitiveness to evil, which makes sin abhorred and loathsome; which resists its snares under every name and form; which trembles for the future, and is humbled for the past; which sinks in sorrow at the foot of the cross, ashamed, yet forgiven, confounded, yet filled with praise. There must be obedience to the will of our Father who is in heaven; obedience that is habitual and cheerful, under every difficulty, and at every sacrifice.

The Great Object of Preaching

The love of God to his people must be more fully responded to by the love of his people to God; there must be a more affectionate and deeper toned piety; a piety that is less paralysed by earth, and that receives daily and fresh incitements from heaven; a piety that holds all things in subordination to Christ; a piety that in the pursuit of things temporal and eternal has but this one object, to 'glorify God, and enjoy him for ever', and that aspires to the higher regions of the Christian's life. The object the pulpit has in view is no common one. It looks upon the world as it is, alienated from God by wicked works, and under his wrath and curse. The primitive formations of the mass on which it operates, are the sins and miseries of lost men; and forming that chaos of unsightly things, where 'darkness is upon the face of the deep'. There must be new, and better, and purer formations; the Spirit of God must move upon the face of the waters, and he who sits upon the throne must create all things new.

This object also is as single as it is important. When the risen and ascended Saviour appeared to Saul of Tarsus for the purpose of making him a Christian man and a Christian minister, he addressed him in the following impressive language: 'Rise, and stand upon thy feet; for I have appeared unto thee for this purpose, to make thee a minister and a witness both of these things which thou hast seen, and of those things in which I will appear unto thee; delivering thee from the people, and from the Gentiles, to whom now *I send thee, to open their eyes, and to turn them from darkness to light, and from the power of Satan unto God, that they may receive forgiveness of sins, and inheritance among them which are sanctified by faith that is in me.*' From the hour this commission was put into the hands and written upon the heart of Paul, his high distinction was to be a minister of the everlasting Gospel, and his single aim to 'turn men from darkness to light, and from the power of Satan unto God'. Every design that is hostile to this, or in any way inconsistent with it, is at war with the great object of the Christian ministry. God called them to the sacred office, that they might co-operate with his once suffering and now exalted Son, and his mighty and condescending Spirit, in converting a great multitude which no man can number, intercepting their course to the gates of death, overthrowing the empire of darkness and sin, and establishing, extending, and perpetuating the kingdom of truth, and righteousness, and peace, and joy.

Whatever subordinate ends, therefore, the Christian pulpit may secure in this or the coming world, its legitimate, paramount aim is the glory of God in the salvation of men. Its great end is one, and only one. If 'the chief end of man is to glorify God, and enjoy him for ever', the chief end of those who minister his word is to glorify him in that great work with which his manifested glory is most intimately allied. 'Unto me', says the Apostle, 'who am less than the least of all saints, is this grace given, that I should preach the unsearchable riches of Christ, *to the end* that now unto principalities and powers in heavenly places, might be known, by the church, the manifold wisdom of God.' It is God first, God midst, God last, God everywhere, God exalted in the Gospel of his Son. It is to bring forward, and sustain, and magnify the full claims of the adorable Godhead; so that men who do not know may know him; men who despise may have honourable thoughts of him; men who suspect and slander him may look upon him with a trusting confidence. It is not to make them hypocrites, and induce them to put on the show of friendship, and thus prepare themselves for a greater damnation; it is to prevail upon them truly and honestly to give up their controversy with God, and make peace with him through the blood of his Son.

It is not the favour of the people; 'we seek not *yours*,' says the Apostle, 'but *you*.' Nor is it their wealth, nor their honours; it is themselves, and their salvation. It is the *soul* that a faithful minister is thinking of – the deathless *soul*; it is this that he is praying for, and preaching to, that he may present it to his great Lord as 'his joy and his crown'. Such is the high, the grand aim of the Christian ministry, and such it will appear to have been, when such a man as Paul goes up with those who were given to him as the seals of his ministry, to bow themselves before God and the Lamb. It is this which gives such grandeur and power to the pulpit. Such it will appear to have been when the joys of heaven and the torments of hell are felt in their everlasting weight and reality, and when the magnitude of God's redemption, and the wondrous results that have flowed from it, shall be unfolded.

All men do not comprehend this commanding motive and object of ministerial devotedness: would that it were comprehended by all of us who are Christ's ministers! 'Never forget', says the youthful McCheyne, writing to one of his brethren in the ministry, 'that the end of a sermon is the salvation of the people.' We would

The Great Object of Preaching

have our minds imbued with this truth, and are greatly desirous that the minds of others should be as deeply imbued as our own. This is what our pulpits so imperatively demand. In this great object, the mind and heart of the preacher must be concentrated; this great end he must pursue with great singleness of purpose, and great strength and ardour of affection. His efforts will rise as high as his own impressions of the importance of his object, and no higher. He may expect to accomplish very little, unless his own mind is absorbed in his high calling. He need not be afraid of being too much excited in the pursuit of such an end; for it is impossible that the affections of an enlightened and well-balanced mind should be too strong and ardent, where those affections can be gratified only by the salvation of men, and through the instrumentality of God's truth. It is but for the salvation of men to become his great object; his thoughts are but to dwell here, and his desires centre so habitually, so tenderly, so solemnly, on this great object, as to make it the paramount passion; and his pulpit would read different lessons from those it often reads. Let this be wanting, and the preacher's heart freezes, his lips freeze, and his pulpit is but an icy tablet.

There is a fixed and steady aim towards this great object discernible in some ministers, which in others is a very slight and cursory one. It needs not much discernment to discover which are the more powerful preachers. No two men in this land appeared to have the great object of preaching more directly or more steadily before their minds, than those departed and beloved servants of God, the late Dr. Payson, of Portland, and the late Dr. Nettleton of Killingworth; nor do I know of any who were more successful in winning souls. There was a period in the life of Andrew Fuller, when he said, 'I think I never yet entered into the *true idea* of the work of the ministry.' Happy, timely thought! and the subsequent usefulness of this man of God shows how much the power of the pulpit depends upon the aim and end of the preacher.

Many a minister could tell a similar experience; they were new days to him, and, in some sort, a new conversion, when he first 'entered into the true idea of the work of the ministry'. What impulse is like this? What is the pulpit, without this impulse? How can it gain the object of its appointment, if it does not aim at attaining it? Is it any marvel that it should be powerless, when it *seeks* not to be powerful? We ask for the pulpit that engrossing attention, and thought, and zeal, which the great object of it demands, well assured that it has weight and influence enough to take full possession of the soul, to fill it, to exhaust it; and when it has exhausted it to fill it again; to stimulate what it has exhausted, and invigorate and refresh what it has made weak and weary. There is surely no want of motives to such a spirit, nor any lack of aliment to it in the truth of God. For with all the richness and variety of that exhaustless volume, there is not a principle nor a fact it reveals but has a bearing upon the object which the Christian ministry has in view, and which, if their own hearts are set upon that object, may not be so enforced as to aim at this great end.

We hear not a little about *elevating the standard of preaching*, and rendering it more in keeping with 'the spirit of the age'. Is there not some delusion in this matter; and in these efforts to elevate the pulpit, may we not be insensibly depressing it below the high and revealed standard? The age is indeed distinguished for great advances in science and the arts, great enterprise, expansive benevolence, high independence of thought, and freedom of inquiry. This advance in science and the arts has added greatly to the richness of language; it furnishes matter for new and more varied illustrations of religious truth; while it erects new fortresses of defence against the attacks of infidelity, and puts into the hands of God's servants new weapons of aggression and assault. The enterprise of the age does, indeed, call for an enterprising ministry; and its public spirit and independence of thought give the pulpit great advantages for urging the claims of God's truth. It is incumbent on the ministry to stand abreast with these advances, and to make the most of them for the honour of God and the souls of men.

Yet is it a mistaken view, that these advances have made advances upon the Gospel, or disclosed any new method of enforcing its great truths, or discovered any new way to the Kingdom of God. The Gospel is in advance of them all. Modern science and improvements, with all their boasting, will not make men better preachers than Christ and the Apostles. The essential and peculiar power of the pulpit, as we have already shown, consists 'not in the words which man's wisdom teacheth, but which the Holy Ghost teacheth'. The 'foolishness of God is wiser than men'. Give me the power of illustrating and enforcing God's truth, and I care not who has the treasures of human learning.

The Great Object of Preaching

Human learning is valuable only to this end; and that it does not always attain this end is quite obvious from the fact, that the most learned men are not the best preachers, nor the most sought after by the popular mind. When John Bunyan preached in London, he attracted greater audiences than the most learned divines of the land, because he preached with greater power. The celebrated Dr. Owen was often among his hearers; and when Charles II expressed his astonishment that a man of the Doctor's learning could hear 'the tinker preach', Owen is said to have replied, 'Had I the tinker's abilities, please Your Majesty, I would most gladly relinquish my learning.'

The fact is, there are no *peculiar* qualifications for the pulpit required by the age in which we live, above those required by former ages. We have no better preachers than Bunyan, and Baxter, and Owen. Baxter's *Saints' Rest*, and his *Call to the Unconverted*, are not equalled by modern pulpits. Bunyan's *Heavenly Footman*, his *Come and Welcome to Jesus Christ*, his *Barren Fig Tree*, and his *Grace Abounding to the Chief of Sinners*, would now perhaps be deemed far behind the spirit of the age. And so would Doddridge's *Rise and Progress*, and Alleyn's *Alarm*, and Flavel's *Fountain of Life*, and Owen on *The Glory of Christ*. Men have outlived these old-fashioned preachers. They have outrun the Bible; and if ever they wake up to the great and single object the pulpit has in view, it will be by a 'voice *behind* them'.

The spirit of the age is not the spirit of Paul; and were this greatest of human teachers to return to our world, I fear he would be accused as a tardy imitator of the age in which we live, and that the laurels he earned in Arabia, at Jerusalem, at Antioch, at Thessalonica, at Athens, at Corinth, at Ephesus, and at Rome, would no longer be preserved fresh and green upon his brow. I repeat the thought, there is some illusion here, and some subtle snare of the great Deceiver. The Gospel preached by Paul is not less powerful now than it was eighteen hundred years ago; it is still adapted to all ages, all climes, all states of society, every degree of intellectual advancement, and all men. Nor may we doubt, that if preached now just as he preached it, it would furnish exemplifications of the power of the pulpit, 'not a whit behind' the spirit of the age, or the chief of its apostles.

It is a melancholy fact that, so far as it regards the great object of preaching, the American pulpit is not on the advance. Not a few preachers there are whom it would seem captious to complain of, but who at the same time do not satisfy an intelligent and spiritual auditory. There is something wanting in their discourses; they are not full of light and power; the unction of the priesthood is not there. They are not so absorbed in the great object of preaching that their hearers perceive the object they are aiming at; nor so intent upon it that they themselves are cheerful or depressed, joyful or sad, as the pleasure of the Lord prospers, or does not prosper, in their hands.

These are 'hard sayings', and might come better from one who is better authorized to 'cast the first stone'. Nor is it without a painful struggle between a sense of shame and a sense of duty that the author allows himself to utter them. His own conscience smites him; and he feels the glow of self-reproach coming up in his face when he ventures to say, that the great deficiency in the church of the present age is the want of a spiritual and urgent ministry. Older ministers are deeply conscious of this deficiency in themselves; they feel it when they look toward their beloved and younger brethren. Other professions are on the advance, but the pulpit is retrograde. There are more learned things and more beautiful things uttered from it than were once uttered; but it is fast losing its energy. It has more touches of the German artists, but less of plain dealing with the conscience, less of tenderness and love. It has more of transcendentalism, but less of Christianity. Where is the Lord God of Elijah? Where is the mantle of Tennent and Davies, Edwards and Bellamy, Brainerd and Payson?

Yet would we not be misunderstood. It is not absolutely a degenerate ministry that we speak of; it is not an irreligious and corrupt ministry, but an inefficient ministry. The strength of the pulpit has been insensibly and gradually decaying; and not the less so because the youthful ministry themselves are slow to perceive it. In some respects, it has made great and rapid advances, while in the important article of effective preaching, it has become so manifestly retrograde, that I have heard the thought expressed, with great tenderness, by cultivated intelligence and matured piety, 'We know not where the church can look for able ministers!'

This state of things demands sober reflection. Iniquity abounds, the love of many is waxing cold, and the enemy is coming in like a flood. Never, since the days of Luther, was there a louder call for an effective ministry. Ministers may be pious, able, and evangel-

The Great Object of Preaching

ical in their views, yet not be *good preachers*. They may possess talent, competent intellectual furniture, and large measures of theological knowledge; yet not be able ministers of the New Testament. They may be familiar with theology as a science, yet not know how to preach it. And the reason is, their hearts are not ardently set on the great object of the Christian ministry; they are drawn from it to other things, and contemplate the one thing needful with diminished interest. They do not glide down with the current of the world, and allow themselves to become ensnared by pursuits that are purely secular, but they fall in with the infectious spirit of the times, and are slow to elevate their own minds and discourses to the true standard and the great object of preaching.

It is no easy matter to keep the great object of the pulpit distinctly and steadily before the mind; to do so requires great self-denial, spirituality, and imparted grace, and more especially during prolonged seasons of declension in the church, and insensibility in the world. The mind of an active, enterprising minister cannot be idle. If not employed in the most appropriate duties of his vocation, it seeks employment in those pursuits which, while they have a distant, have no direct and immediate relation to his great object. May not many of us 'lay our hand upon our own mouth'? If I were not such a traitor to my divine Lord, right sure am I that I should have the great and commanding object more constantly and more delightfully present to my thoughts, for which 'he counted me faithful, putting me into the ministry'. Oh, it would be delightful to learn that such men as Baxter, and Bunyan, and Edwards, were about to come down upon our churches with a message that would disturb and stir up us placid, self-complacent, dreamy preachers!

Would that better days might dawn upon the church and the pulpit, and that as we sink to the silence of the tomb, better and abler men, men full of the Holy Ghost, might occupy the places which will so soon know us no more!

11: *Ministerial Diligence*

While just views of the great object of preaching go far towards making a useful minister of the Gospel, these alone do not give to the pulpit its true and proper influence. These views must be carried out into practice, and express themselves in a course of diligent devotedness to the labours of the ministerial office. The single thought, therefore, on which we propose to submit several observations in the present chapter, relates to the necessity of *unwearied diligence* in the work of the Christian ministry.

The Apostle Paul, in giving his paternal counsels to a youthful preacher, has the following remarkable passage: '*Neglect not* the gift that is in thee, which was given thee by prophecy, with the laying on of the hands of the presbytery. *Meditate* upon these things; give thyself *wholly* to them, that thy *profiting* may appear to all.' No imparted gifts could avail for young Timothy, unless he himself were wholly devoted to his work. Paul himself was a noble exemplification of the diligence he recommends; accomplishing in one short life more, probably, than was accomplished by any other man. Prepared for his work by an early attention to the liberal arts and sciences in the schools of Tarsus, and accustomed to manual labour in the trade of tent-making, he possessed a well-disciplined mind, and a body that was inured to hardship.

From Tarsus he was sent to Jerusalem, where, under the tuition of that great master of the law, Gamaliel, he made rapid proficiency, 'and profited above many of his equals'. But God, who had destined him for another profession, and 'separated him from his mother's womb' that he might be a preacher of the Gospel, arrested him in his course, and at the time of his conversion, revealed to him that he was the selected individual who should preach the unsearchable riches of Christ to the Gentile world. From that hour he addressed himself to this great work with a steadfastness of purpose, and a diligence that is without any other recorded example; asking only the question, 'Lord, what wilt thou have me *to do*?' and never stopping to consult his own ease, or in any way 'conferring with flesh and blood'. The first three years of his ministry he employed in different parts of Arabia; from Arabia he returned to Damascus, where, in defiance of the incensed and exasperated rulers he preached openly in the synagogue. Thence he went to Jerusalem, where, though he remained but fifteen days, he left the marks of his mighty mind, if not in the conversion, in the conviction and confusion of his enemies. Thence he went to Tarsus, his native city; thence, in company with Barnabas, he went to Antioch; thence back to Jerusalem; thence to Seleucia, and Cyprus, preaching in all its principal cities. Thence he went to Pamphylia, Pisidia, and Iconium, God everywhere giving testimony to the word of his grace; and thence back again to Antioch, confirming and strengthening the churches, and announcing how great a door had been opened for the conversion of the Gentile world.

We need not follow him in his indefatigable course; it was one of unwearied labour and self-denial, at Philippi, at Athens, at Corinth, at Thessalonica, at Ephesus, at Illyrium, at Troas, at Miletus, at Cæsarea, and at Rome. 'Of the Jews', says he, 'five times received I forty stripes, save one. Thrice was I beaten with rods; thrice I suffered shipwreck; a day and a night have I been in the deep. In journeyings often, in perils of waters, in perils of robbers, in perils by mine own countrymen, in perils by the heathen, in perils in the city, in perils in the wilderness, in perils in the sea, in perils among false brethren. In weariness, and painfulness, in watchings often, in hunger and thirst, in fastings often, in cold and nakedness. Beside those things that are without, that which cometh upon me daily, the care of all the churches.' Never was a mind more divinely attempered to its work than his; and never did a minister of the Gospel so magnify his office, by his 'mighty diligence and industry', in season and out of season, by day and by night, by sea and by land; 'running', as one of the Christian fathers remarks, 'from ocean to ocean, like the sun in the heavens, sooner lacking ground to tread upon than a desire to propagate the faith of Christ'. What he could not accomplish by his voice, he supplied by the diligent use of his pen, leaving upon record fourteen Epistles to the churches, and to us, and all subsequent ages, a view of the doctrines and duties of the Gospel, which, for simplicity, weight, urgency, and true, earnest eloquence, are not surpassed in the sacred writings. It is not amiss for us to have such an example of ministerial diligence before our eyes; we may the better see how much can be accomplished by the patient and self-denying efforts of one devoted man of God.

Effective diligence has respect to the whole course of ministerial life, and comprehends the entire devotement of it to this great work. The *time* of a minister of the Gospel is to him, and to the work in which he is engaged, 'more precious than rubies'. If he is a diligent man, there is nothing he economizes with greater care – gathering up the fragments of it, that nothing be lost. There is nothing for which he considers himself more solemnly accountable; nothing he employs either so cheerfully, or so intensely for the cause of his Divine Lord. Like every other man he requires seasons of relaxation and repose; and while he ought to possess true independence of character, to decide for himself when and what that repose shall be, it becomes him to do so with an honest conscience, and even with lively sensitiveness that it is the tendency of the best of men, where the call for labour and the opportunity for indulgence are distinctly before him, to lean to the side of indulgence. He should have independence of character enough, also, in his arrangements for labour, to *secure* the time devoted to it, without interruption. He *must* do this, if he is an effective labourer; and though it may cost him frowns and popular favour, his habits will eventually become known and respected.

It is of great importance to a Christian minister who insists upon the uninterrupted opportunity for labour, to employ that opportunity *intensely*. This is altogether a matter of habit; and the habit is one which is easily acquired. If there are those who are able to accomplish more in eight hours than others accomplish in twelve, it is from the habit of fixed and concentrated labour. Ministers of the Gospel, of all men in the world, have no time to throw away. They may trifle with any thing, and be prodigal of any thing, rather than time. Wisdom in the arrangement of their time, and punctuality and activity in pursuing this arrangement, enter most essentially into the very elements of their usefulness. 'Seize time by the forelock', was the counsel given by a venerable father in the ministry to the writer while he was yet young. The best days of the week, and the best hours of the day are all demanded for our work. We rebuke our hearers who act upon the presumption that there is time enough yet; perhaps we should rebuke ourselves.

How often is the time too far gone which ought to have been redeemed; how often do we stand discouraged on the threshold of duty, when we might have gone to the duty cheerfully, had we known the value of time.

Men of the world husband their time; Christian men, in their secular pursuits, are wise in the employment of their time. We do not read that the Saviour was ever found standing or sitting idle. 'I must work the work of him that sent me, while it is day', says he; 'the night cometh in which no man can work'. He was the most indefatigable of men, from the hour he entered on his public ministry, to that in which he breathed out his life on the cross. God's accepted time with the sinner is *now*; when, if not *now*, is it an accepted time for his ministers to be about their Father's business? 'Go on, dear brother', says McCheyne, writing to Burns, then at Dundee – 'go on, dear brother; but an inch of time remains, and then eternal ages roll on for ever – but an inch of time on which we can stand, and preach the way of salvation to a perishing world.'

This general remark in regard to the diligent employment of a minister's time, deserves, as we judge, special consideration in regard to one particular department of his official labours. Of all the labours of a minister, the most important is *preparation for the pulpit*. The pulpit is his great sphere of action; the work of the pulpit is the great work to which God has appointed him; it is the work in which most is effected for the great object of that appointment. What he is as a man, a Christian, and a minister of the Gospel, and what he accomplishes for the souls of his fellow-men, depends in no small degree upon the careful preparation of his public discourses. Those there are who are not indolent, yet who do not take sufficient time to prepare for the pulpit. This, we are fully persuaded, is mistaken policy; nay, it is worse. A few men there are of extraordinary powers, and great industry, who may be said to be always preparing for the pulpit, and who have little else to do than hastily gather up and arrange a few selected thoughts, in order to be useful and profitable preachers. But they are rare men, and would increase their usefulness tenfold, if their habitual preparations were more definite and elaborate than they are.

We cannot urge too strenuously the importance of diligent preparations for the services of the pulpit. For what services should a minister be prepared, if not for those where hundreds, it may be thousands, are waiting with solemn expectation to hear the messages of divine love from his lips? We are acquainted with some ministers who make their preparations for the pulpit altogether a secondary concern; they do so habitually. We dare not trust ourselves in animadverting upon a habit that is so censurable, so unministerial. To crowd the preparation for the Sabbath into the last day of the week may sometimes be inevitable; and there are those who can sustain this pressure. Men in the habit of careful preparation are the very men to meet this occasional exigency. Where the vessel is full, it will bear a sudden demand upon it; where the fruit is ripe on the bough, it does not suffer if it be hastily gathered. Ministers, if they are wise, will not allow themselves to be often driven to this extremity. 'Beaten oil, beaten oil, for the lamps of the sanctuary.'

It is related of the celebrated Dr. Dick, the fellow-student of Robert Hall and Sir James McIntosh, and the author of one of the best systems of theology, that his discourses for the Sabbath were begun on the evening of the Sabbath preceding that on which they were delivered. The writer is acquainted with a living minister whom he once heard remark, that he had rarely closed his eyes to rest, on a Lord's day evening, for almost forty years, without anxiously turning his thoughts to the inquiry, *What shall be the subject of my discourse for the next Sabbath?* Nor was he satisfied until he had selected it; and when he had selected it, it became the burden of his thoughts, his studies, his prayers, and often, of his conversation for the remainder of the week. Did we all do this, should we not be better preachers? 'How long', said a flippant licentiate, to the late Dr. Strong, of Hartford, 'does it take you, sir, to write a sermon?' 'That depends', replied the veteran labourer, 'on the nature and importance of my subject; sometimes two, sometimes four, sometimes six days; and *sometimes* almost as many weeks.' 'Is it possible?' exclaimed the astonished young man. 'Why, sir, I can write a sermon at any time in *half a day*!' 'Yes,' replied the Doctor, 'and *make nothing of it*!' With few exceptions, this is the whole history of hasty preparations for the pulpit. To make nothing of the toil, is to make nothing of the sermon. As the Frenchman said of the academy, 'We had nothing to do, and we did it.'

There are, no doubt, seasons when a minister is justified in neglecting elaborate preparations for the pulpit, for pastoral visitation, and the more public services of the Church of God in the world. Seasons of sickness, and especially of pervading public calamity, and seasons of the special outpouring of the Spirit of God upon the people of his charge, demand a degree of pastoral visitation that is incompatible with severe study. For such seasons a laborious student is prepared; he is at home in the lecture-room, at the prayer-meeting, and in the domestic circle. Some of his most profitable services then, are those off-hand and off-heart efforts which cost him little labour; he is fitted for them by a course of previous discipline, by much prayer, and by grace to help in the time of need. It is no presumption in such a man, at such seasons, to look to God, and rely on God for the fulfilment of the promise, 'As thy days, so shall thy strength be'. Yet, even in such seasons, he will find it of great advantage, not altogether to neglect careful preparation for the pulpit. The discourses prepared during seasons of great public calamity, and special effusions of God's Spirit, are usually his best and most useful discourses; they are most worthy of being preserved and repeated; there is an earnestness and unction about them in vain sought in ordinary, and even more elaborate preparations.

One of the most thrilling series of discourses found in our language, is a series published by the ministers of London, during the great plague, in the year 1666. The most effective discourses ever written by President Edwards, and the late Dr. Griffin, bear internal evidence that they were carefully prepared during those memorable revivals of religion in Northampton, New Hartford, and Newark, with the narrative of which every minister is familiar. Never did the late venerable Dr. Dwight preach with so much spirituality and pathos, as during those seasons of refreshing enjoyed at Yale College, from the year 1800 to 1805. Yet, with the exception of his Saturday evening lectures to the students, his discourses were carefully prepared and written. There were two very precious seasons of the general outpouring of God's Spirit, under the ministrations of the late Dr. Emmons, at Franklin; yet, with the exception of his *Improvement*, did this indefatigable student and pungent preacher never address even an assemblage of his awakened and anxious people, not in the district school-house, or a private dwelling, without his written discourse.

No minister can be diligent without a solemn purpose to be so. Severe toil is not naturally a pleasure; labour was the inflicted curse. Active as men are, and busy as they consent to be about trifles, calm, serious, useful labour is not naturally their pleasure. Nor will the habit ever be imbibed without strong resolution. Faint resolutions will not accomplish the object; before one short month is gone, they are gone and forgotten. There is a backwardness, a reluctance to severe and *long-continued* toil, which require great hardihood of purpose to overcome. They cannot be overcome without a struggle; and the man who conquers them will find the conflict such as to demand great watchfulness, and many prayers. His great object must be to 'do *the work* of an evangelist'. He must lay his account with toil, undiscouraged by difficulty, unwearied by years; his master purpose must be, that 'Christ should be magnified in his body, whether it be by life, or by death'.

Are there no incentives to such a career? May we not, by weighty motives, and high encouragements, hold up to our own view, as well as to the view of others, the practicability, the importance, the usefulness, the honour of such a course; and the sinfulness, the depression, the dishonour of putting our hand to the plough and looking back?

Contemplate, then, the *great law of man's being in the present world*. 'In the sweat of thy brow shalt thou eat thy bread, until thou return to the ground.' No man can evade the operation of this salutary law, without being the sufferer. Last of all may a minister of the Gospel quarrel with this arrangement of Divine Providence. Yet is it no uncommon thing to hear the complaint from a certain class of ministers, of the severity of their toil. We may not affirm that this is always proof that they are idlers in God's vineyard; yet is it an indication that they do not feel a deep interest in their work. Ministers are not the only men who have selected a laborious calling. Men of other professions are men of toil; not a few of them are men of indefatigable toil, from the dawning of vigorous manhood to a ripe old age. They expect to gain their ends by unwearied effort; and why should not the ministers of the Gospel? How can they hope to gain them by any other means? There is no violation of the law of human dependence in such expectations. It is alike the duty and privilege of a minister 'to trust like a child, and work like a man'.

There is no one feature of the divine government, no one property of the physical or intellectual constitution of man, no one principle of his social organization, no one characteristic in the economy of his salvation, that proposes a bounty for indolence.

Even in the sovereign operations of God's distinguishing grace, where 'it is not of him that willeth, nor of him that runneth, but of God that showeth mercy', men are enjoined to 'work out their own salvation', *because* it is God who 'worketh in them to will and to do'. Their dependence is their great encouragement. They work when God works; and God works when they work. It is true, that 'it is God who giveth the increase'; and this is the reason why ministers should 'plant and water'. The field must be cultivated, else will it remain barren, and God will give no increase. On the part of the labourers, every thing must give way to the diligent planting and watering. This is a labour which may not be neglected, nor carelessly performed, nor performed for a season, and then abandoned. It is not more true, that 'he that tilleth his land shall have plenty of bread', than that a laborious minister is a fellow-worker with God, while a negligent minister counteracts every law of nature, morals, and grace, and wages habitual war with his Maker.

What is *the work itself* in which a minister of the Gospel is employed? If he is what he professes to be, he is a pious man, and is deeply sensible of the wonderful grace of God, not only in making him the subject of his grace, and an heir of his kingdom, but in 'counting him faithful, putting him into the ministry'. If we have given any just view of the power of the pulpit, there is no employment so important to the present and future well-being of men and therefore, none so desirable. Such goodness and mercy as God has expressed towards his ministers in calling them to his service, deserve more than ordinary returns of obedience and love; they impose obligations of entire and exclusive devotedness to the service, to which, in such amazing condescension, he has called them. In accepting such a service, they have solemnly pledged to it before God, angels, and men, all that they are, and have, and can perform. God has made provision for their temporal wants, that their time and thoughts, undistracted by other avocations, may be devoted to feeding his people with knowledge and understanding; and that they themselves, to the full extent of their opportunity and abilities, may be active and devoted ministers.

It is a cold view of the work of the ministry to urge this devotedness as a matter of mere obligation and duty. *Necessity* is laid upon every minister to be diligent in such vocation; necessity of every kind; the necessity of love as well as of law, of affection as well as of conscience, of gratitude as well as covenant bonds, all constraining him to diligence and zeal. He has a high and holy commission to execute, and how can he execute it negligently? The souls of men are committed to his trust; their apathy must be disturbed, their crimes exposed, their sins rebuked, their consciences impressed, their fears awakened, their refuges of lies swept away, and they themselves urged to flee from the coming wrath. May they be negligent in such a work as this?

And who is the *Master they serve?* The Master they serve is he whose 'name is Wonderful, Counsellor, the Mighty God, the Everlasting Father, the Prince of Peace'. He is the Eternal One, who was before all things; the Omnipresent One who walks amid the golden candlesticks, and holds the stars in his right hand, and is with his ministers to the end of the world; the Omniscient One, and all the churches shall honour him who searches the reins and tries the heart. He is the Saviour who made them, and has preserved and blessed them; who owns them, whose property and servants they are; who to rescue them from death, paid the ransom with his own blood; and who, by ten thousand titles, claims all that they have, and are, and can perform. It is the God incarnate, the humbled Deity, the Eternal Son in tears, and agony and death, throwing around him the burden of their offences, the griefs, and darkness, that he might lift them from the horrible abyss of eternal ignominy and suffering, and through them proclaim this dearbought deliverance to their fellow-men. The heaven-born Pearce could say, 'Yes, my dear, dying Lord, I am thine, thy servant; and if I neglect the service of so good a Master, I may well expect a guilty conscience in life, and a death as awful as that of Judas, or of Spira.' Says Whitefield, 'I want more tongues, more bodies, more souls for the Lord Jesus. Had I ten thousand, he should have them all.' Said Payson, 'O what a Master do I serve! Never was preaching such sweet work as it is now.' Such men proved the temper of their heavenly armour, nor did they desire to put it off till they laid it down by the side of their grave.

This diligent devotedness to the duties of his office is what every minister *owes to himself.* He cannot greatly respect himself, nor the office he holds, unless he is a man of exemplary diligence. Paul would have his beloved pupil so conduct himself that 'his *profiting* might appear unto all'. Young ministers are not always aware how much they are capable of accomplishing, until they set themselves in earnest to persevering labour. Unexecuted, their power lies hidden from themselves. It is a fact of great importance for them to ascertain that their course may be *onward*. The simple truth that man possesses the capacity for constant and perpetual progression is of unspeakable value to a minister of the Gospel. Be his present knowledge and holiness ever so small, his object should be progress; his light should 'shine more and more unto the perfect day'. But this is an impossible thing without patient and persevering toil. Severe toil is what he needs. Of no class of men may it be said with greater truth, that their intellectual faculties, their spiritual graces, and their moral virtues need to be so disciplined in the school of hardy industry. They must be inured to effort, to difficult, and not unfrequently discouraged effort, and effort that ultimately rises superior to discouragement; else will they never 'make full proof of their ministry'.

There is a great difference between those men in other professions who are distinguished for their wakeful and patient industry, and those who do not feel sufficient interest in their profession to perform any more labour than happens to be convenient. There is the same difference among ministers. It is of little moment what their talents are; if they are not industrious men, it is impossible they should possess either the intellectual discipline or furniture to be permanently useful. They are not growing men, because they are not laborious men. Not a few ministers there are, men of splendid talents, who were never better preachers than in their youth. This is a sad failure, and the cause of it is their own want of diligence. They have become wearied with labour; and to find relief from it, they have been changing from place to place, and have drawn so freely upon their former stock of preparation, that they are strangers to the habit of untiring application. Others there are who entered upon their work with no other promise than a stable character and a well-disciplined mind, who have been 'growing with their growth, and strengthening with their strength'. But they are men of forethought and system, men of reading and study, men of patient labour; they are men of self-denial, men to whom time, and progress, and usefulness, are more than personal comfort, more than social intercourse, more than money; men to whom the work of the ministry is everything. They were not born eminent, but became so by great labour and severe discipline, and were accustomed to great and long-continued mental effort.

The great difference in the ministers of the Gospel, is, under God, the result of unwearied application. No man has talent without thought; and no man has rich treasures of thought without great labour. God's blessing is with a devoted minister. The minister who dissipates his time in social intercourse, or who lounges away the hours that ought to be devoted to severer studies in works of fiction; or who dreams them away amid the fumes of his cigar, need not be disappointed at his want of power in the pulpit, nor that he is unable to sustain himself in his high vocation.

Every minister ought to aim at distinction. Nor is there more than one way of obtaining it. 'He that would be the *greatest* among you,' says the Saviour, 'let him be the *servant* of all.' It is just this which a minister should aim to become – the *servant* of God, the *servant* of his church, the *servant* of those committed to his care, 'the *servant* of all'.

If there be pride enough in every minister's heart to make capital out of such an aim as this, there is nothing in the service itself that ministers to his pride. It is not forbidden him to aim at such distinction as was awarded to Barnabas, of whom it is said, that 'he was a good man, and full of the Holy Ghost, and much people was added to the Lord'. He need not fear to aim at distinction in all that is good and useful; distinction in the work which God has given him to perform; distinction in converting sinners from the error of their ways, and covering a multitude of sins.

Yet if he aims at this, he must pay the price for it in corresponding effort. It will cost him dear to be an able minister of the New Testament. It will cost him solicitude and toil, prayer and pains, days and nights of care, tears and trembling. Habit and years may alleviate the solicitude, and dry up the tears, but they do not diminish the toil. King Henry IV once said of his son, who was eager to put on the crown, 'He little knows what a heap of cares and toils he snatcheth at.' So we say of the work of the ministry. 'I envy not a clergyman's life', said Dr. Samuel Johnson, 'as an easy life; nor do I envy the clergyman who makes it an easy life.' It is no easy lot; and where it is made so, it is no *ministry*, no service. If there be those who are seeking an idle and easy life, let them not think of the pulpit. Rather may they find it in the harvest-field, or on the ocean, or at the anvil, or at the saw and the hammer; but they will not find it in the faithful discharge of the duties of the pulpit. The service is one of labour; 'we are *labourers* together with God'. Few among the laborious ministry but have found that there are seasons when it has responsibilities that are hard, very hard, to bear. 'If any man wishes to be a successful minister,' says Payson, 'he knows not what he asks; and it better becomes him to consider whether he can drink of Christ's bitter cup, and be baptized with his baptism.' This is, perhaps, too sombre a picture; yet should we all have more sympathy with such a thought as this, did we know by experience as well as this man of God knew, what it is to be a successful minister.

We cannot suppress another thought: a *diligent ministry is the most happy ministry*. 'Blessed is the man', says Carlyle, 'who has found his work; let him ask no other blessedness. Know thy work, and do it; and work at it like a Hercules. One monster there is in the world; an idle man.' Payson found pleasure in the toil, and joy in the very suffering. Ministers are sometimes exceedingly happy in their work; and never more so than when it is most arduous. 'I find', says Whitefield, 'that the more I do for God, the more I am able to do, and the more I am *comforted* in doing it.' 'I am glad', says he, writing to one of his coadjutors, 'that you have sounded the silver trumpet in London. *Crescet eundo*,* must be your motto and mine. There is nothing like keeping the wheels oiled by action. The more we do, the more we may do; every act strengthens the habit; and the best preparation for preaching on Sundays is to preach every day in the week.' 'I wish for no service,' says Henry Martyn, 'but the service of God, in labouring for souls on earth, and to do his will in heaven. I do not wish for any heaven upon earth, but that of preaching the precious Gospel of Christ to immortal souls. I do not know that any thing would be a heaven to me, but the service of Christ and the enjoyment of his presence. There is not a thing in the world for which I would wish to live, except because it may please God to appoint me some *work*.' These are beautiful thoughts; they are the life, the joy of the ministry.

Every active and diligent minister may not indeed be always thus happy; he has his seasons of discouragement from within and from without. His sky is not always clear; but he is comforted even under the cloud. If he mourns that it is not always harvest with him, he rejoices that it is always seed-time. If yellow autumn does

---

*'It grows as it goes' (quoted from Lucretius 6.341).

not always pour its riches before his eye, yet is he cheered with the beauties and the promise of the opening spring, and the arduous summer. That morbid sensibility, that corroding sentimentalism which is the bane of every manly and energetic quality, and every growing grace, and which sinks so many ministers into despondency, has no place in his bosom, because his best, and holiest, and most buoyant desires are gratified in the prospect of responsible effort. The most diligent may, indeed, well feel that they are 'unprofitable servants', yet are they happy servants, and the most happy when most employed. Ministers lose their relish for their work as they relax their toil. There is, there can be no charm in the severer labours of the sacred office for a negligent labourer. He has few pleasant scenes to look back upon; few pleasant recollections waft their fragrance over his languid mind. The joy of a clear conscience belongs not to such a man. Nor is he comforted in his present labour, however intermitted and light it may be. He has a complaining spirit; such a spirit is the natural growth of an indolent mind. He is perpetually making unhappy comparisons; and, instead of rejoicing in the successes of others, complains only of the want of it in himself. And he has no vivid expectations to cheer him; there are few blossomings of hope springing up in his path. It is always winter with him, never seed-time, never harvest; he wanders amid leafless trees, and shivers under the keen, cold wind.

The life and death of the late Dr. Chalmers, presents a most delightful view of that high degree of enjoyment which attends a laborious minister. In all the voluminous productions of his pen, I do not recollect a gloomy or pensive thought. The most grave and weighty subjects he treats, not indeed without solemnity, but with a buoyancy and vigour that indicate a cheerful and happy mind. I love to think of such a man, and to dwell on the undying verdure of his clustering thoughts. Even his stern and struggling career interests me, it was so light and gladsome. I love to think of him, climbing up the sides of Mount Zion, holding on sometimes by the jutting rocks, and sometimes by the green boughs, ever tasking his fortitude as he ascends, till, like Moses on the top of Nebo, he looks for the last time on the plain below, and scarcely conscious of the change, finds himself by the men of light and love, and in the presence of God and the Lamb. I sometimes think of such a man, and say I would not be a Lazzaroni.* 'I have no desire to be a weed on the shore.'

Ministers must soon be *called to their final account*. Those who can look back upon their ministry with thankfulness, can look forward to that day of reckoning with joy. He who has given them grace to be diligent and faithful, has laid up for them an incorruptible crown. 'They that be wise shall shine as the brightness of the firmament; and they that turn many to righteousness, as the stars for ever and ever.' There remaineth a *rest* for God's faithful ministers. Blessed rest! glorious and everlasting rest! where the curse of labour is passed away, and the blessing only remains of serving God day and night in his temple. Will it not be the sweeter to those who in the present world were 'in labours more abundant?' It is not 'a heap of cares and toils they are snatching at', who look for the 'crown of righteousness, which the Lord, the righteous Judge, shall give them at his appearing'.

Are there no misgivings, in view of the judgment, in the bosom of a negligent minister of the Gospel? Can he look forward to it with peace, with hope, with joy, with triumph in that Saviour who so tenderly requires him to feed his sheep and lambs? Has he taken to himself the whole armour of God, and fought the good fight? Has he so run that he may obtain? Is he sensible that there is a day of reckoning, and endless retribution to ministers, as well as their people? Is the thought present to his mind, that when he stands with them at the bar of God, it is no impossible thing for the blood of souls to be found in his skirts? The office of a minister of the Gospel imparts deep interest to this day of final account, in regard to those who are committed to his trust. The words which he has spoken will bear testimony for or against those who have listened to them; while, if he himself has been negligent and faithless, nothing can shield him from the appalling doom of the unprofitable servant.

But I will not pursue these thoughts. There is a reproach attached to the character of an idle minister, the stain of which is not easily wiped away. An idle minister of the Gospel of the ever blessed God – what a paradox! Such a man belongs not to the class of ministers whom the Saviour had in his thoughts, when he said to his disciples, 'The harvest is great, but the labourers are few; pray ye therefore the Lord of the harvest, that he would send forth

---

*Neapolitan beggar.

labourers into his harvest!' He is not of the class of ministers whom the church prays for; he should fear lest he is out of his place, and lest the sentence should go forth against him, 'Cut him down, why cumbereth he the ground!' Instead of standing between the living and the dead, that the plague of sin may be stayed, such a minister is like the dead among the living. He buries himself alive, and is much more fit for the graveyard, than for the busy scenes of God's church on the earth, and her unsleeping conflict with the powers of darkness. And when he dies, he 'leaves nothing behind him but a tomb'.

It is of great importance that we should form a just estimate of the true character and work of a minister of the Gospel. We are not responsible for the number of our talents, but for the diligent use of them. We need not be afraid of toil. There are sufficient inducements to effort, and effective incentives to fear. Ministers may hope for a grateful return from men; but if this is denied, the promise is good, 'Lo, I am with you.' They have the light of God's countenance; there is no such pleasure in any of the toils of earth; this world cannot do for them what God their Maker so often does, when he 'gives them songs in the night'. It is no time to rest on the field of battle. Shall ministers be negligent, when their mighty and malicious Foe is so indefatigable to gain the victory over them, and the souls committed to their care? Who would not rather labour and die like Payson, than live in inglorious repose in such a work as the ministry of reconciliation? O for such a spirit! O for such a race of ministers – ministers who could say with Paul, as they look back and look forward, 'I have fought a good fight, I have finished my course!'

12: *Every Thing Subservient to the Pulpit*

It is of great importance to the wise and successful prosecution of any object of pursuit, that it be made the great and absorbing object; that the mind be perseveringly directed to it, unobstructed by other pursuits, undivided by an inferior impulse. A divided heart, and a divided intellect are but cumbrous obstacles in the career of usefulness; the object must be single, and steadily pursued, in defiance of difficulties and dangers, be they imaginary or real.

In the selection of his object, every man is under obligations to make choice of one that is worthy, and that God approves; else, if he be a good man, it will be impossible for him to pursue it with a tranquil conscience, and with hearty good will. But when once he has selected it, it should be the object of his life, and the accomplishment of it the fulfilment of his joy.

This is the only true principle of success in any department of labour; it is the great principle acted upon by men who attain any thing like eminence. They select their object; for the most part they select it in early life, and pursue it with unshaken resolution and firmness.

Now this is what we urge upon every minister of the Gospel. His vocation *is* selected, and his great object is to fulfil the ministry which he has received of the Lord Jesus. But there are different departments of labour in this comprehensive profession, some one of which is very apt to have the pre-eminence in his own thoughts and purposes. If we have presented just views of this great Christian institution, and have not given an undue estimate of the power of the pulpit, we have no embarrassment in asserting that the *great object of every minister of the Gospel ought to be to give the* SERVICES OF THE PULPIT *the pre-eminence over every other department of ministerial labour*. He *may* be tempted to make them a secondary concern, and though very far from subjecting himself to the reproach of clerical indolence, direct his most vigorous efforts to other departments of labour.

It were the wiser part for most ministers to come to the conclusion *seasonably*, that they may scarcely hope to excel in every department. If their great object is to be finished and accomplished scholars, it is one which may easily be attained – much more easily than to be finished and accomplished preachers – but it is only by making it the *great object*; anything short of this will at best assign them a secondary rank among literary and scientific men. They may be *good* scholars, and men of highly respectable attainments in all the departments of human learning; and in those departments more immediately allied to the exposition of the sacred Scriptures, they not only may, but ought to be eminent. But if they aim at more than this, the pulpit must be a subordinate object. They may aim at authorship; they may enrich the periodical publications of the age with dissertation upon dissertation, and review upon review, and on subjects which have very little relation to the work of a Christian minister; and though they may do good service to the church and the world, it is at the expense of the pulpit. The press ought not to be the great object of a Christian minister, except as he makes use of it to diffuse the instructions of the sanctuary. The best and most important publications issued from the press by the stated preachers of the Gospel, both on the Continent of Europe, in the British Islands, and in our land, are those which were first prepared and preached to their own people. The published works of Chillingworth, Charnock, Horne, Butler, Pascal, Fénelon, Saurin, Massillon, Robert Hall, Chalmers, Edwards, Davies, Emmons, and Dwight, were selected from the choicest discourses they delivered to the people of their own charge, and were the cream of the pulpit.

Let every minister of the Gospel, therefore, select his object, and let that object be to give the services of the pulpit the first and paramount claim. Every young man, when he enters the ministry, ought humbly, and with a grateful and encouraged dependence on God, to aim at this important end, patiently, and with a strong and undivided purpose. No matter what the temptations to do otherwise, nor what the labour, nor what the temporary mortification, let him be assured of this one thing, that it is only by so doing that he will best accomplish the great end of his solemn and delightful vocation, accomplish most for God and the souls of men, possess an approving conscience, and finish his course with joy.

Every Thing Subservient to the Pulpit

These thoughts suggest the general observation of which we propose to offer some more extended illustrations. The observation is this: that *every thing with which a minister of the Gospel is concerned ought to be made subservient to the pulpit.* Wherever he is; whatever he does, suffers and enjoys; whatever he sees, hears, or understands – everything should have but this single aim.

We often have occasion to refer to the remark of the Saviour, that 'the men of this world are wiser in their generation than the children of light'. The most accomplished and successful in other departments of professional life are in no one particular more worthy of imitation by the Christian ministry, than the painstaking to which they subject themselves in order to render everything subservient to their professional duties and character. They have but one object, and to that every thing gives way, and becomes subordinate.

This is what we solicit for the pulpit, and from those who occupy it. The fruits of their *observation* ought to be consecrated to the service of the sanctuary. Ministers form a part of this great and busy world. There are men and things everywhere about them, both in the sensitive and intellectual creation; there are facts with which they are conversant, every one of which may suggest some appropriate instruction for the pulpit. To observe them, and thus to employ them, ought to be the aim of the preacher; and even if he is curious in observing them, and inquisitive in searching into them, they may be turned to good account for the souls of men. The heavens and the earth, the clouds, the rain, the vapour, the day, the night, the flowers of the field, the crowded city and peaceful hamlet, read affecting lessons to those who are the appointed teachers of their fellow-men. Every individual with whom the preacher associates; every place, every pastoral visit, every chamber of sickness, every house of mourning and every house of feasting; every old man and every youth, every parent and every child may teach *him* something which may the better enable him to instruct *them.* Every pursuit of men, every relation in human life, every change in human affairs; every pestilence, every season of mercy and every startling judgment; every changing period in the life of man, every moral and intellectual revolution; every change either in the strategy or the tactics of the great spiritual Enemy of mankind; and every marked event in the Divine Providence, ought to be made subservient to the pulpit.

There everything should be made to speak, as God would have it speak. It should utter his voice and enforce his claims; should proclaim that 'he is the Lord in the midst of the earth', and call upon high and low, rich and poor together, to 'kiss the Son lest he be angry, and they perish from the way when his wrath is kindled but a little'.

More especially are these remarks applicable to every minister's intellectual attainments. Men there are of enlarged views – men not only of sound and thorough theological training, but men of literature and science, and of extensive and growing research – who, through lack of consideration, or of competent views of the great work of the ministry, or of spirituality of mind, render the services of the pulpit very little the better for all their attainments. There are not a few examples of such men among the living, nor are examples wanting among the illustrious dead, of those who possessed great literary and scientific attainments, but were far from being so able ministers of the New Testament as others of fewer attainments. Isaac Barrow was far inferior to John Newton as a preacher, though so much his superior in human learning. Ezra Stiles, the venerable President of Yale College, though the most learned man of his age, was far inferior in the pulpit to his distinguished contemporary, Joseph Bellamy. The late Samuel Stanhope Smith, the accomplished President of Nassau Hall, eminent as he was in the pulpit, may scarcely be compared with one of his predecessors, Samuel Davies, as an effective preacher of the Gospel, though the former was confessedly the more erudite scholar. This is an unhappiness; it is at least an oversight; it may deserve a harder name. Such ministers are not so successful in 'winning souls' as many of their less learned and humble brethren who lay their little stock of knowledge under constant contribution to the all-absorbing duties of the sanctuary. The reason why the more learned men in the ministry are not always the richest blessings to the church, and the highest luminaries in the world, is, that they so depreciate the importance of the pulpit.

If a minister of the Gospel knows more than he makes use of for the cause of his divine Master, he knows too much. Yet he cannot know too much if his attainments are wisely and devoutly employed. They ought to be of a high order; but they should be sanctified attainments, consecrated to God, and so employed as to promote the great object of preaching. They are of little worth unless they give him additional facilities of illustrating and enforcing God's truth; additional facilities of access to the heart and conscience; and make him a better man and better minister. This is the class of preachers which are so much needed by the church of God in the present age of the world; and they are formed, not by human learning merely, but by this subserviency of all human attainments to the great object of preaching the Gospel.

Human learning is not more the handmaid of Christianity, than the natural ally of the pulpit. It may be made subsevient to the pulpit without preaching *learnedly*. A discourse that is truly and strictly learned, is rarely called for, while the simplest and plainest exhibition of God's truth, other things being equal, is very apt to be exhibited in the best way from learned lips. It is a beautiful remark of the great Archbishop James Usher, 'It will take all our learning to make things plain.' The true value of human learning in a minister of Christ depends upon the character of the minister himself. The biographer of that eminently godly man, John Brown, of Haddington, who had few superiors in classical, oriental, and theological lore, remarks that 'he never showed his learning in the pulpit, except by bringing down the great truths of God to the level of common capacities'. In a brief autobiography, Brown says of himself, 'Notwithstanding all my eager hunting after all the lawful learning that is known among the sons of men, God hath made me generally to preach as if I had never read any other book but the Bible.' There have been distinguished preachers like John Bunyan, and Paul Couch, of New England memory, who had very little learning save what they drew from the Divine Oracles in their mother tongue; but they were men of no ordinary intellect and piety, and they possessed peculiar fitness for their work. Here and there God raises up such men, that 'no flesh should glory in his presence'. He has given them personal qualifications which, in some instances, are of more value than all human learning, and which no human learning can give. Such men form exceptions to the general law of his Providence.

It is far from the intention of the preceding remarks to discourage the vigorous prosecution of learning in a preacher of righteousness. Those there ought to be among this large class of men, who are not only able to give a Christian literature to the world, but who, from the eminence and the opportunities they enjoy, as the professed teachers of theological science, are under obligation to give an elevated and right direction to the minds, even of severely studious pastors. We gratefully acknowledge our obligations to such teachers; their names are an ornament to the American church; they have not toiled in the field of biblical knowledge and sacred geography in vain; and we fondly hope that the sheaves they have gathered are but the first-fruits of still more luxuriant harvests. No matter how extended the researches of the pastors of the churches, so long as their attainments subserve the great object of preaching the Gospel. The limit imposed upon them must be imposed by an honest conscience, and with an eye single to the glory of God in the salvation of men. If the preacher himself be a true-hearted man, this great object will impose the right limit. The work itself in which he is employed, cannot be magnified beyond its intrinsic greatness. It is directly allied to that Gospel to which all things are subservient, both 'of things in heaven, and things that are on the earth', to that Saviour 'for whom are all things, and by whom are all things', and whose triumphs involve the 'subjection of all things under his feet'. Never is the human intellect, in all the extent and minuteness of its researches, so honoured as when its brightest thoughts blend and mingle with the pure rays of God's truth. Whether it expand itself over the vast extent of human inquiry, or penetrate into deep caverns, or soar to the loftier firmament of thought, never is it more profitably or delightfully employed than when the pulpit makes it subservient to the exalted Saviour. Philosophy and sound thinking; chronology, history, and biography; science and the arts; poetry, music, and painting; the languages and characters of men both among the living and the dead, are then in their true place, when they are made to serve and honour Jesus Christ. Cultivated and accomplished habits, embellished and forcible diction, every resource and every acquisition the preacher can command, have their highest adornment and greatest practical utility when they are made tributary to the cross of Jesus.

To a much greater extent than is sometimes supposed may the intellectual attainments and general information of the preacher exert this propitious influence upon the services of the pulpit. Every book he reads may furnish some aliment for the pulpit, because it may furnish some illustration of God's truth. But to secure this end requires thought and prayer and pains. When he takes a book in his hand, or even an inconsiderable pamphlet, let him inquire, *What is there in these pages that may be turned to good account in the service of my Divine Master?* He may find a single fact only, a single character, or a single date, or it may be a single thought, which he may break up into many thoughts, and profitably spread over a wider surface. He may find matter for a series of discourses, in some prolific thought that is contained within three lines of the author he is reading. Original authors, like Bishop Butler, Dr. Samuel Clarke, and Dr. Nathaniel Emmons, if he know how to make a wise use of them, will not only furnish him with thoughts, but give him the power to think, and to strike out trains or associations of thought that are new to his own mind.

It is one of the most mistaken notions in the world for a preacher of the Gospel to lay himself under a sort of devout interdict from an acquaintance with the teachers of error. His business is to become acquainted with all sorts of error. More especially will he find great advantage in cultivating a familiarity with the published works of the great champions of error. I would not like to be ignorant of the writings of those great masters of infidelity, Hume and Bolingbroke, Voltaire and Herbert; nor of the philosophic views of Price, nor of the researches of Priestley, on the great question of the Saviour's character; nor of the able and subtle discourses of John Taylor of Norwich, and Whitby; nor of the works of Hartley, Chauncey, and Winchester. Modern infidels, Unitarians, Arminians, and Universalists, have done little more than repeat the thoughts of these original thinkers. There is a class of ministers who never preach truth so clearly and forcibly as when they have been reading error; there is so much that is *antagonistic* in their temperament, that they are never better qualified to urge the more positive claims of God's truth, than when they come disgusted and sickened from their interviews with its enemies. If an evangelical preacher be a strong man, he will make the enemies of truth subserve the truth itself; more especially if they be strong and powerful enemies, and men of original powers of mind, he will make the eater bring forth meat, and find honey in the carcase of the lion.

It is one thing to read cursorily, and for amusement; another to enter into the spirit of the author, and sympathize with the operations of his cautious or ardent mind. It is by pursuing the latter course that we read to advantage, and that the minds of men of a higher order than our own, become for the time our own minds, and are employed in the work of our Master. It is much easier to do this than it would appear to be at first view; though it may not be done without a good degree of intellectual discipline, nor without tasking the invention of the reader, and developing his powers of thinking and discrimination. It is recorded by the biographer of Robert Hall, that 'a page to him was more serviceable than a volume to many. *Hints* from reading, or discourse, *passing through his great mind*, expanded into treatises and systems, until the adopted was lost in the begotten; so much so that the whole appeared original'.

There is an exemplification of this remark, in that beautiful discourse of Mr. Hall's, entitled, *The Vanity of Man apart from his Immortality*. Every reader sees that it is a discourse which bears the marks of the author's great mind; yet is it very difficult to resist the impression that he had caught the flame from the burning thoughts of John Howe upon the same topic. Nor is it difficult to see that Dr. Emmons, with all his powers of original thinking, had diligently studied the sermon of Dr. Samuel Clarke, on the 'Unchangeableness of Good and Evil', before he wrote his masterly discourse on 'The essential and immutable difference between Right and Wrong'. Some of the most original thinkers, and best preachers, have been led to strike out trains of thought for themselves, and to put their own genius to the greatest efforts, by being familiar with authors of the same cast of mind with themselves.

A thinking man too, if he understands and relishes an original author, though he be far inferior to the author he is reading, will often perceive important trains of thought on topics that are *altogether foreign to the subject of religion*, but which are equally fitted to illustrate and enforce some great principle of Christian truth and duty. And he will mark them. By dwelling on them, imbibing their spirit, and catching the enthusiasm of his author, he can scarcely avoid making them his own; and when he does so, he will find them of great service, especially in his more extemporaneous efforts. There is many a fine train of argument, illustration and appeal in the writings of Cicero and Edmund Burke, which, though the authors 'meant not so, neither in their heart did they think so', is, for the spirit of it, applicable to more hallowed themes than those to which they were applied by the great Roman and English orators.

Every Thing Subservient to the Pulpit

We see for ourselves with what ingenuity and adroitness distinguished men in other professions turn their reading, and their *hearing* too, to good account. Who has not heard splendid arguments at the bar, which, though truly original, were not a little indebted to the pulpit? The same may be said of some of the best efforts of statesmen, poets, and artists. The writer well remembers a remark made to himself by a distinguished Christian statesman, who at the time to which the observation refers, was a member of the Cabinet at Washington, that in preparing his own mind and heart for one of the most important discussions that ever came before that body, he took pains to fortify himself by reading one of the discourses of Robert Hall. Would that statesmen were all thus pure, and thus influenced by Christian principle! And if statesmen and lawyers and poets and artists may learn something from the ministers of the Gospel, why may not the ministers of the Gospel learn from artists, poets, lawyers, and statesmen?

I will venture to emphasize *artists*, because the products of the pencil are too much overlooked by Christian teachers. The writings of Sir Joshua Reynolds are not more important to a professor of rhetoric, than the productions of his pencil are to the preacher. There are scenes in the Academy of Fine Arts in New York and Philadelphia, and more in the Louvre, in the gallery of the Luxembourg, and of the Prince of Orange, and in the Vatican, on which a preacher might dwell for hours, and from which he might retire to his closet and his study, with sensible benefit to his hearers. The historical associations which a well-informed artist throws upon the canvas, as well as the impressiveness of the lessons he teaches, possess great interest for the mind of an enthusiastic advocate of God's truth. What the artist holds up to the eye, the preacher may proclaim to the ear. I would go far to see such a man as Whitefield, in the Louvre of Paris, or the gallery of the Vatican, at Rome, and then to have heard him preach!

The danger to which a well-furnished preacher is exposed is to make his varied attainments serve himself, rather than the Master to whom he owes allegiance. The temptation is subtle and powerful; for the 'sin that dwelleth in him' is not subdued, and he has many a sinful and corrupt tendency to struggle with. Many a laurel is entwined around the Saviour's brow more for the sake of showing the skill with which the wreath is formed, and the grace with which it is thus entwined, than for his sake whom it professes to honour, and on whose brow it is so gracefully placed. It is not always that an accomplished preacher gives the adorable and ever-blessed Jesus the first place. To do this is one of the ordeals of a self-sacrificing spirit, with which he must lay his account; it is one which nothing but large measures of grace, intimate fellowship with things unseen, and probably frequent and severe personal trials, will enable him to endure. His duty is to merge the man of letters in the humble preacher of the Gospel; his danger, that of merging the preacher in the man of letters. Human learning is the natural auxiliary of God's truth; nor is that minister to be envied who overlooks this relation and forces it to honour himself rather than him to whom all honour belongs.

But they are not only the observation and attainments of the preacher that ought to be made subservient to the pulpit; the cause he advocates has strong claims on his own *personal experience.* It is not so much his experience of men and things to which reference is here had, as his own spiritual experience as a child of God, and the minister of his Gospel. There are emotions of which he is conscious, which relate to his own eternal well-being and to the state of his own soul, which ought to exert a very important influence on his usefulness. If he is a child of God, and his heavenly Father has truly called him to preach the Gospel of his Son; and more especially if he designs to make him eminently useful, he will fit him for his work by those experiences of his faithfulness which show that 'he leads the blind by a way which they knew not, and in paths that they have not known'. It is most delightful to mark the hand of God, and observe his abounding grace toward his ministers in training them for his service, even from their youth. He thinks much of them, even when, like Saul of Tarsus, John Newton, and Henry Mowes of Prussia, they are thinking little of him. He is preparing them for the hardships, and even the peculiarity of their spiritual warfare, and shaping their course with a view to the field of labour they are to occupy, even when he is not in all their thoughts.

When it pleases him to call them by his grace, and reveal his Son in them, that they may preach the unsearchable riches of his grace, his dealings with them are generally more observable and strongly marked. They have much to learn of themselves; much of the varied workings of their own deceitful and wicked hearts; much of the subtle and powerful temptations of the great Adversary; much of God and the fulness of his grace in Jesus Christ, if they become able and faithful ministers of the New Testament. And they have no such teacher as their Divine Lord. He well understands what they most need to learn, and when, and by what means to instruct them most effectively. There is a remarkable adaptation in his teaching to the temperament, and character, and associations of his ministers; to their internal spirit and their outward condition; to their experiences and their weaknesses, and to the peculiar labours which they are called to perform. 'I girded thee,' says God to Cyrus, 'though thou hast not known me.'

In a qualified sense, this is true of all the faithful ministers of Christ. Their ignorance of what God is about to do with them, and for them, and by them, is a veil woven by heavenly mercy; and had it been removed, many a time had their heart sunk within them. No small part of their history is one either of painful or agreeable disappointments. Often they are disappointed in their fears; and at the very crisis when their apprehensions are most excited, and their hopes most depressed, God gives them 'the oil of joy for mourning, and the garment of praise for the spirit of heaviness'; and instead of the depression they looked for, they are enabled to say with the Psalmist, 'Thy right hand hath holden me up, and thy gentleness hath made me great.' On the other hand, they are often disappointed in their hopes. The providence of God toward them seems to have scarcely an immingling of light with darkness; their cup is bitter, and full of wormwood and gall. Sins oppress them; Satan ensnares them, and his fiery darts compass them about on every side; terrors take hold on them as waters; God hides his face, and they are troubled; and they know not how to speak in his name. How various, and often how wonderfully mysterious, are the ways, the dark and intricate paths by which he leads his ministers! Sometimes it is by being left to great sins, and sometimes by being subjected to great afflictions; sometimes by the sins of others, and sometimes by the sweetness and richness of their graces; sometimes by friends, and sometimes being left friendless; sometimes by honour, and sometimes by dishonour; but always by methods which may be employed for their usefulness as the dispensers of his truth.

If a minister would give the pulpit its appropriate energy, he will make all his varied experience subservient to the duties of the sanctuary. The *burden* of every man's preaching will be very apt to be that which most interests his own mind and heart. It is the obvious design of God, both in the dispensations of his providence and grace, to lead ministers' minds to feel an interest in subjects and thoughts which it is of special importance they should present to their hearers. Hence the importance of their observing his dealings with them, and making the best use of their own experience in the instruction of those committed to their charge. If God smiles or frowns upon them; if he suffers Satan to have them that he may sift them as wheat; if he gives them unwonted and humbling views of their own sinfulness; and with great experience of their own wickedness, great experience also of their Saviour's love and mercy; if he covers them with darkness, or enables them to walk in the light of his countenance; it is not for their sakes only, but for those to whom they minister. When we read the life of the Apostle Paul, how obvious is it, that it was the gracious purpose of God to teach the world by the religious experience of this his chosen servant. Or when we read the life of Edward Payson, we cannot repel the conviction that it was for their sakes to whom he preached the glorious Gospel that his religious experience was so strongly marked, and so various; that he was so often plunged into the horrible pit and miry clay, and that his feet were so firmly set on the Rock of Ages, and a new song put in his mouth.

There are shades of difference in the experience of God's ministers in different periods of their history. Youthful ministers are more apt to be severe and objurgatory; the more aged are more persuasive. Youthful ministers breathe the atmosphere of Sinai more freely, and more fully utter forth its thunders; while, in a few passing years, these same preachers dwell more on the matchless love of Christ, and in melting and simple strains beseech men to become reconciled to God. It is not often that you hear a man in the vigour of matured years, representing in all their terrors the torments of the damned; he alludes to them, he affectionately affirms them; but he knows too much of the terrors of the Lord to dwell upon the fearful theme. Youthful preachers make less of a single topic, while older ones throw around it the scattered rays of thought, and collect them together in richer and brighter, though less gorgeous constellations. Youthful preachers have more to do with argument and demonstration; older ones assume what they have so often proved, and are more familiar with the duties of the Gospel than its doctrines. Men require both these kinds of preaching; there must be sons of thunder, and sons of consolation; duties as well as doctrines must occupy a wide space in that system of religious instruction which is to regenerate the world; nor would the pulpit become the full and round echo of God's truth if it did not partake of all that variety of instruction, and those changing shades of thought, which form the counterpart of the preacher's own experience.

Not only does God prepare his servants for this well-adapted and effective teaching, but, if they are 'wise, and will observe these things', they will learn of him who thus 'teacheth them to profit, and who leadeth them by the way that they should go'. They never preach with so much simplicity and power, as when they come to the duties of the Sabbath, with the lessons which the Spirit, or the providence of God, or both, have been instilling into their own minds during the week. They are sometimes precious Sabbaths then, and they are sometimes fearful Sabbaths; but they are effective Sabbaths; there is a solemnity, a tenderness, an impressiveness, and even a *peculiarity* attached to them not soon forgotten. 'In my preaching of the Word,' says John Bunyan, 'I took *special notice* of this one thing, namely, that the Lord did lead me to begin where his Word begins with sinners; that is, to condemn all flesh, and to open and allege that the curse of God by the law, doth belong to, and lay hold on all men as they come into the world, because of sin. Now, this part of my work I fulfilled with *great feeling*; for the *terrors of the law and guilt of my transgressions lay heavy on my conscience*. I preached what I felt, what I *smartingly did feel*; even *that under which my poor soul did groan and tremble to astonishment*. Indeed I have been as one sent to them from the dead. I *went myself in chains, to preach to them in chains*; and carried *that fire in my own conscience* that I persuaded them to beware of. I can truly say, and that without dissembling, that I have gone *full of guilt and terror even to the pulpit-door*; and there it hath been taken off; and I have been at liberty in my mind until I have done my work.' Just think of Bunyan's preaching such a discourse as the one we find in his published works, entitled 'The Barren Fig Tree,' with such a state of mind as this! Listen, while he represents the angry God as saying, 'Death, come smite me this fig tree. Fetch away this fig tree to the fire; fetch this barren professor to hell. At this, Death comes with grim looks to the chamber; yea, and hell follows with him to the bedside, and both stare this professor in the face – yea, begin to lay hands upon him. And now he begins to bethink himself, and cry to God for mercy. Lord, spare me! Lord, spare me! Nay, saith God, you have been a provocation to me these three years. How many times have you disappointed me? How many seasons have you spent in vain? How many sermons and other mercies did I of my patience afford you, but to no purpose at all? *Take him, Death!* O! good Lord, saith the sinner, spare me but this once; raise me but this once; try me this once, and see if I do not mend. Well, saith God, let this professor alone for this time; I will try him a while longer. But by the time he hath put on his clothes, and come down from his bed, he doubleth his diligence after this world, and the heart of this poor creature is fully set in him to do evil. Now God takes hold of his axe again, and heaves it higher; for now indeed he is ready to smite the sinner. His fury comes up into his face; now he comes out of his holy place, and is terrible; now he sweareth in his wrath, that they shall never enter into his rest. I exercised toward you my patience, yet you have not turned unto me, saith the Lord. Because I have purged thee, and thou wast not purged, thou shalt not be purged from thy filthiness any more, till I cause my fury to rest upon thee – cut it down, why doth it cumber the ground? And now Death is at work, cutting of him down, hewing both bark and heart – both body and soul asunder. The man groans, but Death hears him not; he looks ghastly, he sighs, he trembles; but Death matters nothing. He that cuts him down sways him as the feller of wood sways the tottering tree; now this way, then that; at last a root breaks, an heart-string snaps asunder; out goes the weary, trembling soul, down to the chambers of death.'

But it was not always thus with this remarkable preacher; he himself refers to other and more delightful seasons; different words from these often dropped from his lips. To the trembling and heavy-laden sinner, he could say, 'Christ hath everlasting life for him that cometh to him, and he shall never perish. He hath everlasting righteousness to clothe him with; and precious blood, that is like an open fountain for him to wash in; and precious promises, and he shall have a share in them; and fulness of grace for him, and wonderful love, bowels, and compassion. He is open and free-hearted to do thee good; he hath prepared a golden altar for thee to offer thy prayers and tears upon; he hath strewed all the way, from the gate of hell to the gate of heaven, with flowers out of

Every Thing Subservient to the Pulpit

his own garden. Behold how the promises, invitations, calls, and encouragements, like lilies, lie round about thee! Yea, he hath mixed them all with his own name, his Son's name; also with the name of mercy, goodness, compassion, love, pity, grace, forgiveness. Coming sinner, hast thou not now and then a kiss from the sweet lips of Jesus Christ; I mean, some blessed word, dropping, like a honeycomb, upon thy soul to revive thee? Hast thou not sometimes, as it were, the very warmth of his wings overshadowing the face of thy soul, that gives thee, as it were, a glow upon thy spirit, as the bright beams of the sun do upon thy body, when it suddenly breaks out of a cloud, though presently it is all gone away? Well, all these things are the good hand of thy God upon thee, to constrain, to provoke, to make thee willing and able to come, that thou mightest in the end be saved.'

Speaking of the seasons of terror to which we just now referred, Bunyan says: 'After which the Lord came in upon my soul with some sure peace and comfort through Christ; for he did give me many sweet discoveries of his blessed grace through him. Wherefore I now altered in my preaching, for I still preached what I saw and felt. Now therefore, did I much labour to hold forth Jesus Christ in all his offices, relations, and benefits to the world, and did also strive to discover and condemn or remove those false supports and props on which the world doth both lean, and by them fall and perish. And when I have done the exercise, it hath gone to my heart to think the Word should now fall as rain on stony places; still wishing from my heart, that they who have heard me speak this day, did *but see as I do* what sin, death, and hell, and the curse of God is; and also what the grace, love, and mercy of God is, through Jesus Christ.'

There is a *tact* in some ministers in thus making all their observation, learning, and experience subservient to the services of the sanctuary. George Whitefield probably possessed this faculty more than any other preacher since the days of Christ. His biographer remarks, 'that it was no difficult matter to see on what subjects he had been reading during the week; for, *whatever they were*, they would be sure to give freshness and novelty to his illustrations of divine truth on the ensuing Lord's Day'. And we may add, that his habits of *observation* seemed all to have this single aim. And so did his own religious *experience*; for he frequently narrated it from the pulpit, and with a freedom that would appear unbecoming in our fastidious age. These were some of his great excellences as a preacher. He made 'the things that be of men savour the things that be of God'. His 'hands dropped with myrrh, and his fingers with sweet-smelling myrrh upon the handles of the lock'. He seemed to carry the 'bundle of myrrh' within his own bosom. He had an aptitude and skill which were most remarkable, in seizing upon the last author he had read, and upon passing events, and his own recent experience, and applying them with prodigious power to the great object of preaching the Gospel. But the remark may not be omitted, that he did not acquire this facility without effort; his mind and heart were trained to it by great vigilance and much prayer.

We may be allowed to furnish a single example of this last observation. On his first visit to Edinburgh, soon after his arrival, there was an unhappy man to be executed. On the day of the execution, Whitefield mingled with the crowd, and was deeply impressed with the decency and solemnity with which the awful scene was conducted. On the next day, he preached to a very large assembly in a field near the city, on the subject of the *Saviour's crucifixion*; and in the course of his sermon adverted to the scenes of the preceding day. 'I know,' said he, 'that many of you will find it difficult to reconcile my appearance yesterday with my character. I went as an *observer of human nature*, and to see the effect which such an example would have on those who witnessed it. I *watched the conduct of almost every person present on that awful occasion*; and I was highly pleased with their demeanour, which has given me a very favourable opinion of the Scottish nation. Your sympathy was visible in your countenances, particularly when the moment arrived when your unhappy fellow-creature was to close his eyes on this world for ever. Then *you all, as if moved by one impulse, turned your heads aside and wept!* And those tears were precious, and will be had in remembrance. *How different was it when the Saviour of mankind was extended on the cross!* The Jews, instead of sympathizing in his sorrows, triumphed in them. They reviled him with words even more bitter than the gall and vinegar they gave him to drink. *Not one* of all that witnessed his pains turned aside his head, even in the last pang! Yes, my friends, there *was one*; heaven's glorious luminary *veiled his brightness, and travelled on his course in tenfold night!*'

The effect may well be believed to be electrical. But it was no casual remark of the great preacher; nor was it from the impulse of the moment. It was premeditated; he took time, and pains, and even subjected himself to obloquy in order to make the execution of this poor criminal subserve the claims of him who was crucified.

Few men are equal to this. Yet ought every preacher to do all that in him lies to give effect to his preaching, and make every thing subserve the pulpit. The pulpit is his place. There is his work. There he stands as God's ambassador to guilty men; and just in the measure in which he magnifies his office, will he make all that he is, and all that is committed to him, tributary to the work which God has given him to do.

13: *The Preacher's Interest in His Immediate Subject*

Where everything on the part of the preacher is made subservient to the duties of the pulpit, he will be very apt to feel an interest in the work which is more immediately before him. An able advocate at the bar, not only feels an interest in the law, as a profession, and makes every thing subordinate to his professional advancement; he feels a special interest in his client and in his cause. A good physician not only feels an interest in the science of medicine; he feels a deep and absorbing interest in his patient, and in the specific disease which is under his treatment. So, to give the pulpit its appropriate power, it is necessary, that the preacher possess a *deep interest in the subject of every particular discourse*. I do not mean by this, a general interest in the great object of preaching the Gospel; of this I have already spoken; but a special interest in the *subject itself* which forms the theme of the discourse which he is actually uttering.

The subjects which form the themes of discourse from the Christian pulpit are in themselves *capable* of producing and sustaining a very high degree of interest in the mind of the preacher. We have before referred to them; nor are there to be found topics of thought within the wide range over which the human mind expatiates, to be compared with these. The highest intensity of feeling ever brought to the truth of God falls below the great and exciting theme. Whatever is lucid in statement, vivid or great in conception, powerful in argument, accurate in discrimination; in a word, all that is concentrated or discursive, which the preacher himself is able to command, may be employed and exhausted on the great and varied subjects with which his mind is officially familiar. There is no vigour of thought, and no tenderness of heart and feeling, however elevated, subdued or subduing, but here finds an appropriate place. Every passion of the human mind may here be expressed, from the more tranquil to the more agitated; from the tears of compassion and grief, to the thrilling emotions of joy and triumph; from hallowed indignation to transporting complacency. It is not possible to feel too deeply, too intensely on such themes. Moses, when he came down from the mount, with his face radiant, and shining from the power of sacred thought and sentiment, and Paul in the third heavens, were but exemplifications of that state of mind which the truth of God is capable of producing, even in creatures whose 'foundation is in the dust, and who dwell in houses of clay'. It is one of the great peculiarities of God's truth, that the most vigorous and sensitive minds never become weary in contemplating it, except from their own infirmity. The more and the longer they pursue these mighty thoughts, and the more labour they devote to the pursuit, the greater the interest, the freshness, with which the pursuit is conducted. Angels stoop down to look into these things; their mighty minds cannot fully grasp them; they are amazed and confounded before them, and in the contemplation of them, cover their faces with their wings.

It is not so with error: error, in the course of a few years, becomes tame and spiritless. Enterprising minds become weary of it, and after a few bold and strong efforts are very apt to abandon the appropriate duties of the pulpit, if not the pulpit itself, for other employments that are more congenial to their high intellectual impulses. The reason why the enterprising mind of such a man as Dr. Priestley employed itself so extensively on subjects foreign to Christianity, no doubt was, that he did not find enough in the meagre and bald Christianity of which he was the advocate, to interest his own masculine thoughts and emotions. If the true secret were known, this would probably be found to be the reason why not a few of the most accomplished men of the Unitarian School, in our own land, have sickened of their work, and directed their thoughts to more exciting scenes and labours.

The preacher's subject is never a bad one, so long as it is taken from the Bible. All that is necessary to give the more, or the most trivial, sufficient interest, is to make it the matter of sufficiently thorough inquiry. Be the theme what it may that is selected from this inexhaustible treasure-house of thought, there is not one among them all but is capable of imparting deep interest to the mind of the preacher; while the more important impart to it an interest, a solicitude, which are sometimes actually too great for flesh and blood to bear.

I have heard preachers – poetical, *beautiful* preachers – whose tongue was smoother than oil, and whose pencil was cold and faint as 'the star-beams that dance on the icy sea'. I have also heard those whose heart was so absorbed by their theme, that they hurried along the minds of their hearers till they kindled a congenial enthusiasm. Griffin did this, and so did Larned. Brainerd and Payson were *victims* to the deep and unrelieved interest which they felt in the subjects which they presented with so much success to their people. It actually crushed them to a premature grave. No man could long survive this intensity of solicitude, were it felt to the full extent which the subjects themselves are capable of imparting. I may not affirm that such intensity of feeling as this is the duty of ministers; yet were it a great privilege to be more deeply imbued with this divine life. It will not be felt in all its power until this mortal puts on immortality; but we may well long to feel it more. It were, indeed, high blessedness to feel it more deeply. Breathe, blessed Spirit! O breathe, not only upon the dry bones of the valley, but on us who prophesy to them in thy name, that we may live!

We are not in much danger, in this age of declension, of that interest which shall diminish our usefulness by curtailing our period of labour. Our minds and our hearts are sufficiently sluggish; inertness of spiritual thought and feeling is our besetting sin: we have no fear that the machinery will be overworked by a too powerful stimulus. On the other hand, there are so many difficulties in maintaining that interest in the services of the sanctuary which their importance requires, that the danger lies in dying rather from the opposite cause, or lingering under a slow paralysis of all right and vivid emotion.

The youthful ministry have not, indeed, so much to struggle with, in this respect, as those who are in the heyday of human life, and those whose sun is going down. The first vivid impressions of truth are still fresh upon their minds; there is no such decay of that natural ardour which, when brought into the service of Christ, is so beautifully impressive and enchanting; the novelty of their work is not gone; and even deficiencies in grace are ostensibly supplied by the redundancies of nature. Yet are we all deficient here; we are guilty, both young and old, of this strange insensi-

The Preacher's Interest in His Immediate Subject

bility to the claims of God's truth upon our best and warmest affections and most ardent zeal.

It is no unimportant inquiry, How shall a deep interest in his subject be produced in the preacher's own mind? The answer to this question one would think the simplest thing in the world. So far as human means and efforts are concerned, it is by just such a process as that by which the mind of Edmund Burke was interested in his most impressive speeches before the British House of Commons; it is just by those means by which the mind of Guizot was interested in the debates of the French Chamber of Deputies; and just as the minds of Macaulay and Sir Sidney Smith were interested in some of those rich and enthusiastic discussions in the Foreign Reviews, which emanated from their pens. It is by looking at this matter as one worthy of consideration, and by *taking pains* to feel that interest. Does it cost thought, it must have thought; does it cost reading, it must have reading; does it cost great self-denial, self-denial it must have; does it cost conversation with men, or intercourse with God; these must not be denied. Sometimes it may come over the preacher's mind, like an unexpected cloud in a clear sky, and he may feel its refreshing influence; but for the most part, it does not visit him unsought. He strives for it, because he deeply feels the need of it; he seeks it, because it is *given*; and he more usually seeks it most earnestly and most successfully in the seasons of his greatest depression.

We cannot but have observed the various degrees of interest which different minds take in the same subject; and which the same minds feel at different times. And it is most encouraging and gratifying to observe the high degree of interest which humble prayer and patient thought often impart. When the mind is earnestly directed toward any important subject; when it is turned over and over again in the thoughts, and viewed on every side; and when investigation, ingenuity, and prayer, and unwearied application are devoted to it, that it may be seen in its clearest and strongest lights, and felt in its true power; it is ordinarily thus seen and felt. To consent to feel this interest; to labour for it, and to practise the self-denial which is necessary in order to cherish it, is never a useless effort. To carry the subject in our thoughts through the week, or even the *weeks* of preparation; to associate it with our toil and our relaxation; to allow it to go out with us when we walk, to haunt our pillow, and creep unseen within the folds of thought when we sleep; to wake with us when we wake, and to be, for the time, the master impulse; *this* is it which gives to the preacher's mind a deep interest in his subject, when he goes to the sacred desk.

These are not unhallowed views; nor are they designed to make any appeal to the preacher's vanity. We do not speak of interest in his subject for the preacher's sake, but for his *subject's* sake. Nor do we mean by taking pains to feel this interest, a desperate and agonizing effort to prepare and preach *a great sermon*; but so to preach what God has enabled him to prepare, that the precious truths of the gospel may not be denuded of their power through the preacher's listlessness.

It is recorded of Henry Mowes, the celebrated Prussian preacher, that a sermon, with him, 'was not the work of a day. It was not a mere outward act; it was an expression of himself. It occupied the whole week. He had it almost daily in his mind. Often would he be found with his first sketch before him, *with his eyes filled with tears*'. Here is the secret of good preaching. A listless week and a Sabbath of interest are just those things which God has not joined together. Spirituality in the pulpit and the want of it in the study of the preacher never dwell together in the same bosom. Ministers may not look for miracles. The kingdom of grace does not set itself against the kingdom of providence; nor does the Spirit of God in any of his operations, ordinarily counteract the laws of man's intellectual economy. The sovereignty of divine influences is wont to put honour upon all the institutions of God's appointment, both in the natural and spiritual world.

The men of the world are absorbed in their *object*; the rich in their pursuit of gain; the ambitious in their pursuit of power; the literary in their pursuit of fame. They are immersed in their object, almost to madness; and their burning zeal attracts every thing around it to feed its flame. Their favourite schemes and projects are scarcely ever absent from their thoughts. Now, it is something like this engagedness, this animation and earnestness, which the pulpit needs, in order to give it power. The preacher must be in earnest; he must lose himself in his subject. He must have a longing, heartbreaking desire to impress the truth he is uttering upon the minds of his hearers.

Nor is it enough for him to feel the *importance* of his subject; he must feel its *peculiarity*. I knew a preacher once, more than twenty years ago, who employed one entire week in writing a discourse on

The Preacher's Interest in His Immediate Subject

the words, 'And in hell he lifted up his eyes, being in torments.' The fearful subject was not absent from his thoughts an hour, till he laid his head upon his pillow on the evening which preceded the Lord's Day. No, nor even then. It was a solemn week to his own soul, a solemn night, but it was a bright and glorious Sabbath which followed it. There are those among the living who remember that day. It will be remembered in eternity.

Let the preacher thus feel his subject; let him feel it to the last hour of preparation, and the last prayer he offers before he enters the sanctuary; and he will go to his work under a high-born and heavenly impulse. When such a preacher goes into the pulpit, he stands there as the dignified, earnest, faithful, affectionate messenger of God, and pours forth the fulness of his thoughts, the strength and ardour of his emotions in some sort worthy of the cause he advocates. He is full of his theme; for days and nights he has been thinking of it, and poring and praying over it. He is imbued with it; what his subject is, that *he* is; he is baptized with it; he has the unction of it, and it is an unction of the Holy One. Such preachers are, in the true sense of the phrase, *great preachers*. They are great preachers, because it is not *they* who preach, but their *subject*; it is not *they* who speak, so much as *Christ* speaking in them and by them. The *men* are little things; their *subject* every thing. *They* are nothing, *Christ* is all.

Every minister loves to preach to an *attentive* auditory. There must be two great constituent elements in the preacher himself, without which the attention of his audience cannot be secured; they are the subject-matter of his preaching, and the interest which he himself takes in what he utters. The late Dr. Emmons was once asked, by one of his brethren, *What was the best remedy for an inattentive audience?* His characteristic reply was, *Give them something to attend to!* But this is not all. He must feel his subject. It is as marvellous as it is mournful, that the weighty and thrilling truths of God's Word lose so much of their force from the little interest the preacher himself feels in his theme. George Whitefield was probably the most remarkable man, in this respect, whom the world has seen.* Rich as his discourses were, they do not compare

---

*This remarkable man was ordained by Bishop Benson. In an interview between the bishop and the Countess of Huntingdon, after some earnest expostulations on the part of her ladyship, the bishop rose up in great haste to depart, bitterly lamenting that he

with the discourses of some other preachers in richness of thought. But in intensity of feeling, he had no equal. He enchained his auditory by his intense interest in his subject. A ship-carpenter once remarked, that 'he could usually build a ship from stem to stern, during the sermon; but under Mr. Whitefield he could not lay a single plank'. It is of themselves ministers should frequently complain, rather than of their hearers; it is they who are cold and inanimate. A drowsy pulpit makes an inattentive and drowsy congregation. Let a strange preacher enter any pulpit in the land, and from the attentive, or inattentive habits of the people, he will not fail to form some just conceptions of its settled ministry.

A preacher who feels an interest in his subject will always be listened to. His hearers may not believe his doctrine; they may be captious, critical, fastidious; but they *will hear*. He cannot have an inattentive auditory; the thing is impossible. Few eyes will wander, few minds will be listless, few hearts will be indifferent. Those to whom he preaches may complain; they may hear and hate; but they will hear. No preacher can sustain the attention of a people unless he feels his subject; nor can he long sustain it, unless he feels it deeply. If he would make others solemn, he must himself be solemn; he must have fellowship with the truths he utters. He must preach as though he were under the eye of God, and as though his own soul were bound up in the souls of those who hear him. He must preach as though he were in sight of the cross, and heard the groans of the Mighty Sufferer of Calvary; as though the judgment were set, and the books opened; as though the sentence were just about to be passed which decides the destinies of men; as though he had been looking into the pit of despair, as well as drawing aside the veil, and taking a view of the unutterable glory.*

---

had ever laid hands upon George Whitefield. 'My lord,' said the Countess, 'mark my words: when you are on your dying bed, that will be one of the few ordinations you will reflect upon with complacence.' The bishop indeed verified her prediction; for when near his death, he sent ten guineas to Mr. Whitefield as a token of regard and veneration, and begged to be remembered by him in his prayers. The poet laureate, Southey, in his Life of Wesley has, little to his credit, related the former, but suppressed the latter part of this anecdote.

*'The bishops,' said George III, 'are very jealous of such men.' When a distinguished prelate complained to him of the zeal of the ministers under the patronage of Lady Huntingdon, he replied, 'Make bishops of them; make bishops of them!' 'That might be done,' replied the prelate, 'but we cannot make a bishop of Lady Huntingdon.'

More than this. He must preach as though *eternal realities were suspended on the passing hour*. This is a thought which ought to be deeply inwoven with the preacher's views and emotions. I have often asked myself why it is that a congregation assembled for the worship of God are, for the most part, less interested in a discourse from the pulpit, than a jury are interested in an argument from the bar! It is not because the bar is always more eloquent than the pulpit, though it often is so; nor is it altogether because the pulpit speaks of unearthly things, and the bar of things earthly. It is mainly because the speaker and the hearers in the courts of law speak and hear with the view of coming to a *present decision* on the subject submitted to their consideration. This *responsibility rests upon them*, and they may not be listless. Let but the thought be present to the mind of the preacher and the hearers, that in the progress and at the close of his discourse *decisions* are to be made that will affect the destiny of men, for weal or for woe, through interminable ages, and this listless hearing, and this insensate preaching, will exist no longer. I say, this *insensate preaching*, because, so far as I have been able to observe, the people are in advance of their preachers in the all-important duty of wakeful and interested attention. It is a very remarkable fact, that God is giving men the hearing ear. They are doing just what they ought to do – expecting much from their ministers; and well it may cause grief of heart that it is an expectation which, with all their increased opportunities, the ministry of the word does not more frequently gratify. There is sin in the pulpit in this matter: would to God that the writer had not so much cause to lay his hand upon is mouth!

One of the effects of a due interest in the subject-matter of the pulpit would be, the happy influence it would exert upon the *elocution and manner* of the preacher. He would not utter his discourse carelessly, nor with the rapidity with which a school-boy recites his lesson. He would not become an *imitator*, but utter God's truth in his own way. There is no air of pretence about him; no craving after effect, no swelling accomplishments. There is earnestness, but there is simplicity and truth. The artificial, the

---

'Well, well,' said the king, 'see if you cannot imitate the zeal of these men. I wish there was a Lady Huntingdon in every diocese in the kingdom.' To which words the queen added, 'As for her Ladyship, you cannot make a bishop of her, it is true: it would be a lucky circumstance if you could, for she puts you all to shame.'

studied, the theatrical, has little sympathy with that chastened feeling which flows from deep interest in his subject. He may be all action, and will be if it is his nature to be so;* but it is possible he may have *very little action*, and yet be a powerful preacher. He would come down upon his hearers, sometimes like the wind, sometimes like the earthquake, sometimes like the fire, and sometimes like the still, small voice. The elder Edwards had no action at all; yet such was his *interest in his subject*, that crowded auditories burst into one universal weeping under his discourses.

Such a preacher may not be accomplished, but he will be forcible; there may be classic embellishment, where the heart is cold as marble. He may even be awkward, but if his subject first live in his own heart, he will be effective. He will not be vain, nor ambitious of distinction of any sort, save to win souls. He will not go out of his path in search of adornment and flowers; though he may pick them up when they lie in his way. He goes forth weeping, bearing precious seed; they are the sheaves that he is looking after, and he brings them home with rejoicing. If his sickle is not tipped with gold, it is of well-attempered steel; it is like a two-edged sword, and he uses it manfully, and as though he was wielding the 'sword of the Spirit'.

The biographer of Archbishop Leighton remarks, that 'he was too intent upon his *subject* to be choice of words and phrases; and his works discover a noble carelessness of diction, which in some respects enhances their beauty. His language is better than mere correctness would make it; more forcible and touching; attracting little notice to itself, but leaving the reader to the full impulse of the ideas of which it is the vehicle. It is great by the magnificence of thought, by the spontaneous emanation of a mind replete with sacred knowledge and bursting with seraphic affections, by that pauseless gush of intellectual splendour, in which the outward shell, the intermediate letter, is eclipsed and almost annihilated,

---

*The late Dr. Stonehouse is said to have been one of the most correct and elegant preachers in the kingdom of Great Britain. When he entered into holy orders, he took occasion to profit by his acquaintance with Garrick, the actor, to procure from him some valuable instructions in elocution. Being once engaged to read prayers and preach in a church in the city, he prevailed upon Garrick to go with him. After the service, Garrick asked the doctor what particular business he had to do, when the duty was over? 'None,' said the other. 'I thought you had,' said Garrick, 'on seeing you enter the reading desk in such a hurry.' Nothing can be more indecent than to see a clergyman 'set about his sacred business as if he were a tradesman, and go into the church as if he

The Preacher's Interest in His Immediate Subject

that full scope may be given to the mighty effulgence of the informing spirit'.

Such a preacher throws the ornate and scholastic preacher into the shade. He may not be a splendid and pompous declaimer; but he is an earnest preacher of the truth as it is in Jesus, and an able minister of the New Testament. He may not *try* to be eloquent, but he will *be* eloquent; his eloquence will be thrilling and impassioned, and tell on the conscience and heart. Pascal speaks of 'the eloquence that despises eloquence'; and is not this the only true eloquence? 'Eloquence', says he, 'is a pictorial representation of thought; and hence those who, after having painted it, make additions to it, give us a fancy picture, but not a portrait.' Let the preacher utter that which comes in contact with the minds of his hearers, and let him *so* utter it as to establish the correspondence between what he utters and what they perceive and feel; and so far as human instrumentality can do it, he will not fail to carry the hearts of his auditory. This is his object; it is his sole object. Like an able and effective advocate at the bar, who is more intent on gaining the cause of his client, than on making a pretty speech, or a splendid argument, he delivers himself to the purpose. His obligations as a minister of the Gospel are present to his thoughts; he feels for men who are so soon to become the tenants of an unalterable eternity; and, like Paul, he is 'pressed in spirit to testify to them that Jesus is the Christ'. He does not *affect* an interest in his subject he does not feel; he has that deep experience of God's truth which teaches him how to feel and how to speak. He 'speaks that which he knows, and testifies that which he has seen'. There is honesty in his spirit, and nature in his manner; and therefore is there impressiveness and urgency. And there is great variety, too. Sometimes he is plain and argumentative; sometimes authoritative; in his rebukes sometimes tender, and sometimes terrible; but more often a weeping suppliant, beseeching men to be reconciled to God.

This is the highest style of the pulpit; especially if the preacher have gifts as well as graces, and possesses a vigorous and comprehensive mind. Even men of ordinary endowments, with

---

wanted to get out of it as soon as possible'. He next asked the doctor, 'What books he had on the desk before him?' 'Only the Bible and Prayer-book.' '*Only* the Bible and Prayer-book,' replied the player; 'why you tossed them backwards and forwards, and turned the leaves as carelessly as if they were those of a day-book and ledger.'

such a spirit, are effective preachers. We have known many such; may the Lord of the harvest multiply them! He himself is with such ministers; and when his presence goes with them, the pulpit has power. It does execution; it saves; and where it saves not, it most fearfully damns the soul. It is this that makes the light of the pulpit shine, and its ministers a flame of fire.

14: Ministers Must Be Men of Prayer

An occasional remark has been thrown out in the preceding pages, intimating the importance of prayer in the ministers of the Gospel. The thought is one which may not be passed over lightly.

The appropriate vocation of a minister of the Gospel is one which has much to do with God; it is a spiritual, and not a secular vocation. His own soul may indeed be greatly ensnared by this very circumstance; he *must* be familiar with spiritual things; this is his *business*, and he *may* be familiar with them as a *matter of business only*. If it be so with any of us, we are of all men most to be commiserated; because, 'after having preached to others, we ourselves shall be cast away'. If it may be said of any man in the world, that he lives very near to heaven, or very near to hell, it may be said of a minister of Jesus Christ. If he is not a pious man, he is among the most obdurate of the wicked; and though his feet may stand on the highest mountains of Zion, he stands on slippery places, and shall slide in due time. If he is not a man of prayer, he is not a man of God, and had better be anywhere else, than in the pulpit.

Yet is the thought a pleasant one to the mind of a good man, that he is occupied in a religious, and not a worldly vocation; and that the privileges as well as the obligations of the sacred ministry have this great peculiarity. 'We will give ourselves to prayer and the ministry of the word.' This is the law of the pulpit. Ministers are 'labourers together with God'; and their intercourse with him ought to be unembarrassed and intimate. Their life is one of continual, and in some respects, peculiar dependence on him; and on him their eye ought to be steadily fixed. This is their great support and comfort. Their personal trials are sufficiently numerous; and if they have not a refuge in God, and hide not beneath the shadow of his wings, the Comforter is far – far away. To no class of men is the thought more welcome and precious that God is their friend, than to the trembling heart and jaded mind of his ministers. 'More is he that is for us, than they that are against us!' Who better than they know how to appreciate the inviting summons, 'Come, my people, enter thou into thy chambers, and shut thy doors about thee; hide thyself as it were for a little moment, until the indignation be overpast.' Who more than they have need to appropriate the promise, 'For in the time of trouble he shall hide me in his pavilion; in the secret of his tabernacle shall he hide me; he shall set me up upon a rock.'

But these are not the precise thoughts which we desire here to enforce. We speak rather of that intercourse which ministers have with God as his commissioned servants, sent by him to perform a great work, and one in which they constantly need his assistance and direction. We would fain urge upon ourselves and our fellow-labourers that delightful *habit* of prayer, in the cultivation of which the commissioned servants of God go to him under every exigency, and in which there is such an exceeding great reward.

There are ministers who are by no means slothful, and who possess a deep interest in their work, who yet labour to very little purpose, *because their time* is not *profitably* employed. Their course of reading and study is not so useful to them, as preachers, as it might be; and their out-door labour is not always so arranged as to subserve the pulpit. In this matter they need to be directed by wisdom that is from above, and should seek that direction as constantly as they ask for their daily bread. Youthful ministers especially, are not always sensible of the importance of so employing their time, and arranging their labour as to accomplish the most for the cause of God and the souls of men. Yet this is their great object; and in the prosecution of it they must just submit themselves to a heavenly guidance.

In their *selection of subjects* also for the instruction of their people, ministers are often most unwise, and expend no small amount of strength to very little effect. I have heard many a discourse which produced the impression on my own mind, that if the same amount of thought and labour had been bestowed on a more useful topic, the preacher would have better answered the expectation of his hearers, and the great object of preaching the Gospel. There is not a little preaching which, from this cause alone, profits no one; it is not to edification. While listening to it, an intelligent and devout hearer can scarcely help saying within himself, What then? What if it is all as you say? What good comes of all this? Do we say more than we are warranted in saying when we express the fear that too many preachers select their subjects 'without asking counsel of God'? It is no small relief, in prosecuting his studies for the week, for a minister to have the consciousness that his divine Master approves his work, and that the discourse he is preparing is upon a topic which has been assigned him, and given him in answer to prayer. Nay, there is confidence; there is courage and hope; there is joy; his own mind is stimulated by the thought, nor does the sacred excitement pass away until he has delivered himself of the burden, and his appointed message is made known.

More than this. It is no uncommon thing for the preacher to be *greatly embarrassed* in the choice of his subject; the embarrassment is not unfrequently a serious one, and occasions loss of time and effort. Sometimes it arises from the poverty of his own resources; sometimes from the difficulty of deciding between the conflicting claims of more subjects than one; and sometimes from the sluggish operations of his own mind. It is often a profitable embarrassment to the preacher, and constitutes a part of that intellectual and spiritual discipline, by which he is made a better man and a better minister. By it he is taught to think and feel and pray, and he is brought to a deeper sense of his own littleness. He learns to have recourse to the Master who sent him; and he finds it available. The promise is good, 'If any man lack *wisdom*, let him ask of God, who giveth liberally and without upbraiding.'

The writer has now in his thoughts a youthful minister of Christ, who had occupied almost an entire day in searching for a subject for the following Sabbath. He had sought direction apparently in vain; he had turned over page after page in the Bible; he had inspected his commonplace-book; and could find no subject in which he felt sufficient interest to induce him to select it as the topic of his forthcoming discourse. His mind was depressed; he felt as though he could never write another sermon, and doubted his fitness for the ministry. Toward the close of the day, he fell again on his knees, and the first sentence he uttered was, 'O Lord, I am as a *beast* before thee!' The thought he had uttered made a deep impression on his mind, and at the close of his prayer, he turned to his folded manuscript, and began a discourse from that passage in the seventy-third Psalm: 'So foolish was I and ignorant, I was as a beast before thee!' God had heard the voice of supplication.

We have no doubt that this is substantially the history of thousands and thousands of some of the most profitable discourses that are ever preached. We who ought to know so much of God know very little of his bounty; very little of his faithfulness and condescension as a prayer-hearing God. We too often pray as though we thought him unwilling to give. What amazing words are those – 'O THOU THAT HEAREST PRAYER!' Subjects that are thus given in answer to prayer ought always to be accepted, be the subsequent labour they cost what it may. God is pleased that we should ask, and pleased when we accept and employ his gifts. He will continue to give, if we furnish this proof of our honesty in asking.

Still further. The same spirit of prayer should attend us in the *preparation* of our discourses, as in selecting the subjects of them. If we are not satisfied with the method and arrangements of our thoughts, or if we are not satisfied with a page we have written; let us betake ourselves to our knees till we are satisfied. Let us not only *think out* our subject, but *pray it out*. Those views of divine truth which are enjoyed under the influence of prayer are very different from those in which prayer has no part. Without prayer, even the more spiritual truths will be very apt to be studied as a science merely, and our increasing acquaintance with them will not minister to our spirituality. With it, we shall acquaint ourselves more with the adorable and ever-blessed God, and with every view of him shall sink in the dust before him, and make his service our joy. It is not the view of the naked eye that discovers God's truth in its beauty; it is the view taken through the telescope of prayer, in which distant objects are brought near and magnified. Things unseen elsewhere are seen at the mercy-seat, and in new aspects, and new beauty and loveliness. They stand out in their celestial brightness, they cluster like the stars in the Milky Way. The delighted eye dwells upon them, the swelling bosom feels them, and when we speak of them it is with glowing lips. We have often read of those who studied the Bible upon their knees. Would not our sermons be more appropriate and effective, if more elaborate with prayer? Would not the weak parts of them be stronger, the barren more rich, the cold more ardent, the objurgatory more persuasive, and the whole more pungent and faithful, were it more imbued with the spirit of prayer?

Nor is this all. If from the toil of the study we advert to the *devotional* services of the sanctuary, what minister will venture upon them without prayer? For every part of this public service, the spirit produced at the mercy-seat is a qualification that is absolutely indispensable; but in no one thing are ministers more deficient than in the *devotional* exercises of God's house. We sometimes listen to prayers from the pulpit which are absolutely chilling: they have no connection of thought, and no spirituality of feeling. While listening to them, they seem to us to partake very little of the character of religious worship: were there no relief from such prayers, we would gladly take refuge in the formularies of an established liturgy.

We are no advocates for forms of prayer in the pulpit: the Scriptures set us a different example. The nature of the service itself requires a more spontaneous and free, and full, and varied expression of Christian feeling than any forms can furnish. Piety itself very often requires the free and spontaneous expression of a full and gushing heart. Those who are, on principle, most attached to forms, are not unfrequently constrained to lay them aside. Archbishop Secker, when laid on his couch with a broken thigh, was visited at Lambeth by Mr. Talbot, the vicar of St. Giles, in Reading, who had lived in great intimacy with him, and received his preferment from him. 'You will pray for me, Talbot', says the Archbishop, during the interview. Mr. Talbot rose and went to look for a prayer-book. 'That is not *what I want now*,' said the dying prelate; 'kneel down by me, and *pray* for me *in the way I know you are used to do*'; with which command this zealous man of God complied, and prayed earnestly from his heart for his dying friend, whom he saw no more.

An instance of episcopal candour like this is well worth recording. Grace is stronger than forms, and in the time of need must have utterance in its own way. A most beautiful sight is this – a devout clergyman of the Church of England kneeling at the bedside of the dying Primate, and at his request offering an extemporaneous prayer in the Archbishop's palace at Lambeth! There is no need of argument in favour of spontaneous prayer, after this. A rich and spiritual prayer, coming from the well-furnished mind and glowing heart of the preacher, forms one of the great excellences of our own directory for religious worship. We have on one occasion, and in accommodation to the usage of the place, publicly made use of the forms of prayer of our Episcopal brethren: but it was new wine – the old is better. We greatly prefer our own usages. These spontaneous devotional exercises with us decide the character of the whole service. We know how a minister will preach, after we have heard him pray.

Never shall I forget some prayers I have listened to during seasons when God was pouring out his Spirit upon the church of which I was a member before I became a minister of the Gospel. Often have I felt since, that these services are the most responsible and most difficult part of a minister's duty. Oh, the trembling of heart which sometimes comes upon us when we stand up to address the Infinite God! Our hearers, for the most part, think little of this part of our public duty; but once let the most devout and most intelligent of them ascend the sacred desk, and spread forth his hands to pray, and he will at least have some sympathy with those on whom this solemn responsibility is devolved. And where do they learn to pray, but in habitual and intimate fellowship with God, in the secret of his presence? It is by praying, that we learn to pray. No matter how much we have otherwise learned, if we have not sweet and happy intercourse with God in our closets the lesson is forgotten. But there is a halo of glory around the mercy-seat, in the midst of which it is impossible long to remain in secret, without reflecting its radiance when we stand in the presence of the 'great congregation'.

If from the devotional part of the service, we turn to what is more properly its *instructions*, there is not a devout minister in the world but would bear testimony, that there is no preparative for preaching like that which is made in his closet. Nowhere else will his mind become so imbued with the spirit of his errand; or so deeply impressed with a sense of the Divine presence; or so touched with love to Jesus Christ and the souls of men. Whence too, comes that power of the Holy Ghost, which renders the truth powerful, but from the same exhaustless source? No minister has done his utmost to give power to the pulpit, who has not tried the power of prayer. Shame on us that our preaching is so powerless, when God has said, 'Ask, and ye shall receive!' Is it so, that we may always go into the pulpit fully furnished for our work, and have the Spirit of our Master with us, simply for the asking, and shall we ever go alone?

It was a terrible reproof to men of other times, 'There is none that calleth upon thy name, that stirreth up himself to take hold of thee.' It is indeed a wondrous thought, that worms of the dust may thus have free access to God, and are actually rebuked for not 'stirring up themselves' to take hold on him. There are *no* discouragements in our work when we can go to God's throne. We need be careful for nothing, if 'with a true heart and full assurance of faith', we can come near even to his seat and fill our mouth with arguments. We may, indeed, often go with heaviness, but we shall often come away with tranquillity and joy. We may go as slaves, but we shall find our chains knocked off there, and have the liberty of children. We may fear and tremble; we may agonize; but we shall prevail. Jacob, as a prince, wrestled with the Angel of the Covenant, and had power with God. O what an illustration of the power of prayer was that! *Let me go! let me go!* No, no, *I will not let thee go; I will not let thee go unless thou bless me!* How little do we know of the power of prayer! a power to which even the power of God condescends to be subjected, and which divides with him the government of the world! Others may think as they will; but for ourselves, we cannot reconcile the form of prayer with the power of prayer. Just think of Jacob reading from a prayer-book, when he wrestled with the Angel of the Covenant; or Elijah when he bowed his knees on the mount! It lessens its power just in the measure in which it depends on form. The atmosphere of prayer is not that factitious atmosphere which is evolved by the screws of a printing press. Where the heart feels deeply, and prays effectively, it throws away its forms; it has desires of its own and must express them.

We scarcely know what different men, what different ministers, we should be, did we know more of the power of prayer. We should see in God's light, labour in his strength, repose in his love, be filled from his fulness, reflect his glory, live in and for him. He who hears the young ravens when they cry, would not shut his ear against us when we go at his bidding and on his errand. When Moses complained that he was 'slow of speech, and of a slow tongue', his Maker replied to him, 'Who made man's mouth? Now, therefore, Go; I will be with thy mouth, and teach thee what thou shalt say!' We may be compassed about with infirmities; but 'with the petition in one hand, and the promise in the other', we may be 'strong in the Lord, and in the power of his might'.

It is narrated in the life of Andrew Fuller, that at a meeting of several very distinguished ministers at Northampton, the question was discussed very much at length, 'To what causes, in ministers themselves, may much of their want of success be imputed?' The answer 'turned chiefly upon their want of personal religion; particularly *the neglect of close dealing with God in closet prayer*'. The probability is, that every collection of judicious and godly ministers would come to the same conclusion. The prophet seems to express the same thought when he says, 'Their pastors have become brutish; they *have not sought the Lord*; therefore they shall not prosper, and their flocks shall be scattered.' The time was, when the pastors of the American churches valued the privilege of prayer. They were not only men of prayer, but they prayed often for and with one another; their reciprocal and fraternal visits were consecrated and sweetened by prayer; nor was it any unusual thing for them to employ days of fasting and prayer together for the effusions of God's Spirit upon themselves and their churches. And they were days of power, days when God's arm was made bare, and his right hand plucked out of his bosom. Nor was it difficult to see, then, wherein the great strength of the pulpit lies; 'he that is feeble among them shall be as David, and the house of David shall be as God'.

15: *The Personal Piety of Ministers*

There is no topic on which the writer addresses his brethren in the ministry, either young or old, with more reluctance and shamefacedness, than that which is here indicated. Yet much as he is constrained to fill his own bosom with reproach, and humbling as he foresees his reflections must be at every step, he may not forego what he hopes may be deemed some appropriate thoughts on a subject so vital to the power of the pulpit. The most discouraging, yet most impulsive thought, in attempting to perform this service, is, that in no part of the present volume does he rebuke the meanest of all God's servants with the same severity with which he feels he must administer rebuke to his own soul.

It was a very bold and presumptuous thing on his part, when as a young man, and but just entering on the third year of his ministry, he ventured to instruct his fellow-men by some published *Essays on the Distinguishing Traits of Christian Character*. Almost forty years in the ministry have taught him that youth and inexperience can write more flippantly on such a theme than maturer years, deeper retrospection, and a more varied, if not more doubtful experience.

It does not require much discernment to see, that if one would be an effective preacher he must be a pious man. He may indeed occupy the place of a minister, and do some good in the world, and be destitute of piety. God may restrain him from overt sins; his religious education and enlightened conscience, his habits of application, and his intellectual orthodoxy may accomplish something toward supplying the deficiencies of imparted grace. His love for moral disquisition may give him an interest in his appropriate work; his attainments as a scholar, and his power over the minds of men as a teacher, may render his work pleasant; while his pride of character, if he is a hypocrite, and his false hopes, if he is a self-deluded man, may give a buoyancy to his mind which shall induce him to fulfil his ministry to the last. Yet all the while he may live and die an ungodly man. His church may mourn over him when he sleeps in the dust; his fellow-labourers in the work of God may stand around his grave, and say, 'Alas, my brother!' and many an honest panegyric may be uttered in commemoration of his fidelity, while he himself is 'lifting up his eyes in hell, being in torments!' He has appeared in the presence of his Judge, and uttered that last plea of a forlorn hope, '*Have I not prophesied in thy name?*' but he has received the final answer, 'I never knew you; depart from me, thou worker of iniquity!'

If we should say we weep while we thus write, perhaps there are those who would not sympathize with us. Yet who would not weep? Oh, is there one of all the race of Adam more to be pitied than such a minister? With its 'poison drop of scorn' he must drain the cup of agony, and taste all the bitterness of death. He has saved others; himself he could not save! Through that very instrumentality by which his mind has become blinded, his heart hardened, and his eternal doom aggravated, others have been brought into the kingdom, while their own once beloved minister is justly cast out into outer darkness, where there is weeping and wailing and gnashing of teeth! He who wept over Jerusalem, I am sure, were he on earth, would weep over such a man. Could angels weep, they would flood the pulpit of such a man with tears. None, none but the sturdiest devil, could be indifferent to such a doom. Yet have there been, and are, such ministers. Oh that we might be more faithful to our own souls! that we might be more faithful to one another, love one another more, and pray for one another, lest we also come to that place of torment! It is a sacred office which the ambassador of the cross holds; but there is nothing in it which will save him from hell.

The evidences of piety in ministers are the same as in other men; they know what they are, and need only the same self-inspection and scrutiny which they urge upon those who hear them. God does not always give them that consciousness of a filial spirit, and that full assurance of hope which are frequently enjoyed by private Christians. They have ordinarily less embarrassment in their view of his truth than private Christians, but more spiritual darkness. Now and then their consciousness of love to the Saviour is absolute, their path is all radiance and joy, and their step firm and strong toward the house not made with hands, eternal in the heavens. In the strength of such a faith they go many days, and even after the noonday brightness is past, and the sun of hope gone down, the twilight lingers long, and as in the frigid zone, sometimes mingles itself with the blushing dawn. Yet is it no uncommon thing for them to pursue their toil under great doubts of the genuineness of their own religion; and if you were to ask them, at the close of some of the most impressive discourses they ever preach, if they had made their own calling and election sure, they might only tell you that they have hoped it is well with them; or they might be silent; or they might be pensive, and turn away to seek some secret place of prayer. Yet they toil on, usefully and often cheerfully, in seed-time and in harvest, through storms and sunshine, on the Sabbath and during the week, under the busy noon and silent midnight, satisfied of the truths of God's holy Word, with a firm and unshaken belief that there is a way in which he can safely and honourably show mercy, and, at the same time, so deeply sensible of their own ill-desert, and the excellence of his justice, that they leave the event in his hands, resolving only to labour on and finish the work which he has given them to do. Paul's state of mind was different; his religion was brighter; his faith in the great propitiation was stronger, and his hopes more cloudless. Yet do ministers often need such a discipline as this, to constrain them to walk humbly before God and the world.

True piety is its own evidence wherever it exists in the soul. There is something in it which is so totally different from all sinful principles and affections, that it is the proper object of consciousness. If a man loves Jesus Christ more than father, or mother, or wife, or children or houses, or lands, or even his own life, the change in his affections, from what he was by nature, is such as to be perceived. The reason why this perception is not always distinct and strong, is, that these gracious affections are so embarrassed by the remains of moral corruption. When we feel the bondage of sin, and so frequently offend the Saviour, as we do, we can not help fearing that we have never given him the first place in our hearts. We may have the fullest conviction of the truth, that indwelling sin does not destroy the evidence of imparted grace; yet where it is strong, in defiance of this conviction, the existence of gracious affections is discovered with difficulty, and the evidence of a gracious state is proportionably obscure. It is a truth of God's word, that *one act of true faith* in Christ constitutes a Christian. But what is true in theory, we are not always able to perceive to be true in our own experience. The voice of the 'inward witness' may be confused, and overpowered, and even silenced by the clamours of other inward and outward witnesses, which conflict with this almost forgotten consciousness, so that the comforts of it are 'few and far between', and the light of hope is almost extinguished by the oppressive darkness. I repeat the thought, the truth is a precious one, that one act of supreme love to Jesus, and one act of saving faith in him, constitutes the Christian. But it is a pregnant and prolific truth, and no abortion. Save the thief on the cross, there is no recorded fact in the Scriptures which warrants the conviction that it is ever found alone. It is a tree in bearing; and on its branches hang every Christian grace and moral virtue. Repentance is pendant with the weight of sin, and bright with the dewdrops of godly sorrow. Humility and meekness are there, those sweet fruits of the Spirit. There is the charity which seeketh not her own, and is the bond of perfectness, blushing like the rose of Sharon and the lily of the valleys, sending forth its fragrance upon this desert world. It is a tree planted by the rivers, whose fruit does not wither, and whose leaf does not fade. It is a growing grace, and though not the uniform, the infallible pledge of persevering and increasing holiness. The kingdom of God is 'As if a man should cast seed into the ground, and should sleep, and rise night and day, and the seed should spring up and grow, he knoweth not how. For the earth bringeth forth fruit of herself, first the blade, then the ear, then the full corn in the ear.' It is not one grace therefore, that we must seek after, as evidence of piety, but every grace.

'Be ye holy in all manner of conversation: because it is written, Be ye holy, for I am holy.' We have much to do with holiness in the abstract: would that we possessed more of it in our own hearts! Ministers have peculiar opportunities and means of a growing conformity to God, because they are familiar with his truth; because their views of it are often so strong and clear; and because their vocation is such, that the motives to this conformity, in all their variety and force, are so often present to their minds. There is nothing which increases the obligations of men to be holy, and which lays these bonds upon them in all their strength and tenderness, but is experienced in the work of a Christian minister. They greatly delight in those clear, connected, and comprehensive views of God's truth which they so often enjoy; but should they not more often be humbled under the reflection that 'to him that

The Personal Piety of Ministers

knoweth to do good, and doeth it not, to him it is sin'? Though inhabitants of this low earth, they dwell in regions of light; they inhabit its mountain summits, where the sun shines bright and clear when clouds and darkness rest upon the valleys below. God expects that his ministers should be holy men. 'Be ye clean that bear the vessels of the Lord!' *Holiness to the Lord* was inscribed in deep and legible lines on Aaron's forehead. Ministers expect holiness of themselves; the church of God expects it of them; the world that lieth in wickedness is disappointed unless it discovers in them a piety that is both genuine and eminent.*

For reasons just suggested, *genuine* piety in ministers will be, for the most part, above the ordinary measure of piety in other men. They dwell nearer the sources and springs of it; and if they drink not of them, can they say in truth, 'My soul thirsteth for God'? A man who spends his life in the contemplation and study of things that are unseen and eternal, must have one of two very opposite characters. If his contemplations be devout, he must attain to greater than ordinary spirituality of mind; if undevout, he must be a most wicked man. He will be a man to be admired and imitated, or one to be abhorred and shunned.

In determining the true genius and nature of piety, the writer has but one remark to offer to his brethren, who, on such a subject, need no instructions from his pen. The longer he lives, the more is he persuaded, that the sum and substance of true religion consists

---

*As an exemplification of this last remark, I transcribe the following letter of George III to the Archbishop of Canterbury:

'MY GOOD LORD PRELATE,

'I could not delay giving you the notification of the grief and concern with which my heart was affected, at receiving authentic information that revels have made their way into your palace. At the same time I must signify to you my sentiments on this subject, which hold these levities and vain dissipations as utterly inexpedient, if not unlawful, to pass in a residence for many centuries devoted to divine studies, religious retirement, and the extensive exercise of charity and benevolence; I add, in a place where so many of your predecessors have led their lives in such sanctity as has thrown lustre on the pure religion they professed and adorned.

From the dissatisfaction with which you must perceive I hold these improprieties, not to speak in harsher terms, and on still more pious principles, I trust you will reform them immediately; so that I may not have occasion to show any further mark of my displeasure, or to interpose in a different manner.

'May God take your Grace into his Almighty protection!
'I remain, my Lord Prelate,
'Your gracious friend,
'G.R.'

in *obedience to the commandments of God*. 'This is the love of God, that we keep his commandments, and his commandments are not grievous.' Oh it is a great matter, in heart and in life, to abstain from those things which God has forbidden, and to do those which he has required. It alters not the importance of this remark, that such a righteousness is not a sinner's justification, is all his *religion*. Impulses of fancy, animal emotions, vague and dreamy sentimentalism may inweave themselves with the intellectual temperaments and habits of good men, and give their piety its lights and shadows; but they form no part of their piety. That fervour which glows only to obey, and those impulses which impel to do and suffer the will of God, are alone worthy of confidence. Men are dead in trespasses and sins, because they never obey God; devils are devils, because they live in disobedience. And Christian men and Christian ministers are Christian just in the measure in which they are obedient. Faith is as obedient as it is confiding; love is as dutiful as it is affectionate; humility is as submissive as it is lowly; penitence is as much afraid of sinning as it mourns for sin; joy is as quick to do the will of God, hearkening to the voice of his Word, as it is enraptured and transporting; and zeal is as warm and steadfast in giving battle to all that is wrong, as it is when it burns with its boldest and most active spirituality.

It is a dry doctrine, a dead orthodoxy, and no more resembles true piety than a marble statue does a living man, that does not express itself in obedience. There is amazing force in that remonstrance of Samuel to Saul, 'To obey is better than sacrifice, and to hearken than the fat of rams.' Afflictive fastings and fervent prayers, devout contemplation, eloquent sermons, fitting religious conversation, and commended sanctity are sounding brass and tinkling cymbal, compared with cheerful obedience to the will of God. Nor, in saying these things, do we forget that the 'Lord looketh on the heart' and requires a spiritual religion. The religion that is all internal, and the religion that is all external, are upon the same footing; both are bad: the former all emotion and alternate rapture and grief, and empty imagination; the latter, the form of godliness without the power. What is piety, but that state of mind and moral feeling which regards God as God; which loves him as God; which obeys him as God, and honours him as our Lawgiver and our Redeemer? What is piety, but the love of the creature so responding to the love of the Creator, that in defiance of every opposing claim, whether of corruption within or the world without, and in opposition to every other master, it makes the Redeeming Saviour its Lord, and perfects holiness in his love and fear? What is piety but that great astounding principle, which, while it is the main-spring of action in the heart, has the vigour and efficacy to make itself felt in every artery, and vein, and muscle, and delicate nerve of the moral man? Strong spiritual exercises, under the powerful impression of Scriptural truth, are characteristic of a healthful state of moral feeling, only when they are sufficiently strong to make us love and perform the will of our Father which is in heaven.

This is the piety which the pulpit solicits in order to give it power. It is goodness. It is loveliness. Yet is it that energy of purpose which arises from an imperious conviction of duty: that humility which makes the minister 'as one that serveth'; that self-denial and public spirit which distinguishes him from those who are 'lovers of their own selves'; that love of God which consists in keeping his commandments; that love of man which pities the apostate, and goes after the lost sheep; that faith which takes strong hold of God's promises; and that conscious dependence which relies upon his all-sufficient grace.

There is no part of a minister's work that is not immediately affected by his piety. The object at which he aims, his own personal qualifications, his firmness and stability in the faith, his perseverance in toil, his comfort in trials, and his whole spirit, and even manner in the pulpit, are influenced by his fear of God, and his love of Jesus Christ. Light and love are distinct things. His embassy is an embassy of love. Before Peter was sent forth, after his lamentable fall, his affection and sincerity were put to the test before many witnesses, 'Lovest thou me? lovest thou me more than these?' Happy minister who like him can say, 'Lord, thou knowest all things; thou knowest that I love thee!' We have but to read the life of Whitefield, and Payson, and McCheyne, in order to be convinced that the secret of their success was their piety. The Earl of Bath says of Whitefield, 'Mocked and reviled as Mr. Whitefield is, still I contend the day will come when England will be just, and own his greatness as a Reformer, and his *goodness* as a minister of the most High God.' Whitefield died in 1770, and in the town where the writer of these pages was born. The churches in Newburyport, to the present day, preserve the remembrance of his preaching, not more than the remembrance of his piety. He sometimes preached in the evening, and in the open air to great multitudes. On one of these occasions he says, 'All was hushed and exceedingly solemn. The stars shone bright; and then, if ever, by an eye of faith I saw him who called them all by their names. My soul was filled with a holy ambition, and I longed to be one of those who shall shine as the stars for ever and ever.' Just think of a man who has even the common gift of utterance, holding forth the word of life in such a state of mind as this! At another time he says, 'I lead a pilgrim life; you will pray that I may have a pilgrim heart. Ere long I hope my Heavenly Father will take me home. I am ambitious: I want to sit upon a throne. Jesus hath purchased and provided a throne in heaven for me.'

That beloved man of God, too, Henry Martyn, was a lovely exemplification of personal piety. 'Let me praise God,' he would say, 'O how great is his excellency! I find my heart pained for want of words to praise him according to his excellent greatness. I look forward to complete conformity to him as the great end of my existence, and my assurance was full.' Again he says: 'Nothing seemed desirable but to glorify him: all creatures were as nothing.' And again, 'O my God, it is enough. Hasten, O hasten the day when I shall leave the world, and come to thee; when I shall no more be vexed, and astonished, and pained at the universal wickedness of this lost earth. But here I would abide thy time, and spend and be spent for the salvation of any poor soul, and lie down at the feet of sinners, and beseech them not to plunge into an eternity of torment.'

There is something in such a state of mind as this, which gives to the pulpit that which nothing else can give. To be effective, its ministers must live near to God, be filled with his fulness, and reflect his glory. Men must take knowledge of them that they have been with Jesus, and that it is not they who live, but Christ who lives in them. It was the remark of one who was familiar with Archbishop Leighton, 'If none shall go to heaven but so holy a man as this, what will become of me?' It is easy to see that the religion of such a preacher is the most effective preaching.

> When one that holds communion with the skies,
> Has filled his urn where these pure waters rise,
> And once commingles with us meaner things,
> 'Tis e'en as if an angel shook his wings;
> Immortal fragrance fills the circuit wide,
> And tells us whence his treasures are supplied.

The Personal Piety of Ministers

It is this which makes an able and powerful preacher. Such a man will always be listened to, and prove himself a commanding and authoritative messenger of the Master who sent him. The spirit of his office rests upon him, and he will make impressions upon the conscience and heart, even though he may not excite admiration and applause. Even though he be not great, he will be greatly useful. His ardent piety will give a charm to his preaching even beyond that which is imparted to a less pious but more consummate orator.

While the personal character of the American ministry will not suffer in the comparison with that of any other portion of Christendom, it is quite obvious that the present is not the age of pre-eminent piety. The piety of our fathers puts us to shame. The church participates largely, not only in the prosperity, but the spirit of the world; and her ministers, because they have not more faithfully rebuked this sin, have themselves become infected with it. It is not with us now as it was 'in the kindness of our youth, in the love our espousals, and in a land that was not sown'. Our hearts are not softened in the fountain of God's love. We do not live as holy men of God were wont to live, 'as pilgrims and sojourners on the earth', and declare plainly that we seek a city that hath foundations, whose builder and maker is God. God himself is too much a wilderness to us, a land of darkness, and the world too much our home. Would that we mourned over this state of mind with bitter tears! We grope in darkness, sometimes in thick darkness; and we lose our relish for our work, because we savour so much of the things that be of men. The Gospel we preach has not its counterpart in ourselves. We teach others what we ourselves have not practically learned. Our outward man perishes, but our inward man is not renewed *day by day*; our renewed nature does not become newer and fresher as we go onward. Oh, it is dreadful to live thus, to preach thus, with the dead weight of our corruption dragging us down to the earth! It is unworthy of the Master we serve, and of the cause we advocate; it is unworthy of ourselves. This inconsistent piety is the plague-spot of the pulpit. It is the polluting, the infectious thing. It makes the preacher ashamed to look his people in the face; his conscience smites him; his heart trembles; and he may well feel that he can never more open his mouth, because of his shame. His energy is weak and pusillanimous; his holy daring is faint-hearted; his affectionate tenderness is fled and gone, because the words he utters do not find a distinct and full echo from his own heart.

It ought not, it must not be thus with the ministers of Christ. God will try us, and make us holier men, or he may abandon us. If he has indeed chosen us and ordained us, it is that we should go forth and bear fruit, and that our fruit should remain. If we are indeed his, he will assign more to suffer, as well as more to do; until we can say with Paul, 'I count not my life dear unto myself, so that I might finish my course with joy, and the ministry which I have received of the Lord Jesus, to testify the Gospel of the grace of God'. The preacher and the man must be one. His heart must be a transcript of his sermons, and then will he be a chosen vessel to carry to lost men his name who was crucified. It will be no inconsiderable evidence of the truth and power of Christianity, when such are its preachers, and such the power exerted by its pulpits.

16: *The Example of Ministers*

We need not stop to introduce the subject of the present chapter by any exordium. In order to give the pulpit power, *ministers themselves must enforce its instructions by a life and conversation in keeping with their high vocation*. This is so obvious a truth that any illustration of it would seem to be needless; yet are there some things in relation to it which have been too frequently suppressed, and which, perhaps, may subject him who utters them to obloquy. It were no more than the sober truth, were the writer to say, that in expressing his thoughts on this topic, he does so in the deliberate expectation of rebuke from some of those whom he highly respects, but who, in his judgment, have mistaken views.

It is too much to expect that the ministers of Christ should be perfect men; defects in their character are what the church and the world must always look for. We have no objection to perfect ministers, if we could find them; but all whom we have ever seen, had something to confess and be forgiven, and much need to grow better. 'There is not a just man upon earth that sinneth not'; there is no living minister, and none who ever did live, but those who knew him best were able to detect some discernible blemish, some weak spot in his personal character. We are not apologists for human imperfection; yet do we pity the man who, in this fallen world, expects to find every thing in his minister, to gratify either his piety or his pride. He can have little knowledge of himself, and little of that charity which hopeth all things, and covereth a multitude of sins, if he cannot appreciate true excellence because it has blemishes. It were a rare combination, to find any one man possessing all the personal qualifications that are to be desired in those who are set apart for the Lord's service. The *beau-ideal* may be a very agreeable picture to the imagination; but it will never be realized. It was, indeed, once realized; but it was too unearthly for this low world, too pure for men to look upon; they defiled it, yea they spat upon it, and smote it with their hands, and exclaimed, 'Let him be crucified!'

There are two ways of estimating the character of God's ministers; the one is by making their imperfections prominent, the other by giving prominence to their excellences. A minister may have some good qualities, and be deficient in others. He may be distinguished for prudence, and not for zeal; or if distinguished for zeal, be exposed to imprudencies. He may be unsocial, but studious; or if not studious, he may make some amends for this deficiency by the familiar acquaintance he cultivates with his fellow-men. He may be heedless of his secular affairs, and you may reproach him for making perpetual exactions upon the bounty of his people; or he may be careful of them, and you may accuse him of worldliness. The man will find enough to do who sets himself to search and hunt out a minister's imperfections; he will find them in plenty. He may triumph in them, and live upon them, as those do who 'eat up the sins of God's people'; but he will not, I am thinking, on that account, enjoy a more thriving spirituality. A happy man he cannot be; how holy he is, must be left to the decisions of his own conscience, and of another day. But it would not be surprising if his humility, his contrition, his self-diffidence and meekness were somewhat questionable, and if he were not exposed by his own spiritual pride to fall into the snare of the devil. I am acquainted with men, who are in the habit of sitting in severe judgment upon the character of ministers; but they are suspicious men, rash men, and men whose word would be taken with some grains of allowance in a court of justice. It would certainly seem to be a more pleasant and profitable employment, and would savour more of Christian *equity*, in forming an estimate of the ministerial character, to give its acknowledged excellences their due weight.

Not a few of the moral defects of ministers depend upon their natural temperament. Those who have the fewest imperfections are not always the best men, and for the obvious reasons that they may have the fewest excellences. They may not be capable, from their natural temperament, of possessing strong and striking excellences; and on this account, their imperfections may be comparatively few. It may be difficult to detect them in an imprudent or an idle word; because their disposition is naturally retiring and taciturn, and they rarely speak at all, except in the pulpit. You may not be able to reproach them with rash or

The Example of Ministers

imprudent conduct, because they are men of shrinking diffidence, and instead of throwing themselves amid scenes of exciting interest, they leave such scenes to men of a different spirit. Well do I remember a minister in this community, now gathered to his fathers, who, if judged by his imperfections, would meet a severe verdict; but who, when estimated by his excellences, has scarcely left his equal behind him. I loved and honoured him, because, whoever else was backward, he was always ready, with his hand, his heart, his time and his money, for every good word and work.

There may be quite as much of the power of godliness in the more animated, as in the more tame; while there may be, and ordinarily are, more visible imperfections in the former than in the latter. Men there have been who have deeply mourned over these constitutional exposures; while it is quite obvious they would not have possessed the manly and vigorous piety for which they were distinguished, nor have achieved that which they were raised up to achieve, without them. There were natural traits in the character of the Apostle Peter which rendered him rash and presumptuous, and which led to his fall; yet had he been more phlegmatic and cold, while he would have avoided the infamy of denying his Master, he never would have so proved himself his self-denying and enthusiastic disciple. Imperfections there were in the character of Martin Luther; and they were imperfections which a certain class of men in our own day would have severely rebuked; nay, some modern churches would have called him to account for them. But without the natural temperament to which they are obviously to be attributed, he never would have been the distinguished Reformer. We forget his errors when we read his Commentary on the Epistle to the Galatians, and see him before the Diet at the city of Worms. He might have been as mild and circumspect as Melanchthon, and Protestantism might have been strangled in its cradle. There is a buoyancy of mind and heart which God has given to some of his ministers, for great and important ends; and though it may expose them to indiscretions, they ought to be thankful for the gift, and instead of abusing it, only labour to devote it to his glory. Their Heavenly Father has a work for them to do for which he has fitted them; he lays burdens upon them which men of a different temperament are not able to bear; and in his own time and way he will make it his care, that while his gifts promote their usefulness, they do not ensnare their souls.

We are no believers in an unsocial Christianity, nor do we desire to see its ministers unsocial and cheerless. This might be in keeping with the dark ages of Rome, but it has no alliance with the cheered spirit of the Gospel. Cheerlessness is not piety; gloom and depression are not piety. They are precisely that artful counterfeit of piety which the devil imposes upon many a minister of the Gospel, for the purpose of blasting those fruits of the Spirit, which are 'not meat and drink, but righteousness, and peace, and joy in the Holy Ghost'. There is a worldly joy, a joy that is found only in the world and from the world; but it is 'like the crackling of thorns under a pot'. But there is too a 'joy of the Lord', which is the strength of God's ministers, as well as the strength of his people; it is joy in God, and joy from God, through Jesus Christ. Some of the best, and most devoted, and most successful ministers I have ever known, have been distinguished for their attractive cheerfulness.

There are not wanting those who impugn the character of the Christian ministry, because they do not carry the *solemnity* of the pulpit into all the scenes of social life. Many indeed are the scenes of social life where the solemnity of the pulpit is called for; nor in any of them are the dignity and proprieties of the ministerial character unfitting. But as well might secular time be transformed into the Sabbath, and the busy scenes of the world into the formal services of the sanctuary, as the emotions of the pulpit pervade the uniform intercourse of a minister, either with the people of God, or the men of the world. Levity and worldliness are sufficiently out of place in him who is an ambassador of God to guilty men; but affected solemnity is even worse. Ministers there are who are so solemn that you never see a smile, or a pleasant expression upon their countenances; they are absolutely *fearful*. There is no piety in this. Were an angel from heaven to dwell with men, his spirit and example would be perpetual rebuke to such ministers. Christianity, though of divine origin, is not the religion of angels; it is ingrafted on the human nature. Angels would delight to be its preachers; but the treasure is committed to men; the whole arrangement is adapted to what is human; and while its great object is to purify and elevate, it is no part of its design to terrify. It is not a sort of personified apathy, nor is it some ghostly messenger that lives only among the tombs; it moves among men as the messenger of heaven's tenderest mercy; and though wherever it goes, it rebukes iniquity, its footsteps are radiant with light and love. It multiplies the joys of men, and only admonishes them that they may not be sinful joys.

'Wisdom is justified of her children.' John the Baptist was accused of unsocial severity even to madness; while Jesus Christ himself was called a glutton and a wine-bibber. Let ministers, in their intercourse with the world, have a conscience void of offence. They are human; nor is there any generosity in denying them the relief of those occasional relaxations from toil, amid the interchanges of cheered thought and chastened feeling, which the better fit them for their appropriate work. We need not fear the influence of such men, but rather stand in fear of those who slander them, and whose severer piety expresses itself most spontaneously in the dark jealousies of a suspicious mind. Who would not prefer to stand in the place of Robert Hall, than in the place of some of his fastidious accusers? Much as the pulpit was indebted to the intellectual superiority of this wonderful man, it was not less indebted to his moral superiority. He was, by the universal consent of the devout and godly, himself an eminently devout and godly man. He had his faults. He was censorious, and sometimes abusive; he was occasionally so, even to excess, and witty and sarcastic almost beyond endurance.*

But we should do great injustice to ourselves and our subject, were these animadversions all we have to say on the subject of ministerial example. While we do not look for faultless conduct in the character of ministers, yet do we look for traits of character which carry conviction to the public mind, that they are men of God. The Apostle Paul, in enumerating the qualifications of a bishop, says, 'Moreover, he must have a *good report* of them that are without.' While he may not be the slave of popular opinion, he should commend religion by the influence of that 'good name', which is 'rather to be chosen than great riches'. We have seen him in the closet, in the study, in the pulpit, at the bed-side of the sick and dying, and at the grave of the departed; but there are other

---

*On being very gravely reproved for his faults by one of his brethren, and in a manner not a little dictatorial and solemn, he sat for a while in perfect silence. At length he replied, 'I suppose, brother W., it is just as you say. There is a difference between you and me. And it is just this: I let off all my nonsense in the parlour, and you keep yours for the pulpit.'

scenes where his Christian graces and moral virtues ought to honour the sacred name by which he is called. His family has claims upon him, and so has the social circle; nor unless he go out of the world, can he be wholly unmindful of the responsibilities of business. In all these spheres, he ought to maintain a reputable character in the view of the world; every part of his conduct ought to be truly estimable; so that every beholder shall be constrained to acknowledge, not only the sincerity of his profession as a Christian, but his superior practical influence as a minister of the Gospel. His office demands this; it is worthy of it; if he has habits, or practices that bring it into disrepute, his preaching loses much of its power, and the pulpit sometimes receives a dangerous wound.

The Bible is given to men to be the rule of their conduct. This important truth every minister preaches, and insists upon; he is constantly calling upon men to acknowledge its authority, and to pay to it that practical deference which its supremacy requires. But what if, in the sight of all the world, he fails to make it the rule of his own deportment? May he persuade himself that men have not discernment enough to perceive his inconsistency? What if he is remiss in the observance of the Sabbath; what if he is not strictly moral, temperate, pure, and honest; what if he is not punctual in his pecuniary engagements; what if his promises are violated, and it is understood that he is not always true to his word; what if he is extravagant in his statements, and habitually allows his imagination to give such a colouring to facts, that he cannot be confided in; are these things no reproach to the pulpit? Far otherwise. If the imperfections of his character are such, that they are continually rising up to the remembrance of his hearers, he preaches almost in vain. He may indeed be accused of wickedness of which he was never guilty; but if he has failed even in that circumspection which would have protected him from the imputation, or suspicion of evil; or if there is any thing in his deportment which is obnoxious to misconception; his character may have received a dangerous wound. But if *he is* a wicked and immoral man, though he speak with the tongue of an angel, men revolt from his teaching. Or if he is a good man, and has been betrayed into secret sin, how are the difficulties and trials of his work augmented! His own soul becomes estranged from God; his bosom is agitated by the thought that he is a suspected man; he trembles before 'the shaking of a leaf,' and a 'fire not blown consumes him.' In the midst of laughter his heart is sorrowful: God hides his face, and he is troubled; he loses his relish for his sacred employment; clouds settle on his path, storms gather; he has lost his courage, and feels that he has no shelter from their fury. And if his sin be not secret, and amount to some gross immorality, though he *may* be a good man, and a true penitent, men feel that he has unfitted himself for a preacher of the Gospel; he feels so himself; and the greatest honour he can do his office is to put off its robes.

There is great weight in Paul's injunction to Timothy, 'Take heed to *thyself*; be thou 'an *example* to the believers, in conversation, in faith, in purity'. A bishop 'must be blameless as the steward of God; not self-willed, not soon angry, not given to wine, not greedy of filthy lucre; but sober, just, holy, temperate'. He must furnish living convictions of the importance and power of a virtuous life, of an example that will bear inspection, and disciplined by care and watchfulness.

But there must be a great advance upon all this, in order to give the example of ministers its due influence. There are distorted exhibitions of the religion they preach, as well as those distinctive influences to which we have just referred. There are foibles which discredit and degrade the pulpit; there are minor immoralities which scarcely have a name, which have a bad aspect in a Christian minister, which stain his name, and make it of bad odour in the world. There are habits also, which have been long indulged in defiance of the convictions of judgment, the reproofs of conscience, and the settled persuasion that they are a barrier to usefulness. There are worldly indulgences which are justified by the example of some ministers, which are highly injurious to the cause of Christ. While they preach faithfully, they *live* as though they were slaves of the world; slaves to its fashions, its example and influence. They court its smiles, they imitate its manners, and they meanly cringe to its dictation. They rob God, in order to save the means of indulging in the pomp and glitter of worldly pride. They expend more upon the decoration of their own persons, and the persons of their families, and upon splendid furniture and paintings, than their profession of supreme love to Jesus Christ will justify. The scenes of worldly pleasure often echo to their voice, and are graced with their stately step. Nothing is more obvious than that they wish to be on good terms with the world, and to be well spoken of by the rich and the fashionable, even though at some occasional sacrifices of principle, and a good conscience. But the world itself does not honour them for these things; it often despises them, and if they themselves are not despised, the contempt due to them visits the cause they dishonour. We have known ministers who, if they were to be judged by their preaching only, would rank high as men of rare attainments; but who, if followed elsewhere, would be found, in more respects than one, to be very different men. We ask for the pulpit greater consistency than this. We ask for it the upright and delicate judgment of a well-informed mind, and a sound conscience; we ask for it the verdict of a cultivated sense of propriety and consistency; we ask for it the qualities that are in estimation with men of probity and honour. Things there are that are somewhat beyond the rigid Christian virtues, that never fail to adorn it. There is a transparent simplicity of character, a freedom from dissimulation, a superiority to the meanness of artifice and management, a command of the temper, and a command of the tongue, and a determined adherence to the principles of honourable intercourse, which, because they are possessed by so many who make no pretensions to religion, when neglected by Christian ministers, throw the pulpit into the shade. The ministers of the Gospel ought to surpass the best specimens of morality and honour among mere worldly men; and when they do so, obloquy will close her lips, and a thousand tongues will move in their defence.

Nor is this all which they ought to exemplify. It was to his ministers that the Saviour uttered the thought, 'Herein is my Father glorified, that ye bear *much fruit.*' Hurtful indulgences may be restrained, and the more moral and honourable virtues may be cultivated, where there are none of the rare and peculiar excellences of the Christian character. Ministers of the Gospel, of all other men, ought to live to *do good.* The pulpit always has power, when, in addition to a full and faithful exhibition of God's truth, those who occupy it, like their Divine Lord, 'go about doing good'. It is a delightful view, when, through every opening channel, they send forth the expressions of Christian benevolence upon this world of sin; when, in their plans and efforts, they comprehend all the evils of suffering humanity, sympathizing with its griefs, and not overlooking its perplexities and cares. Their character should shine in works of love. These give them a passport to the confidence of men; they commend the religion they preach as something beyond a mere system of doctrine, or mere professions of good will. An ostentatious display of active goodness is not what they should seek, while they need affect no studied concealment of it, and may be willing to be known as the friends of their race. It is characteristic of the religion they preach, to do good 'unto all men, especially to those who are of the household of faith'.

But it stops not here. If we look into our own hearts, we shall find it is no easy matter to 'love our enemies', to 'bless those who curse us', to 'do good unto those that hate us', and to 'pray for those who despitefully use us'. How easy it is to shut our hearts against them! Yet this is not the part of those who preach his Gospel, who loved us when we were dead in sin, and when enemies, died for us. The man who harbours resentment, treasures up the remembrance of wrong, and refuses to forgive, reflects no honour upon the Gospel of Jesus; men may be pardoned for refusing to confide in it on his testimony alone, who furnishes so uninviting an illustration of its practical influence. Ministers must exhibit more of the spirit of Christ; when they do so, men will see and mark it, and not withhold from it their respect and confidence. Nor should they always wait for opportunities of doing good, but go in search of them. They must ascend in order to reach those who are above them; they must descend to those who are below them; they must seek to do good to all. They ought to be careful how they erect a wall of separation between themselves and any man, or any class of men to whom they may be of any service for this life, or that which is to come. Nor should we ever feel that we have done enough, until the means and opportunity of doing are exhausted.

There is also another topic which relates to the example of ministers, on which I will venture to make a few suggestions; I allude *to a due attention to the decorum and proprieties of their social intercourse.* It was not beneath the Apostle to instruct the Corinthians, that 'charity doth not behave itself unseemly'. If ministers were more mindful than they sometimes are, of the demands of courtesy and kindness; if, while they rise above the formalities of frivolous and unmeaning etiquette, they were solicitous also to avoid the imputation of a rugged and unfeeling barbarism; if, in their treatment of one another, and their treatment of other men, they were influenced by the spirit of mild forbearance, and the charity which 'thinketh no evil'; the pulpit would be not a little the gainer by the change. They should be 'of gentle blood'. If in all their deportment they were gentle, as Christ was gentle; if they were accommodating without weakness, amiable and indulgent without crime, and dignified without constrained and artificial ceremony; their influence as preachers would be increased many fold. The reputation of the pulpit has often suffered by the coarse disregard of the thousand nameless proprieties of social life, which are far more truly the natural fruit of Christianity, than the product of any conventional impulse or restraint. Ministers need not be rude in order to be faithful; rather do they need to be kind.

Christ is our great model. He was all that was courteous. Let any well-bred and observing man read the narratives of his life, as given by the four Evangelists, and he will mark the perfectness of good-breeding; there is not a single action in all the vicissitudes of his course that was not in perfect good taste. He was never distant and cold, nor rude and obtrusive; he was never terrible, save to wickedness. The minister who possesses most of his spirit, comes nearest to a genuine philanthropist and a true gentleman. If there were more of this spirit among those of us who preach his Gospel, many things not perhaps positively sinful, but nowise honourable to piety, would be restrained. There would be less contention, less of the bitterness of party strife, less chilling alienation and neglect, fewer local and sectional difficulties, less freedom with one another's reputation, less meddling with the private concerns of others, and more regard to their feelings in matters that are unimportant. Our ecclesiastical judicatories would present different scenes; we should have less occasion to congratulate ourselves that the laws of duelling and private combat are unknown in the church of God.

But we need enlarge on such a topic. Whether so serious a cause of complaint or not, as we have supposed, it is certain that the disregard of Christian decorum has impeded and impaired the influence of Christian ministers, and brought the name of the pulpit into anything but good report.

We shall with difficulty be persuaded, that we have given too much importance to these thoughts on the subject of ministerial example. It is in vain to talk about piety where there is not sterling

The Example of Ministers

virtue, and an example that is worthy of the Gospel we preach. I would allow a minister every indulgence that is not sinful, and that is not hurtful to the souls of men. I would be bound by the code of a high morality, and hold myself responsible for every breach of it; but I would not be bound by the caprices of men. We should be watchful, even in things that are lawful, not to throw a stumbling block in the way of others. 'All things are lawful for me,' says Paul, 'but all things are not expedient.' He would not eat the flesh, nor drink the wine offered in oblation on heathen altars, no, not 'while the world standeth', if 'it caused his brother to offend'. There is no part of a minister's example that may be deemed unimportant, which seriously affects the interests of religion in the world. We may think little of these things abstractly; but they are of great moment in their bearing upon the cause of God. Men may be fatally led astray by the wrong impressions they receive from the heedless and untender walk of Christian ministers. We may sometimes complain of restricted influence, when the fault is our own. If all the disciples of Christ ought to be 'living epistles, known and read of all men', much more his ministers. We depreciate this method of teaching. Men are not to be instructed by records and proofs merely; they reject the divine testimony even when it is spread before their minds. But there is one species of evidence which they find it hard to resist; it is the consistent example of its ministers. There is no preaching like a holy life. It is a death-blow to the Church of Rome, that so many of its ministers are ungodly and wicked men. No church can prosper without an exemplary ministry. Mitred heads and apostolical succession are little matters compared with 'the things that are of good report'.

We are humbled in view of some of the thoughts we have suggested, and therefore dwell on them perhaps to the weariness of our readers. It is not enough for ministers to be men of piety; it must be a piety that lives, and acts itself out. Preaching is not piety. Men will not give the pulpit credit for a religion which it does not exemplify, nor ought they to do so. It is not the eloquence of the pulpit alone that they look for. It is the silent eloquence of a heavenly example. The short epitaph inscribed by Nazianzen on the tomb of Basil, was, 'His words were thunder, his life lightning.' Where the life of a minister is conformed to the law of God, and illustrates the power of his Gospel; where the truth of Christ shines out in the walk and conversation; where the *whole* testimony which a minister bears is in favour of the Gospel he preaches, and no part of it is arrayed against another part, but all bears the same witness; it is not easily denied. The pulpit needs no more efficiency than that which, under the favour of its great Author, it possesses the means of exerting. Let it faithfully apply itself to these, and it lives only to bless the world. Its light is destined to shine not more in acts of splendid brilliancy, than in that steady uniform brightness, which is lighted at the altar which is within the veil.

17: *The Responsibility of Ministers*

The true influence of the pulpit will be found to be intimately connected with deep impressions of responsibility on the part of those who occupy it. Everything that has been suggested in the preceding pages, is fitted to enforce this solemn thought. Nor is it one which the ministers of the Gospel can ever feel too deeply. The office they bear, the Master they serve, the interests committed to them, and the influence and power they exert, throw upon them a burden of responsibility which is borne by no other class of men, and will render their account at the bar of the Supreme Judge, solemn beyond any thing which the tongue of mortals can utter. It were no marvel if a deep sense of this responsibility should have deterred many a man from entering the pulpit, and made more tremble who have ventured to enter it and have occupied it long. It is a responsibility which diminishes not with growing years; and which, could the whole extent of it have been anticipated, would have presented an affecting, if not a fearful view to many a youthful aspirant for the sacred office.

There is responsibility in being clothed with an immortal existence; and in being gifted with powers and facilities of doing good in the humblest sphere. There is responsibility in the successful cultivation of those faculties and powers, by familiarity with the works, and providence, and truth of God, and in the communicated grace that calls the foreigner and exile into the divine family, and gives him a name better than that of sons and of daughters.

But how is this responsibility enhanced, when to all these is added the call of Heaven to a work of which the holiest are unworthy, and Heaven's investiture with an office which might well constrain a seraph to exclaim, 'Who is sufficient for these things?' Which of us who serves at the tabernacle, is awake to just apprehensions of this single thought! What a trust is this ministry! How solemn the account which must be given for it! If ministers remind others of their responsibility, may they not, in their turn, be also reminded of theirs? If they charge home their accountableness upon men of station and wealth, men of lofty calling, high associations, commanding authority, and controlling influence, shall not the solemn charge be brought home to their own bosoms, who stand before their fellow-men as God's ambassadors, and in his name show them the way of life? But for him who has called us and whose call we may not disregard, but for his grace that is sufficient for us and his strength that is made perfect in human weakness, the office of a Gospel minister would be too heavy to be borne. God grant, that none of us may find to our cost that we had better have been any thing else; that it had been better for us to have been intrusted with the two talents, rather than the five; better for us to have exchanged our responsibility even with the wicked and slothful servant, who hid his talent in the earth, because it is the one talent only for which he is responsible! Better, far better, to be the humble and unnoticed door-keeper in God's house, than to have occupied the most enviable pulpit in the land, either for selfish and vile ends, or not to have occupied it with honesty, care, and pains.

There is nothing which Christ's ministers are called upon to watch over more cautiously, to cultivate more assiduously, and to exert more wisely and benevolently, than the power of the pulpit. What effort, what study, what prayer – what faithfulness, what devotedness to God and their work – unwearied, repeated often, and repeated long and undiscouraged, become those who, from their vocation, exert so much influence on the character, the usefulness, the deathless destiny of their fellow-men? Ministers will meet this responsibility at the bar of God. It will run parallel with their eternity.

When I say that I tremble for the ministers of the Gospel, I can truly say, that I tremble for none more than for myself. I would not be released from the responsibility; but I should be afraid to counsel any man to *seek* it, who has a hesitating conscience or heart. The harvest is great, 'and the labourers are few'; and I would 'pray the Lord of the harvest to *thrust* forth labourers into his harvest'. I would have no man enter the pulpit, whose heart and conscience will allow him to keep out of it. If, with an honest conscience, and a loving and satisfied heart, he can keep out of it, let him stay where he is. But if conscience *urges* him, if a loving heart to his redeeming God and King, and to the souls he has purchased with his blood, *constrain* him, so that he cannot turn a deaf ear to God's call, in the strength of the Lord God, and making mention of his righteousness, and his only, let him go to that sacred calling. If the Master thus 'thrusts him forth', he *must* go. With all the responsibilities of the work, he *must go to it*, and trust implicitly, trust constantly, trust cheerfully to the Master's promised grace.

That pulpit! What an attractive, what a delightful, yet what a fearful spot! That preacher's breath is constantly touching some secret spring that shall set mind after mind in motion, whose pulsations shall be felt when the scenes of earth are forgotten. It is but a single spot, yet it speaks to a thousand generations. The living testify to its influence, and generations of the dead lie scattered around it, who will one day rise up and bear witness to the mighty power which it has wielded. What a scene will that be, when they thus rise! Who is prepared for it? Who can abide it? Who may abide 'the day of his coming' and 'who shall stand when he appeareth'? On that vast mass of minds, and through all the narrow pathway of this low world, that pulpit is exerting its silent influences, and as God is just, he who exerts them shall give account. Some of the most solemn and affecting disclosures of the Great Day of reckoning will consist in the discoveries it makes of the influence of the pulpit. Such a day will be a fitting winding up of these earthly scenes. Small and great, ministers, and their people, shall stand before God. Yes, it will be a fitting winding up of the scene, where this world has been the selected spot for man's education for eternity, and where the sanctuary and the pulpit have been the selected means of forming the characters of men.

The inquiry as to why the pulpit is often so powerless is one of great interest to a laborious preacher. We have no desire to find relief from the responsibilities which God has thrown upon his ministers; yet are there some thoughts in relation to their want of success, which may furnish some relief to that depression of mind to which they are sometimes subjected.

The Scriptures teach us, that wherever the Gospel is faithfully preached, it produces widely different results. It is in perfect accordance with the nature of the Gospel, that it should be so. The truths which it discloses cannot be faithfully exhibited without making impressions, either for good or for evil, upon every mind to which they have access. Such is man's intellectual and moral nature, that where these truths are once resisted, they are more easily resisted afterwards, till eventually the human heart becomes impregnably fortified in its obduracy, and is abandoned of God. The same truths repeatedly uttered and rejected serve only to excite and invigorate unhallowed emotions, to disturb lurking enmity, and to awaken slumbering wickedness. Men never sin so fast and with such vigour of thought and emotion, they never become so precociously ripe for destruction and prematurely fuel for the flames, as when their dry and fruitless branches are spread out under the resisted light and scorching heat of heavenly truth. 'We are unto God', says the Apostle, 'a sweet savour of Christ in them that are saved, and in them that perish. To the one we are the savour of death unto death: to the other we are the savour of life unto life.'

This representation is abundantly confirmed by facts. In all ages thus far in the history of the world, there have been more who have treated the Gospel with indifference, opposition, and contempt, than have received it with confidence, gratitude and joy. From the preaching of Enoch to the preaching of the Apostles, and from the preaching of the Apostles to the present time, so far has it been from having had unmingled success, that while it has healed spiritual maladies in all lands, it has left more unhealed. Its ministers have met with disappointment, even where they had the most sanguine expectations. Like their Divine Master, they have been 'set for the fall and rising again of many'. It is not in their power to give it success. God is a Sovereign in the dispensation of his grace; 'the wind bloweth where it listeth'; and he hath 'mercy on whom he will have mercy'. There are instances in which, strive as much and earnestly as they will to fasten a sense of guilt on the conscience, they leave it unaffected. They can make no impression upon the levity and carelessness, the callousness and insensate obduracy of the carnal mind. Even where solemn impressions are made, the cares of the world spring up and choke the word, and the fairest promise is blighted in the bud. They wield a two-edged sword, and where it does not wound to heal, it wounds but to destroy.

Nor may this want of success be always attributed to their unfaithfulness. The incense of Paul's services was acceptable to God, even where it was the savour of death unto death. Where the message is the message of God's truth and grace, the message itself is acceptable; and where it is faithfully delivered, and attested by a consistent life and conversation, the Divine approbation is not withheld from the messenger. The field yields flowers and fruit that are swollen with the dew and redolent with the odours of heaven, even when trodden under the foot of men. And though in gathering the harvest, but here and there a sheaf may be found, while the field is covered with tares, the reaper shall come home with rejoicing. He has done a work for God which will not be forgotten, even though his sweetest hopes have suffered defeat. Other objects have been obtained by his ministry besides the salvation of men; nor shall his faithfulness lose its reward.

Jesus Christ has nowhere commanded his ministers to *convert* men. He has commanded them to preach his Gospel; to declare the whole counsel of God, whether men will hear, or whether they will forbear. This is their great concern, and for this they are responsible to their own consciences, to those who hear, and him who sent them. It is a sad result indeed, where their message is rejected, and one over which ministers may well weep in secret places. But notwithstanding this, their preaching has not been lost. His great and glorious character who sent them shines forth; his claims have been asserted; and all that is pure in his rectitude, alluring in his mercy, fearful in his wrath, and discriminating in his sovereign dominion, have, through their instrumentality, been seen and acknowledged. God is glorified in, and by his faithful ministers, though they make hard hearts harder, and blind eyes more blind. Every faithful exhibition of his Gospel makes known to this thoughtless world the manifold wisdom of God, according to the eternal purpose which he purposed in Christ Jesus, and makes it known to, even where its results are so lamentable, to principalities and powers in heavenly places.

But while we say these things, we may not suppress the remark, that the powerlessness of the pulpit is in too many instances to be attributed to ministers themselves. If in so saying, the writer reproaches himself, he has no wish to repel the reproach which may be due to him in common with others, or even byond them. Men may preach the truth with all plainness and fidelity, whose own bosoms are not warmed by it. They may preach for sinister and selfish ends, rather than that God may be exalted. They may be weak and uninteresting preachers, because they bestow little time, or thought, or prayer upon their preparations for the pulpit. They may loiter the week away, and the blessed day of God which they ought to hail with joy, finds them embarrassed and unfitted for their work. Weeks and years, and a life of toil, is what they may not think of; their great object may be to avoid the more weighty responsibilities of their calling, and their ingenuity is tasked to its utmost to find out expedients by which they may meet these responsibilities with the least labour. Or if they are men of toil, it may be for themselves they are toiling; it may be for place, for fame, for care and competency, and not for Christ and the souls of men. They have no heartfelt impressions of the condition of those who are living without God and without hope, and no deep solicitude to lead them to repentance. Or if they have these sympathies, they are evanescent as the dew. They have little confidence in God, and little of that joy in him which is the strength of his ministers, as well as his people. The great object of their holy vocation does not fill their minds, engross their thoughts, and draw toward it their strongest and most ardent affections. And it is no marvel that such preachers complain of little success.

These are affecting and humbling thoughts. Were those of us who are set apart for the Lord's service more in the habit of inspecting ourselves and searching our hearts, we should have less difficulty in ascertaining the causes of a fruitless ministry. But everlasting thanks to him to whom they are due, it is not in the unbelief of his ministers, to 'make the faith of God of no effect'! His gracious designs will not be frustrated. Let the thought encourage his ministers that they plead for God, as well as for the souls of men. So far as they are faithful, his aims and theirs are one. O that we might more deeply feel the importance of the position we occupy, the work to which we are called, and the vows that are upon us! Paul said to the Corinthians, 'I was with you in weakness, and in fear, and in *much trembling.*' Little do they know the heart of God's ministers, who do not suppose that it habitually responds to this consciousness. If ministers are made to feel their own insufficiency, and if the churches are made to feel the insufficiency of their ministers, it is that both may learn that their help cometh from God.

There is great, nay, unspeakable joy in the work of the ministry when it is attended with the power of God; but let it not be said that it is ever joyless. It were indeed a privilege to be able to say with Paul, 'Thanks be to God who always causeth us to triumph in Christ, and

The Responsibility of Ministers

maketh manifest the savour of his knowledge by us in every place.' And had we his spirit, we should oftener say with him, 'as sorrowful, yet always rejoicing'. If we may forget ourselves in thinking of our work, much more may we forget ourselves in thinking of our Divine Master. We should be happy ministers then, even though not always successful. And should we not be more successful? And then what joys! – no longer transient, no longer few and small, but rich and plenteous, dropping from heaven like the dew, coming down like the rain, flowing like rivers whose banks are full to the brim!

When ministers are most discouraged, they rarely utter their discouragements to the ear of man. They often feel that they stand alone, but rarely do they burden their people with their apprehensions; their course is a silent and uncomplaining course. But never ought it to be a discouraged one – no, never! Let none of these things move us, neither let us count our lives dear to ourselves, so that we may finish our course with joy, and the ministry we have received of the Lord Jesus, to testify to the Gospel of the grace of God.

It is a wise arrangement of Divine providence, that 'one generation passeth away, and another generation cometh'. The time cannot be long before the writer must retire from the field of labour, and leave it fresh and ripe for a glorious harvest. He knows the distance he has journeyed, and the path he is treading. He has bright anticipations of what is to take place when he himself is numbered with the forgotten dead. These days of declension and darkness will not continue long. If it were right that he should do so, he could envy the youthful ministry of reconciliation, who are entering upon their work at a period so rich in promise. The clouds of mercy are gathering thick over this lost world; the times are full of promise; this long protracted slumber is breaking up; there are those now alive, and on the earth, who will see the signs of the Son of Man coming in power and great glory. Such a scene as is allotted to those who are just putting on their armour, is cheerless only when it is neglected. Nothing so certainly as cheerful toil, and a cheerful faith in things not seen as yet, will become a sweeter, and yet more sweet preparative for the joy of their Lord.

18: *A Competent Ministry to be Procured*

The remaining topic of discussion introduces us to a series of observations of a different character from those to which our attention has been thus far directed.

If what has been already suggested be true, it is truth of no small importance. If the pulpit has the influence which has been attributed to it; if by Divine appointment, it possesses constituent elements of influence which belong to no other institution; if by a wise, diligent, and humble consecration of themselves to its appropriate services, those who occupy, may employ it in securing the noblest results ever effected through the instrumentality of creatures; there are *obligations* resting upon the church of God, and upon the world, in relation to the Christian ministry, which have not always been appreciated, nor even duly considered. What obligations rest upon the ministry themselves, we have seen: they are weighty beyond measure. Ministers are often tempted to shrink from the responsibility, and many a time feel that is is a burden too heavy to be borne. But are they alone in this responsibility? Are there no corresponding obligations resting upon the church, and the world around them? The *people* and the *ministry* are correlative terms. They compose the entire population of Christian lands; nor is there any obligation resting upon the latter, without a correlative obligation on the former. *What then are the obligations of the people, in view of the relation they bear to the Christian ministry?*

The most general and comprehensive thought which suggests itself in reply to this inquiry, is, that *the ministry must, from time to time, be supplied by the people themselves.* We look over the earth, and see that it is most imperfectly supplied with ministers of the Gospel. Death is making perpetual inroads upon the number of living teachers: 'your "fathers" – where are they? and the prophets, do they live for ever'? In a little while the present generation of ministers will have passed away; nor will any be found to take their places, without suitable forethought, prayer, and effort, on the part of those to whom the duty of procuring this supply belongs. The all-wise and gracious God made provision for this supply under the Hebrew dispensation, by making the priesthood *hereditary*; but this law is no longer binding; the high privilege is now offered to all the families in Christian lands, to aid in furnishing a perishing world with a competent supply of Christian ministers. No department of the Christian church possesses this exclusive privilege; nor does the obligation rest exclusively on any one tribe, or family, or man. It is a common privilege, and a common duty; and becomes specific only as the thoughts, and prayers, and efforts of any particular community, or individual, are directed to this great object, or the providence of God imposes upon them peculiar obligations. But whose thoughts, and prayers, and efforts *ought not* to be directed towards it? Who shall ask to be released from the obligation of directing his inquiries, to a subject of such interest? I know not the church, nor the family, nor the man who can be released from this obligation.

It may not be unseasonable to enter here somewhat into detail, and specify those classes of persons, and those individuals, on whom this obligation is most sacredly imposed.

It rests, in the first place, *on Christian ministers themselves*. That great law of the Jewish church, that the priesthood should be hereditary, though abolished, is yet not without meaning. It is in some sort, *the law of nature*, that the child should follow the calling of his parent. He may be supposed to have facilities and a training for such a vocation which are peculiar, and such as are not enjoyed by other classes of men. To what extent the Christian ministry in other lands has been supplied from the families of Christian ministers, I am not extensively informed; the history of the American church abundantly indicates, that this has been one of the greatest sources of this supply. Let any man carefully inspect such a work as Allen's *Biographical Dictionary of the Lives of Eminent Men in North America*, or the *American Quarterly Register*, and he will be both surprised and gratified to see, to what extent the Christian pulpit has been supplied from the families of ministers of the Gospel. Not far from seventy ministers in the American church can trace their lineage to the elder Edwards; he himself was the son of a clergyman; and his earliest known ancestor was a preacher of the Gospel, settled in London in the reign of Elizabeth. There are ministers now living among us, who can trace their genealogy to five, and some to six generations, in a direct, unbroken line, to the house of Levi. Others there are, who have been permitted to introduce, some two, some three, and some five of their sons, to the same sacred vocation with themselves. We should probably be not a little surprised by our inquiries into the lineal descent of the *living* ministry, to ascertain that such multitudes of them are the sons of those who themselves served at God's altars.

After some considerable research and correspondence on this subject, I have come to the conclusion that more than one-fifth part of all the ministers in the Presbyterian and Congregational churches in this land are of ministerial descent. Here then, this obligation, as it seems to me, primarily rests. Ministers of the Gospel have peculiar opportunities for meeting the claims of the world in this great article of its exigencies. From their birth, their sons should be devoted to God for the work of the ministry; for this great work they should be offered to him in holy baptism; for this they should be cared for, and educated, and become the subjects of earnest and ceaseless prayer. It is a great privilege, and wondrous mercy, when the Lord of the harvest condescends to *accept* the offering; the most faithful and devoted minister is not worthy of this high honour; while they from whom such an offering is not accepted, and whose prayers in this particular remain unanswered, and whose highest hopes for their sons are not realized, can only 'lay their hand upon their mouth'. There is no breach of God's covenant faithfulness in denying us this distinguished blessing: nor is it sovereignty merely that denies it; it is equity, it is justice; and we have only to bow to it in submission and silence.

It is no unimportant part of the official and pastoral supervision of ministers also, to look over the young men of their respective charges, and seek out, and direct, and encourage those who give evidence of piety and fitness for the work of the ministry. It was one of the indications of God's presence with the people whom the writer of these pages has been permitted to serve in the Gospel, that for a series of years, not a few beloved youth among us were in constant training for this great work; and from year to year, went out from us to preach the everlasting Gospel. And it is among the indications of our mournful declension, that for a series of years last past, there has been but a solitary individual. Every church in the land ought to have at least one young man of their own number, who enjoys the benefit of their sympathy, their counsels, and their prayers; and who, under these delightful and covenanted influences, goes forth to proclaim the 'unsearchable riches of Christ'. That church cannot be in a healthful condition which can find no individual of suitable character for the ministry of the Gospel among them; or who if found, is suffered to languish through lack of their Christian sympathy.

But while this duty begins with those who minister in God's sanctuary, it ends not there. There are *not a few Christian families in every congregation*, whom it becomes to devote some one or more of their sons to the work of the ministry. This is the second great source of supply. Were all the sons of all the ministers in the land, to become ministers, the supply would still be inadequate. And where shall the great Head of the church look for it, but to the families of his own people! The Bible defines who are the families of his own people: they are the families where both or *one* of its united head, is the professed disciple of Jesus Christ. The believing husband may not say, the Saviour does not expect this offering from *me*, because he is associated with an unbelieving wife; nor may the believing wife say, he will not accept it from *me*, because she is associated with an unbelieving husband. Such is the bounty, the generosity of God's love, that the *covenant* relation to him and his church, of every such family, is decided by the *believing*, and not the unbelieving parent. This is a most wonderful and gracious arrangement, and so full of encouragement, that the believing parent cannot hope too much from God for his or her children. The irreligion that is in a family may throw obstacles not a few to the religious culture of the rising generation; but because the religion that is there is of God's planting, his faithfulness is pledged to sustain and give it influence. How certainly, and how much more does this obligation rest upon families whose hearts are bound together not only by the purest of all earthly love, but by the common bond of that love which is heaven-born and unearthly? He who 'sets the solitary in families and makes their children like olive plants round about their table', may peradventure claim some one of those he has given you for the ministry of his Son. It may be that the 'Lord hath need of him'. Is there not one among them all whom you can cheerfully consecrate to him for this self-denying and high service? and of whom you can say, with Hannah, when she stood praying in the temple, 'He shall be lent to the Lord, as long as he liveth'?

Are they more ambitious views that you are indulging, and a more lofty station that you are looking for on behalf of the son of your vows? For one I cannot sympathize with you in such views. Had I a son qualified for this high service, self-denying as I know it to be, I would rather see him an humble, and faithful minister of the ever blessed Gospel, than at the head of the bar, or the most distinguished professor of the healing art, or at the head of the most successful mercantile house in the land. It is incumbent on Christian families deliberately to look at this grave subject. The church of God is dear to him as the apple of his eye; yet how few are 'there to guide her among all the sons whom she hath brought forth: how few to take her by the hand of all the sons that she hath brought up'! God may not accept your offering; yet go, in the humility of faith, and in the strength of dependence on his grace make the offering at his throne. Nor let your child long remain ignorant of these secret transactions between you and your Maker. Let him know that if he breaks away from God, and refuses to enter the ministry of his Son, he countervails your most ardent expectations and vows. Often remind him that he is 'lent to the Lord'; educate him in his fear; and who shall say that he will not abundantly bless your offering, and in 'filling his poor with bread' through your instrumentality, also fill your own heart with joy.

19: *Ministry Compared with Other Professions*

A third source of supply for the Christian ministry, must be found in *those young men of piety and talent, who are already educated, or in a course of education for the other learned professions*. When God commanded Moses to deliver his message to Pharaoh, Moses replied, 'O my Lord, send I pray thee by the hand of him whom thou wilt send'; but by this answer the anger of God was kindled against his timid and reluctant servant. We have no desire to see every pious and well-educated man employed in the ministry of the Gospel, nor is every such man qualified for the service. Such men are needed elsewhere, as well as in the sacred ministry. Yet ought the question to be deliberately presented to the mind of every well-qualified young man, *Whether he can the better serve God and his generation by engaging in some one of the other learned professions, or in the ministry of his Son?* This is the only question which a conscientious man will look at. Private interests must be laid aside and this single question considered, in the light of God's truth, God's providence, and the realities of eternity.

There is no miraculous call at this age of the world, to the work of the ministry. Whether one is called to it, is neither more nor less, than whether, upon a full view of the subject, it is his *duty* to enter it. Like every other question of duty, this is to be decided by those leadings of Divine Providence, which indicate to an ingenuous and obedient mind, what his Heavenly Father would have him to do. What are these indications? Are they not a heart sincerely devoted to the service of God, an honest purpose of living to his glory, a willingness to be devoted to him, in that way in which we may probably perform the most essential service, together with those natural talents and opportunities and means that fit us for this employment. To be conscious of these things, or to have a prevailing consciousness of them, must go very far toward producing the conviction in every honest mind, that the best service he can perform, is to honour his Maker by preaching the Gospel of his Son. It will be very difficult to keep such a man out of the ministry; his conscience calls him to it; his heart calls him to it; God calls him to it; and unless obstacles which cannot be surmounted obstruct his path, he must obey the call.

Yet is this conviction not the creature of mere impulse, a mere *impression*, produced by supposed supernatural influences. It is just the deliberate conviction of a devout mind, adopted in full view of all the light it can obtain, after having sought counsel of God and man, and after no small schooling and self-discipline. Many a young man has entered the ministry under the influence of mere impulse, whom a little experience has taught that he is not fitted for this laborious employment. It may be with reluctance and some mortification that he abandons it; but if he perseveres in a service to which God has not called him, it must be with a discouraged heart. What the Saviour said to those who followed him without anticipating the sacrifice of so doing, may with stronger propriety and greater emphasis, be said to every young man who is directing his thoughts toward the Gospel ministry: 'Which one of you, intending to build a tower, sitteth not down first and *counteth the cost?*'

These remarks may not be turned to good account by all who read them. The object of them is not to discourage young men from entering the sacred office; but rather to encourage. The unhappiness is, that they may present *discouragement* to the very minds which they ought to *encourage and stimulate*. Like the discriminations between genuine and spurious piety, the dart which was aimed at the false professor is felt most deeply by the more diffident and humble. Self-diffidence is no proof that a man is not called to the sacred office; on the other hand, it is one of the more welcome and delightful indications that God designs him for a service in which 'he that planteth is nothing and he that watereth is nothing'.

Among the considerations which ought to operate on every man who is balancing this great question, we place in the foremost rank *the power of the pulpit, and the intrinsic importance of the Gospel ministry*. We do not depreciate other departments of human labour, nor other professional vocations; we would that they were all occupied by godly men. We honour them all and have reason to honour them. There is a vast amount of splendid talent, and acquirement, and not unfrequently acquirements, and talent, that are sanctified and devoted to good ends, brought to all the learned professions.

It is greatly desirable that our universities and colleges should be under the teaching of men deeply imbued with the spirit of Christianity. Where this service has attractions for the Christian mind, we would be slow to entertain the doubt, if such a mind is in its proper place, in the instruction of the young. It is a most delightful fact that so many men of high qualifications for their office, are found in our seminaries of learning, who are not less the honoured professors of Christianity, than of literature and science. Nobly in our youthful land are such professors doing their exalted work, and winning their unwithered laurels. Long may they do so, and cast their honours at his feet who was crowned with thorns!

The medical profession in all its branches, has deserved attractions. From the dexterous management of magical incantation of ancient times, to the more sober investigation of times less ancient, and the still more solid deductions of the inductive philosophy which have been extended to the study of the animal economy in our own days, this department furnishes a beautiful and brilliant comment upon the spirit of accurate observation and unwearied research, of which there are so many living and illustrious examples. A Christian physician is an ornament to his race, and treads in the steps of that great and Almighty Healer, whose miracles of healing were the precursors and attendants of his miracles of salvation. Many there are of this character in the land; it is deeply to be regretted they are so few; and that in so learned a profession, they are so many who exert a neutralizing influence upon Christianity.

Of *Law*, says the great Hooker, 'there can be no less acknowledged, than that her seat is the bosom of God, her voice the harmony of the world: all things in heaven and earth do her homage, the very least as seeking her care and the greatest as not exempt from her power. Both angels and men, and creatures of what condition soever, though each in a different sort and name, yet all with one uniform consent, admiring her as the mother of their peace and joy.' I have wondered how there could be an unchristian lawyer. If the poet could say, 'an undevout astronomer is mad'; what shall be said of the man whose professional vocation leads him to define and vindicate the rights of his fellow-men, who is heedless of the rights of his Maker? What shall be said of him who best understands those great rules of action, commanding what is right, and forbidding what is wrong, who, in his vast range of thought, overlooks the law of God?

I well remember the time when the profession of the law was not so exalted and honoured a profession as it now is. It is, and ever since the Revolution,[*] has been a large body of men, embracing a great variety of moral and religious character; so that no general affirmation relating to it would be free from exposure to plausible criticism. If the men of eminence in this profession may be regarded as the most probable representatives of the mass, the lawyers of the two generations which have passed since the Declaration of our Independence, may fairly be distributed as those who were in the height of their influence for the twenty years immediately after the Revolution, and those who now, and for the last twenty years have been prominent. Of the earlier class it may be said, that they were highly educated; were polished gentlemen; were very learned and of remarkable ability. But they were not men of the highest and purest morality, and were very greedy of the gains of the profession. This is not universally true, but it is true in the main; and every one who will inspect the character of the class will satisfy himself of the truth of the remark. As to the prominent members of the bar of the last twenty years,[†] and the present day, we may say with truth that in integrity, in purity of life, in general moral character, and in consistent religious profession and conduct, they are far superior to their predecessors. They are not inferior in ability; they are scarcely their equals in learning, finished manners, or in that brilliancy which attracts the general admiration.

The improvement in the character of the bar, in this country, has probably been greatly promoted by the Law Schools formed in various parts of the country after the model of the Institution in Litchfield. All these schools have exerted an elevating moral influence, and some of them an influence that is truly Christian. Reeves, Kent, and Greenleaf deserve well of the American churches. Young men thus destined to the bar have been placed at once at the pure fountains of those legal principles, and those considerations of truth, justice, public policy, and refined equity,

---

[*] 1776–83, when the American Colonies broke away from Britain.
[†] 1828–48.

of which the science of the Law is composed. Their intimacy with these principles has most favourably influenced their character. In no aspect has scientific education produced better results than in the influence it has exerted on the bar of the United States; which, for its high position in moral and religious character, has no superior. In no land does this profession deserve the name of a Christian profession, so truly as in our own. To an extent altogether unknown in the English and Scottish courts, the most distinguished jurists, in very many of these States, both on the bench, and at the bar, are professedly Christian men, and exert an influence in favour of Christianity. As a useful and benevolent employment a Christian may well confess that this profession has strong allurements; while, as an employment for cultivated intellect, it possesses, in the extent of its researches, and in the accuracy and precision of its discriminations, elements of a most enviable kind. Few subjects present a more noble expression of the comprehensive, and at the same time the analytical powers of the human mind, than the study of the law in all its branches, and in its gradual advancement.

If from the law, we look to the profession of a *Statesman*, we may not deny that it has attractive inducements. An enlightened Christian statesman, I am very sorry to say, is a rare character among the men of our own times. There is too much in the profession that is corrupting to the human heart, too much to fire ambition, and generate intrigue, too much to cherish the love of money and the love of power, too much of rivalry and party strife, to render it a safe position for a follower of Jesus Christ to aspire after. A Christian man may be a statesman; but if he aims at this perilous position, he transplants himself from a soil refreshed by the waters of the sanctuary, to a mountain of snow, or to the bleak rock that is washed by the spray of the ocean. He will scarcely flourish like the palm-tree, or grow like the cedar in Lebanon. The arena of political agitation must be a different thing from what it is, to allow us to say of it, that for the gratification of enlightened intellect, enlarged views, and more than all, that public spirit which is the prominent feature of Christianity, the science of government furnishes a desirable sphere of thought and labour.

We are not unwilling that the claims of other professions should be canvassed, while we have ventured to speak as we have spoken for God and his sanctuary. Do we need to crave indulgence from our learned and professional readers, when we say, that with all the attractions of other professions, it is the privilege, even of the humblest, and the meanest occupant of the pulpit, to claim for it a superiority over them all.

This superiority belongs to it, if for nothing more than the wide range of thought which it presents to the human intellect, and the interest it imparts to mere intellectual investigation. If the intellect is ever interested in what is great, it is interested here. If it is philosophical and metaphysical disquisition that interests it, or the natural sciences, or refined and elegant literature, here it may revel as in the richest banqueting house of thought. If it be the thorny field of controversy with the foe that it seeks to travel over, or the garden of flowers, or the matured and yellow harvest as it waves in the sunlight, here is all that can gratify it. It will be very difficult to find the men in the literary world whose enthusiasm has been more ardent, and whose intellectual enjoyment has been more pure and more intense, than theirs whose life and soul have been wrapt up in the pursuit of theological science.

If from this intellectual interest which the great subjects of natural and revealed religion excite, we turn to the *moral* interest, and look at the benevolent motives which address themselves to the heart of every honest preacher of the Gospel, we shall see our office still more magnified. What these are we have already specified. And is there no interest in a course of investigation, and of public instruction, argument, and appeal, where these great objects form the impulsive power? I need but submit the inquiry to a Christian mind. Is there interest in those wondrous achievements which the mind, the eye, and the hand of man have compassed for the social and temporal benefit of our race; and is there none in the mightier achievements of the Gospel of the grace of God? Is there any thing to attract the heart in those philanthropic efforts, which have thrown over the ruder nations, and the more rude states of human society, the charms of civilized and polished men? And is there none in turning them from dumb idols, to serve the living God? Is the pride of man gratified in erecting pyramids, building towers, and founding empires; and shall not his humility be gratified by his favoured and undeserved instrumentality in building up the walls of God's temple, and extending the empire of his gracious Redeemer over the souls of lost men? Is he gratified when he scans the heavens, penetrates the bowels of the earth, navigates unexplored seas, converts deserts into cities, makes islands in the ocean, and turns in the sea upon the solid land? And has he no heart to rejoice when he makes the moral desert blossom as the rose, and the wilderness like the garden of God; when through his humble efforts, the abundance of the seas is converted unto the Most High, and when, from an abyss deeper than all the deep places of the earth, he is the selected instrument by which the deathless soul is raised to celestial mansions? Does he dwell with gratified and grateful complacency on his successful efforts in healing the sick, in defending the innocent, and redressing wrong, in pleading his country's cause before the elders of the land; and shall he have no gratified and grateful emotions when he pleads the cause of the King of kings, when he asserts the rights of the Eternal Lawgiver, and when he conducts the poor and wretched and blind, the corrupted, degraded, palsied, and dead in sin, to the great Author of holiness and life?

An anonymous writer in *Blackwood's Magazine* remarks, 'I know of no profession more capable of fulfilling all the objects of a vigorous mind. I am not now talking of mitres; they can fall to but few. I speak of the prospects which it opens to all; the power of exerting the largest influence for the highest purposes; the possession of fame without its emptiness, and the indulgence of knowledge without its vanity; energy turned to the most practical and lofty uses of man; and the full feast of ambition superior to the tinsel of the world, and alike pure in its motives, and unmeasurable in its rewards.'

In which of these noble spheres, then, will a well-qualified young man accomplish the most for the God that made him, and the generation he lives to serve? In which will he do the most good, and accomplish the great end for which his being, and his piety, and his qualifications were bestowed? Where will his soul find the richest aliment, and his conscience be most at ease, and his heart most tranquil? *Where is he most needed?* Not in the crowded profession of the law; nor in the overstocked and suffocated department of the healing art; nor in the professor's chair, for which there are twenty aspirants to one vacancy.

So much has been said and done of late years on the subject of educating *poor and pious young men* for the Gospel ministry, that the obligation of furnishing the pulpit from any other classes of society seems to be in a great measure lost sight of. Now we enter our solemn protest against some modern views of this doctrine. It were a calamity greatly to be deplored, should we act upon the principle that *poverty and low birth are essential qualifications for the Christian ministry*; and that a well-bred man is disqualified from becoming a minister of the Gospel because he is well-bred, and the son of a rich man disqualified because he is rich. Yet such is the strong tendency of the public mind: the church of God and ministers themselves scarcely think of looking for men to serve the Lord Jesus in his sanctuary, save to the poor.

It is true that the Saviour selected some from the poor to be his Apostles. *Peter, Andrew, James,* and *John* were fishermen; yet ecclesiastical historians inform us, that James and John were of noble family. *Matthew*, though an Hebrew of the Hebrews, was a Roman officer, a broker or money-changer; an office which was indeed of bad report among the Jews, but among the Romans accounted a place of power and credit; so much so that it was ordinarily conferred on none but Roman knights. William Cave, in his *Lives of the Apostles*, states on the authority of Suetonius, that Titus Flaminius Sabonus, father to the Emperor Vespasian, was a publican of the Asiatic provinces of Rome, and highly respected in his character and office. *James* the less was related to the priesthood, and was kinsman to Zacharias, the father of John the Baptist; so was *Judas* his brother, and both of them belonged to the royal family of David. Simon Zelotes belonged to one of the most honourable sects of the Jews; and though it became subsequently degenerate, was in the days of the Saviour of high repute and authority. Of *Philip, Bartholomew, Thomas,* and *Matthias*, we learn nothing from the New Testament, except their vocation to the apostleship.

Paul, the distinguished Apostle, called so miraculously, was eminent from his youth in the learning and philosophy of the Gentile world; educated in the metropolis of Cicilia, renowned as it was for its schools, and even rivalling Alexandria and Athens. Having laid the foundation of his attainments in the sciences at Tarsus, he was sent by his parents to Jerusalem to perfect himself in the study of the law, under the celebrated Rabbi Gamaliel. He himself takes particular notice of his honourable descent, nor is it any impeachment of his high standing and consideration in society that he was by trade a tentmaker, because the sons of the highest families were brought up to a trade. It is a well known fact that the most learned among the Jews were, in early life, trained to some branch of manual and useful labour. It was a maxim among that people, that 'he who teaches not his son a trade, teaches him to be a thief'.

Thus much of the Apostles. If we inquire after others, and during the Apostolic age, we find *Mark*, a descendant of the priesthood; and *Luke*, the physician educated in the metropolis of Syria, the 'very lap of the muses', and familiar with the learning of Egypt and Greece. We find *Barnabas*, also a descendant of the priesthood, the son of rich and pious parents. We find *Timothy*, his father a Greek, his mother a Jewess, fitted by his early education, as soon as he was converted to the Christian faith, to be employed by Paul. We find *Titus* of Crete, the common account of whom is that he was of the blood royal of the Island. We find *Dionysius* one of the judges of the Grecian Areopagus; *Clement*, the son of Faustus, who was near of kin to the Roman Emperor; and *Justin Martyr*, a highly educated young man, and greatly accomplished by foreign travel. We find *Irenæus* the Greek, the successful pupil of Papias, and prepared by his liberal and extensive training for the important post he afterwards occupied in the Church of God. We find *Theophilus* of Antioch, a young man, versed in the writings of all the great masters of learning in the heathen world; *Tertullian*, descended from the Gens Septimia, a regal tribe among the Romans, and maintaining consular and patrician honours. We find *Origen, Cyprian, Gregory*, and others not a few, all descended from wealthy parentage. Dr. M'Crie, in his *History of the Reformation in Italy*, the best which I have seen, states that the *Italian Reformers*, who performed and suffered so much in resisting the corruptions of the Church of Rome antecedently to the days of Luther, and who fled to different countries of Europe, were men of high and noble descent. So far as I have been able to ascertain, the great mass of Christ's ministers, in Europe, Asia, and Africa, have been descended from parentage that was *above want*; and who, if they were not affluent, have, by the force of their own character, found their way to the pulpit without the aid of charity.

Until within a few years past this is equally true of the American clergy. Nothing is hazarded by the general remark, that the brightest constellations in all lands, and the men whose light has shone to distant ages, have been from families respected and honoured for their station in human society. But there is one example that outshines them all, and that may well cover the face of the young man with blushes, who is tempted to regard the office of the Christian ministry as beneath his rank. I allude to the only Son of the acknowledged and reigning Monarch of all worlds. Wealth he had, for the riches of the universe were his; honours he had, for angels bowed at his footstool; power he had, for all power was his; high and exalted parentage he had, for he was the Son of God, the Father's equal. O blush, and be ashamed, that He whose honours make all earthly honours wither, should lay aside his sceptre, and put off his crown, and come down to this low earth, for the sake of becoming a Minister of that Gospel, whose service is not sufficiently lofty and elevated for thee, his creature, his pensioner, his child!

It were enough honour to resemble him, who 'though he was rich, for our sakes became poor, that we through his poverty might become rich'! Yet he condescends to solicit that very youth to come into his vineyard. His church needs him. The poor and the destitute need him. Important churches, which have long looked in vain for men of combined piety, talent, and some consideration in society, need him. His Divine Lord has need of him – he has need of *him*. It is that young man of Christian nurture, of early piety, of cultivated talent and habits, and of accomplished character that he needs. It is that youth of promise, who is looking toward the council-chamber, and the forum, and that has qualities that will shine amid the bright lights of the land. His church, in the pressure of her wants, will seek out others: she will find them in the highways and hedges; but she will not *seek* for *him*. Him the Master calls more directly. Jesus, who died for him, calls him to forsake all, and become his ambassador to dying men. There are those whom *he* must guide, and none else. O there is a lamentable destitution in the ministry, of such men! Thousands there are who are praying, and looking for the time when *such* men shall not be ashamed to be enrolled among the ambassadors of their despised Lord. It is a sorry day this, in which men of distinction shun the sacred ministry. Where it will end, we do not know; but we implore them to look at this great question in the light of eternity.

There is an affecting anecdote related of that memorable Italian reformer, *Filippo Neri*, and the youthful student. 'Filippo was living at one of the Italian Universities when a young man, whom he had known as a boy, ran up to him with a face full of delight, and told him that what he had long been wishing above all things in the world, was at length fulfilled, his parents having just given him leave to study the law; and that thereupon he had come to the law-school, and meant to spare no pains or labour in getting through his studies as quickly and as well as possible. In this way he ran on a long time; and when at last he came to stop, the holy man, who had been listening to him with great patience and kindness, said, "Well! and when you have got through your course of studies, what do you mean to do then?"

"Then I shall take my doctor's degree," answered the young man.

"And then?" asked Filippo Neri again.

"And then," continued the youth, "I shall have a number of difficult and knotty cases to manage, shall catch people's notice by my eloquence, my zeal, my acuteness, and gain a great reputation."

"And then?" repeated the holy man.

"And then," replied the youth, "why then, there can't be a question, I shall be promoted to some high office or other, besides, I shall make money and grow rich."

"And then?" repeated Filippo.

"And then," pursued the young lawyer – "then I shall live comfortably and honourably in health and dignity, and shall be able to look forward quietly to a happy old age."

"And *then*?" added the holy man.

"And then," said the youth – "and then – and then – then I *shall die*."

'Here Filippo lifted up his voice, and again asked, "AND THEN?" Whereupon the young man made no answer, but cast down his head, and went away. This last *And then?* had pierced like a flash of lightning into his soul, and he could not get quit of it. Soon after he forsook the study of the law, and gave himself up to the ministry of Christ, and spent the remainder of his days in godly words and works.'

It is true there are trials in the Christian ministry; and some of them are peculiar and severe. But are they too many, or more than these servants of God need? Nor is the ministry the only profession in which there are trials; yet is it the only one which has such promises, and such a reward. What a day will that be, when a faithful and laborious minister stands before God! When the mighty God, even the Lord, shall say, 'Gather my saints together unto me, those who have made a covenant with me by sacrifice': and when before 'the general assembly and church of the First Born', and in presence of assembled worlds, he shall present the fruits of God's grace and his fidelity, to his Father and their Father, to his God and their God, and say, 'Behold I and the children which thou hast given me', trials will be forgotten. Disclaimed honours will then be restored, and look bright again. Yea, toil, weariness, watchings, fastings, penury, reproach, and frowns, will all be forgotten in the fulness of the joy.

There is a remaining source of supply to the Christian ministry, when all these are found to be inadequate. The American Republic has introduced a new era, not only in the State, but in the church. The pride of family is rapidly vanishing away, and personal worth is daily becoming more and more the only standard of character. It is impossible to maintain any thing like an aristocracy in any land without something like the law of entailment. With some few exceptions, the rich in this land were the sons of the poor; while those who are now the sons of the rich, will, with some honourable exceptions, themselves be poor in a few years after their fathers sleep in the dust. The wealthy, and well educated, and honoured among us, have for the most part no high parentage to boast of. They will be much more likely, in tracing up their parentage, to stumble over a carpenter's bench or a blacksmith's anvil or a butcher's stall or a stage coach, than upon a peerage, or a bishop's see. Right or wrong, this is the actual state of things in this democratic land: and with all wisdom and energy the *church of God must meet it*. Men are no longer great by inheritance, but are self-made men. The church is just as democratic as the world; she has few rich that were not once poor, and few poor that will not become rich. In this land, therefore, it is no dishonour in a young man to be poor. Poverty is no barrier to his advancement either in church or State.

There are not a few young men of fine minds and straitened circumstances to be found in our churches, who must, if this extensive country be furnished with ministers of the Gospel, direct their attention to the pulpit. This therefore must be regarded as one of the sources from which those large supplies can be obtained that are demanded by the millions that are perishing for lack of knowledge. The exigencies of the land *justify and demand the effort of selecting and educating this class of young men by the charities of the church.*

There are intrinsic and adventitious disadvantages, and even objections to this great enterprise; and they deserve a candid hearing. But if those that are adventitious may be diminished and removed, it ought not to be fatal to so important an enterprise that those which are intrinsic and inseparable from it remain. 'Where there is a will, there is a way.' A strong young man, be he ever so poor, may find access to the ministry, by the force of his own strong will, and the solicited blessing of God upon his own exertions. Yet is there many a one naturally well qualified for extensive usefulness in this field of such varied labour, who is not thus strong. There can be little doubt that those young men who are physically, intellectually, and spiritually qualified for the ministry, would greatly increase those qualifications by that course of mental and physical toil, so patiently and with such exemplary self-denial endured by some who found their way to the pulpit long before modern Education Societies came into existence. They would 'show themselves *men*', and be more respected and vigorous and useful. The loss of time by such a course of self-training and discipline, would be made up by the accession of influence. Some of the most laborious men who have held their places in the church during the last forty or fifty years, were men of this stamp; and no class of ministers have proved themselves more trustworthy, or have enjoyed a larger share of public confidence.

But such has been the pressing demand of the world for ministers, that this tardy progress has been found to be too slow; and necessity, which knows no law, has driven the churches to the bold experiment of *seeking out* young men, and aiding them in their preparatory course of study. Multitudes have thus been brought into the ministry, who, from sensitive diffidence, or more sensitive poverty, would never have thought of devoting themselves to this great work. They are men fitted for the exigencies of the age, and have done good service; while there are those among them who have shone as stars of the first magnitude, and eclipsed the light that rose amid fewer clouds. Nor is it any marvel, nor ought it to be any serious disappointment that in an enterprise so untried, and conducted upon so large a scale, there should have been some unhappy failures. They have been not a few; we confess they have been unhappy. There is something wanting in this class of men: even not a few of them who have gone as missionaries to the heathen have given more trouble, and more expense, than those who have found their way to the pulpit unaided. They expect too much; they have, to too great an extent, the habit of dependence upon others. If we look over the land too, we shall find the leaders of new measures, and that fearful radicalism which has distracted the churches, among those who were low-bred men; who have been brought up from their youth to be jealous of clerical influence, and who have not grown up with those sentiments of respect for the Gospel ministry which it deserves. Let me not be misunderstood. A poor young man is not necessarily a low-bred man; it is not because he is *poor* that he may not be entitled to high confidence. If we doubt the expediency of introducing *low-bred* men into the pulpit, it is because the 'Ethiopian cannot change his skin, nor the leopard his spots'. It is a sure way to bring the office into contempt, when the church makes to herself 'priests of the lowest order of the people'.

Experience gives wisdom. No class of men have profited more by their experience, than those to whom the churches have intrusted the selection and education of poor and pious youth for the ministry. The enterprise is now probably as well conducted as it can be; and if not, there is but one thing wanted to make the system as perfect as it is capable of being made. That one thing is the *extension of the system of parochial schools* throughout all our churches. These, under a wise supervision, would become not only the nurseries of the church, but the nurseries of the ministry. They furnish the very scenes, and associations, and employments which put the intellectual and moral character of this class of youth to the test; and which, by that gradual development which is most to be relied on, would indicate the most worthy candidates for the church's charity. The report of the Board of Education on the subject of parochial schools, presented to the General Assembly of the Presbyterian Church, at their last annual meeting, does not give undue weight to these thoughts, when it says that the 'parochial system will, with the blessing of God, *give the church a wider range from which to expect ministerial supplies*. She will not only have better ministers, by God's grace, but more of them. In proportion as Christian education exerts an influence on the minds and hearts of the youth of the church, are the probabilities increased of their turning their attention to the ministry.

There is no irreverence in such an anticipation. God employs means in the advancement of his kingdom. As the multiplication of churches secures in the ordinary course of Providence an increase of communicants, so a larger class of youth religiously educated in church-schools, will be likely to furnish an increased supply for the sanctuary. The qualifications of candidates trained up from early youth, under the watchful care of the church, would be well known in all our congregations and presbyteries. From the nature of the case, there would be fewer risks encountered. Character would be formed on a superior model; piety would have a more intelligent basis; the nature of a call to the ministry would be better understood; would be better known, as well as of a better order. Almost all the failures connected with the Board of Education, have been from the class whose *early* education was neglected. The most hopeful candidates of the church are those who have drank in the 'sincere milk of the word' with their nursery rhymes and their mother's prayers, and who have been regularly trained in Sabbath and other schools. It must not be supposed, however, that under the best possible system of church education, we shall be free from failures among our candidates. But we may labour by prayer, and by effort of every kind, to diminish the number; and it is believed that no improvement upon our existing system would be found so radical and effectual, as the education of our future ministers under the care of the church, from the school to the theological seminary.

It is by methods like these, that a competent ministry is to be procured for the church and the world; and if in our former observations, we have not claimed more for the pulpit than belongs to it, it is but justice that it be more abundantly supplied. Whatever means of a different kind may be adopted, the harvest will not be gathered in without the appointed labourers. A voice reaches us on this subject, not from our own land only, but from every part of the world. More than twenty years ago, the American Missionaries in the far distant East, in one of their communications to the churches at home, have embodied the following important thought:– 'Sending teachers without the Bible, was the error of the Church of Rome; let it not be the error of Protestants to send the Bible without preachers.'

If we look to our own land alone, notwithstanding the increase of ministers within the last thirty years, the ratio of this supply by no means stands abreast with the ratio of an increased population. This vast land is to be supplied with the Christian ministry. It is no easy matter to contemplate the number of inhabitants that are to be affected by a preached Gospel in such a land as this. 'The present confederacy of the United States of North America, contains a larger area of cultivated land, and hospitable climate, than any country that has previously existed. Ancient and modern empires sink into insignificance when compared with it. The United States of America contain 2,300,000 square miles, over half a million more than Europe, if we except Russia. Their greatest length is 3,000 miles; their greatest breadth 1,700 miles. They have a frontier line of 10,000 miles; a sea-coast of 36,000, and an inland lake coast of 1,200 miles. The rivers of the United States are the largest in the world. The Missouri is 3,600 miles in length; or more than twice as long as the Danube. The Ohio is 600 miles longer than the Rhine. The Hudson, entirely within a single State, is navigable 120 miles above its mouth farther than the Thames. One of the States has an area of 70,000 square miles, and is about one-third larger than England. From the eastern extremity of Maine to New Orleans, the distance is 2,000 miles, or 400 more than from London to Constantinople. From London to Constantinople, you cross the entire continent of Europe, and through most of its principal kingdoms. The great proportion of the whole extent of the territory of the United States is uncultivated. The population of the country, as rapidly as it increases, would not occupy all the public domain in a cycle of 500 years. So vast, indeed, is the territory of the United States already, that it takes no ordinary mind to contemplate its extent, and few indeed can calculate its resources; and the most comprehensive intellect cannot, even when warmed by a high-wrought imagination, give but a faint glimmering of the future wealth and power to be accorded to the American people. Our population is spreading from the Eastern to the Western Ocean, and in a few generations will constitute the largest nation in the world.'

And if we take into account the unevangelized parts of the earth, how fearful is the destitution of Christian ministers! What an army of young men must be found, and educated, and sent forth ere the Redeemer have the heathen for his inheritance, and the uttermost parts of the earth for his possession. 'Pray ye the Lord of the harvest, that he would send forth labourers into his harvest!' Prayer, prayer, prayer. 'Pray ye the Lord of the harvest that he would send forth labourers into his harvest!'

20: *The Fitting Education for the Christian Ministry*

We have, in the preceding chapter, presupposed, that the duty of the church in regard to the *classical and scientific education* of her sons for the Christian ministry, is in a good measure performed. In all ordinary cases, we insist on such an education. The necessities of the church may justify the setting apart of men to the sacred office who have not enjoyed the advantages of an extended education. After the revocation of the Edict of Nantes, the French Protestants called to the pastoral office some of their most zealous and enlightened members, and are indebted to them for their continued existence. But the instances in which this is called for are rare; necessity knows no law.

We proceed, in the present chapter, to a topic of some delicacy, and implore direction to treat it in the meekness of wisdom. A classical and literary education is not all that ministers need; nor is it all for which the church ought to hold herself responsible. There is *a solid, theological, spiritual, and practical training* of her sons which must be cared for; nor can she throw this responsibility from her own conscience; nor may she stand by, an indifferent and silent spectator, if she sees, or even fears, that her beloved and consecrated youth are exposed to a training which will diminish their usefulness in the service in which she desires and prays that they may be eminently useful.

We have intimated that the pulpit is less powerful than it was in the days of our fathers; and this acknowledgment comes to us from quarters from which it might be least expected. The existing ministry are not backward in announcing the mournful fact. One of the most venerable and experienced teachers in the Theological Seminary at Princeton, makes the following faithful statement on this subject, in an address to the students in that institution, which has been read with great interest, and has given great satisfaction both to the churches and their pastors. I shall offer no apology for introducing these thoughts, expressed as they are with the

The Fitting Education for the Christian Ministry

clearness, purity, and meekness so characteristic of their accomplished author. 'The means of more mature study, and the excitements to more mature study, have been constantly increasing; but both the means and excitements have been lost upon a large number of our candidates. And when a rapid improvement might have been expected, a real decline, if I mistake not, has been silently and insensibly going on. A little more than three quarters of a century ago, there was a considerable number of ministers in the Presbyterian Church in this country, who deserved to be called illustrious. As to the reality of this fact, you will not hesitate, when I mention, as a specimen, the names of President Dickinson, the elder President Edwards, President Burr, the Tennents, Mr. Blair, President Davies, President Finley, and a number more scarcely inferior; men, most of them, at once eminent for the fervour of their piety, the activity of their zeal, the vigour of their talents, the extent of their erudition, and their commanding influence.

The distinguished usefulness of these holy, apostolical men, in giving a tone to the preaching, the discipline, and the character of the church to which they belonged, it would not be easy to estimate. They were felt to be "workmen that needed not to be ashamed", qualified "rightly to divide the word of truth"; and the churches, and their younger brethren confided in them, and looked up to them, and, under the divine blessing, were guided aright. They were men fitted to have influence, and they *had it*, and employed it for the glory of God, and the best interests of mankind. The generation of ministers next to them, were, as a body, little, if any less distinguished. Then we had Strain, and Duffield, and Witherspoon, and M'Whorter, and Waddell, and Wilson, and Rodgers, and Hoge, not to mention others of equal claims; men of wisdom, piety, prudence, dignity, and peace; men who commanded the veneration and confidence of the churches; men, who, whenever they appeared in ecclesiastical judicatories, especially in the higher ones, seemed as if they were sent to enlighten, and guide, and bless the family of Christ.

Of the *present state* of our Church in reference to this point, it is both difficult and delicate to speak. But I ask – Have we an equally illustrious list to show at this hour, in proportion to our greatly augmented numbers and advantages? The ministers of our Church are nearly ten times as numerous as they were sixty years ago; and the facilities for obtaining books, and pursuing study, are also greatly multiplied. Upon every principle of proportion, we ought to be able *now* to bring forward a catalogue of Presbyterian apostles at least ten times as large as could have been produced in the days of Edwards, Davies, and Finley. But can we produce such a catalogue? It would rejoice my heart if I could think it possible. We cannot, however, I think, so far impose upon ourselves as to deem it possible. The most mortifying facts of a contradictory character stare us in the face. How difficult is it, even in this day of theological seminaries, to supply an important vacant congregation with a pastor, in whom the union of eminent learning, talents and piety is considered as indispensable?'[*]

We have the same complaint from the learned Professor who now occupies the theological chair at Andover. 'The effectiveness of the pulpit,' says he, 'in comparison with other efficiencies, has declined among us to an alarming extent, within the last fifty years.'[†]

We cannot but regard sentiments like these, coming, as they do, from the fountain-heads of theological learning, and the highest eminence of observation, as worthy of grave consideration; and the question forces itself upon us, May there not be some latent defect in the modern system of educating young men for the Gospel ministry?

In former days, the training of youth for the pulpit was conducted by the *pastors of the churches*; they were scattered over the land, and amid all the scenes and responsibilities of the pastoral office. Nor may it be denied that there were important advantages in this arrangement. Pastors themselves would feel the responsibility of becoming qualified for the office of theological teachers; and the most eminent learning and ability of the church, instead of being concentrated in a few select localities, would be more widely diffused. Young men were indeed *taught* less than they are now taught in theological seminaries; they heard and transcribed fewer lectures; they were not listeners merely, but were allowed to be inquirers, and even encouraged to be disputants. The consequence was, that while they were *taught* less, they *studied* more,

---

[*]Address of Rev. Samuel Miller, D.D., Professor of Ecclesiastical History and Church Government in the Theological Seminary at Princeton.
[†]Professor Park.

thought more, *wrote* more; and their minds were better disciplined, if not so richly furnished. With less learning and fewer attainments, they were abler men; abler casuists, abler polemics; abler, more instructive, and more practical and acceptable preachers of the Gospel.

One of the great advantages of this system of tuition was found in the *pastoral supervision* exercised over the young men by their teacher. They were members of his family; they took their turns in conducting its daily devotions; their character and conduct, and qualifications for the sacred office were inspected; and while there was great familiarity of intercourse between the teacher and the taught there were not wanting those rebukes, admonitions, and paternal counsels and encouragements that are so much needed even by young men of high Christian character.

Nor was it one of the least of the advantages attendant on this system of education, that the students became acquainted with *men and things*; with good men and bad; with sceptics and unbelievers; with scenes of affliction and scenes of joy; with sickness and with death; with weekly meetings for prayer and instruction among the people, and with the various dealings of God's Spirit with the souls of men.

Students of theology under such a course of education, have also often been made eminently useful; and not a few of those revivals of religion with which the churches in the days of old were so frequently visited, were promoted by their influence, even while pursuing their preparatory studies.

Nor is the suggestion an unimportant one, that it was by such a domestic training as this, that the young men imbibed some just impressions of the proprieties and courtesy of social intercourse. Instead of entering the ministry crude and green, as the mass of young men usually do, who for some eight years have enjoyed little intercourse save that which is found within the walls of a college, and a theological seminary, they entered it with a more subdued and chastened mind, enjoying all the sympathies of a Christian people, and not unfrequently from the fragrant atmosphere of churches on which the rains of heaven had fallen, and the Sun of Righteousness risen with healing in his beams.

It was not unnatural, that in contemplating the change from this system of education to that which is now pursued by theological seminaries, a doubt should have suggested itself to the minds of our fathers, whether, on the whole, it would be a change for the better. I know there were such doubts, for I was personally familiar with the inquiries and discussions on this subject, on the part of the friends of the theological seminaries, both in the Congregational and Presbyterian churches. The experiment has been made, and its results are before the world. *The churches must judge* whether it has, or has not furnished them with a more able and efficient ministry, and whether it has proved itself more effective, either in the pulpit, or from the press. It is quite obvious that *something* has been lost by the change, and it is equally obvious that *something* has been gained. If I were called upon to strike the balance, I frankly confess I should be not a little embarrassed. My own train of thought, and my own convictions of duty, would lead me to something like the following conclusions.

The change is made; it was made by men in whose piety, judgment, and experience we have great confidence, and who often and earnestly sought counsel of God. A large amount of funds has been invested in the existing theological institutions; the age in which we live demands a learned ministry; and the current of public opinion is strongly in favour of the present system of education. To distrust it now, and more especially to propose any radical alteration in the system, would be attended with results that would be mournful. These and other considerations would lead to the conclusion that our theological seminaries *must be sustained*.

But we may not rest simply in this conclusion. If there are evils incidental to this system of instruction, may they not be remedied; and is it not a possible thing to give our theological institutions such a direction, that they shall be better than they are, and more certainly accomplish the benevolent designs of those who founded them? The inquiry is one of great and common interest; the time has arrived when it may receive impartial consideration without injury; and it is pressed upon us by facts which render the consideration of it not unseasonable.

The great solicitude, the agitating apprehension of the pious and venerable founders of our theological seminaries, was, lest the opportunities they should furnish of high intellectual culture should not have the best tendency to raise up a spiritual ministry. It were proof of criminal thoughtlessness to be ignorant of his devices who plots the ruin of the church by infusing into her the spirit of the world; and who, the more effectually to accomplish his purpose, would enervate the vigour, by impairing the spirituality of her ministers. She has survived the shock of persecution; she has proved herself superior to the assaults of infidelity and 'science, falsely so called'; but she has another conflict to engage in, another victory to attain. With her members, it is the all-absorbing spirit of worldliness; with her ministers, it is the same worldiness, only in another and more subtle form. She has yet to survive the conflict with that pride of sacred learning, which is now putting to the test the spirit of her ministers, and by which they themselves are so greatly ensnared, and the truth of God so diluted that it flows too often only from human fountains. Men of letters, men of research, men of taste, and accomplished scholars, who, like the rest of mankind, have the remnants of all that is unhallowed in the pride and ambition of the human heart, may look upon it as a miracle of mercy, if they make not shipwreck of a good conscience in the great work of the Gospel ministry. The age is one in which the love of learning rather than the love of Christ, is easily substituted as the great stimulus to ministerial effort; and in which it were not surprising if men are found occupying the sacred office, whose greenest laurels are gathered from the tree of knowledge, rather than from the tree of life which is in the midst of the Paradise of God.

If what we have suggested in preceding observations, do not produce the conviction that we are no enemies to a learned ministry, that conviction will be produced by nothing which it is in our power to utter. Much as we may, in every view, fall short of our own standard, we are advocates for a learned ministry, and for a spiritual one. The dangers to which we have referred must be obviated at the threshold, and in our theological seminaries. *How must they be obviated?*

In replying to this question, I answer, in the first place, It must be by a watchful eye over the young men who are there pursuing their theological education. The rivalship of *numbers* is unworthy of these seats of sacred science. Numbers may ruin us. It is impossible that a very large number of students should enjoy that pastoral supervision which they need. Many a young man has finished his course in our theological seminaries, who never ought to have thought of the ministry, and whom a faithful pastoral supervision would have so instructed; while more have suffered in their usefulness as ministers, for the want of that personal inspection which, from the multitude of students, it has been impossible to exercise. Give us abler, better, and more spiritual preachers, even if they must be fewer. The three hundred that lapped under Gideon, were more potent than the mighty host of Midian.

Our second reply to the question is, *Let the teachers of those who are being educated for the ministry be men of no inconsiderable experience in the pastoral office.* In the early organization of theological seminaries, the professors were of this character; they came with the experience of settled pastors; not with clear heads only, but with warm hearts, and from the warm bosom of the churches which they loved. Their more early pupils were the flower of the churches; they preached as though they understood and felt the Gospel; and though not a few of them have been called to their rest, their names will be long embalmed in the memory of good men. It is a wise arrangement of the Theological Seminary of the Presbyterian Church, that the professors shall be *ordained ministers of the Gospel*. I need not say, that this designation is ordinarily applied to the stated pastors of the churches. There are exceptions to this rule; but the reasons must be urgent to induce a presbytery to ordain any man, *sine titulo*, or save in connection with a pastoral charge. We say this is a wise arrangement; for there is no such *prima facie* testimony to the personal qualifications of a teacher of young men who are pursuing their studies with a view to the Christian ministry, as that which is furnished, by having usefully and acceptably sustained the responsibilities of the pastoral office. There is no such test of his intellectual and spiritual qualifications, of his tact as a teacher, of his habits of industry, and of his capacity and willingness to 'endure hardness as a good soldier of Christ'. If the deacons must 'first be proved', much more the ministers; and if ministers, much more the instructors of ministers. The more deliberately and impartially the subject is considered, the more it will be found to be one of the absurdest things in the world, to invest a man with the office of a teacher of the sons of the prophets, who is himself no prophet.

It requires but an ingenuous and impartial view of this question, in order to produce the strong conviction, that the rule ought rarely, if ever, to be dispensed with; not even in favour of those departments which, from their own nature, are most purely *scholastic*, and for the competent occupancy of which young men must be specially trained; for there is no part of that training more important than the labours of the pastoral office. We cannot say too much in favour of these more scholastic departments; they are worthy of the best and holiest talents and acquirements of the choicest sons of the church. They are departments in which the best informed mind may task its greatest resources, the most acute mind exhaust all its powers of discrimination, the most safe and well-balanced mind prove its caution by its well-judged conclusions; and where the mind that is most equable and trustworthy in seasons of excitement, of invading errors and stormy conflict, is most needed. And for these reasons, they are departments which call for unsleeping vigilance and supervision. They are the very departments which are exposed to exert a wrong influence; where the wisest men are in danger of imbibing loose and unevangelical views, and proving eventually unsafe guides of the aspiring and unstable minds of the young. It is true, they are departments for which it can hardly be expected that a man should be fully prepared in the ordinary course of pastoral labour; but they are departments for which any scholar-like pastor can easily prepare himself, with much less labour than he devotes to the incessant toil of the pulpit, and for the premature and hasty occupancy of which there is no good and sufficient reason.

There can be little doubt that the founders of our theological schools, by requiring that the professors should be ordained ministers of the Gospel, designed to protect these seminaries from the evils of a mere scholastic influence. The church may be induced to disregard this law; influences may be brought to act upon her from the theological seminaries themselves, of which she herself is not aware, to induce her to disregard it; but in yielding to them she knows not what she does.

We are well aware that we shall be complained of when we say these things. Yet we say them freely, fearlessly and humbly; we say them because life is short, and we may not be able to say them at another day; and we say them, because vast prospective interests are at stake in the practical decision of this great question. Mere scholars, those who know more of books than of men, and more of theological halls than the pulpit, ought not to be invested with the trust of educating a *whole generation of young men* for the Christian ministry. The fact may no longer be dissembled, that the *tendency*, if not the design of our theological seminaries themselves, is to fill the most important chairs with purely literary men; men who neither have, nor expect to have, any relation to the pastoral office; men ordained, not to the work of the ministry, but to their professorship.

It is easy to see that such arrangements once entered upon, are apt to be *progressive* and to perpetuate themselves. Age and experience sleep in the tomb; and those only become the teachers of ministers, who have themselves never been the teachers of the people, and never served the church of God in the ministry of his Son. There are many things that favour such an arrangement, unwise as it is. It is one that is easily made; and the individuals whom it specially regards are men of great attainments and great excellence of character. There is not a little about it, too, that is captivating to congregated youthful minds, who may, without any imputation of wrong doing, be supposed to exert sufficient influence in effecting it. The men are on the spot; they are acquainted with one another, and draw well together. The glare of human learning, and the pride of man, are gratified and exalted by concentrating in the schools of the prophets youthful teachers of the highest promise. But the effects of the delusion will, sooner or later, be bitterly bewailed. It will be a sorry day when the churches are led away by considerations like these.

The history of the past and the example of other churches, may not, on so important a subject as this, be regarded with indifference. In reply to some inquiries on this subject, a very sensible clergyman of the Scottish Church, remarks: 'Among the voluntary dissenters in all the three kingdoms, the union of ecclesiastical charges with professorships, is, so far as I remember, universal.' There is no portion of the earth to which the evangelical churches in this land have been in the habit of looking with greater reverence and confidence than the churches of Scotland and Geneva. Most justly have they done so; there are no nobler examples for our imitation than these churches, from the days of Calvin and Knox, down to those of Merle D'Aubigné, and Chalmers. So far as my information extends, not an instance can be found in these churches – churches where the pulpit has exerted more influence than in any other part of Christendom – in which the training of ministers has been committed to those who were strangers to the responsibilities of the pastoral office. So far from this, the ablest and best professors in the theological schools of Geneva, Edinburgh and Glasgow, have been, and still are, men who, like the great Calvin, have been the most approved pastors of the churches, and not a few of these have not even demitted their pastoral charge. If we look to Germany, we do indeed see a different usage; their professors are for the most part purely scholars, and rarely pastors. Nor is it to the rationalism, the mysticism, the idealism of Germany, nor to its crippled orthodoxy, that the American churches have any desire to look for examples of theological nurture.

Theological science, as a science, has no peculiarity; it is in this respect just like every other science; no man understands it until he has *practised* it. The statesman does not, the jurist does not, the physician does not, nor the navigator, nor the surveyor. Lawyers and physicians do not commit the training of their young men to those who have never been practised in their profession; they would deem it a great blunder. The laws of the land require that some portion of the time of their students should be employed in the *offices* of practised teachers. A man must have been in the midst of his work, and observed and marked with studious care and anxious solicitude, the practical operation of his principles, in order to present those principles in their truest and best light to the youthful mind. No matter what the talents of a theological instructor may be, it is not possible for him rightly to exhibit the truth of God, and teach others to exhibit it, if he himself have not been in the habit of exhibiting it to the *popular mind*. Books and treatises, reviews and single discourses written by these distinguished authors, speak for themselves; they have great excellences, but they have this one deficiency, that they have no savour of the pastoral office. They are not like the works of Leighton and Erskine, Romaine, Witherspoon, and Edwards; nor are they, with all their acuteness and research, what they would have been had their authors seen more hard service. They evince talent and piety, but they are wanting in the knowledge of the human heart; they are wanting in that which men want to know and feel; they are wanting in that impressive, impulsive, practical exhibition of truth which the popular mind demands. They savour of the cloister, but not of the pulpit; they savour of scholarship and intellect, while they ought to be imbued with a richer fragrance. Even as mere biblical commentators, preachers have the pre-eminence; nor do I know that there are to be found any writings of this description superior to the beautiful commentaries of Calvin and Doddridge.

We have sought to ascertain, if the *Scriptures* anywhere contemplate a class of theological teachers, who have not themselves been the acknowledged and honoured teachers of the people. Unless we have overlooked some important fact, the history of the Jewish and Christian Church speaks the same language, from the days of Samuel to the days of Paul, and it is uniformly in favour of the views here expressed.

What is the voice of common sense, and of all the better feelings of our hearts on this very plain question, if it be not that the men whose professed employment is to teach others to preach the Gospel, should themselves be preachers of the Gospel? Is it said, they *are* preachers of the Gospel? They are so, but not to the *people*. And how often do they preach it to their own eclectic charge? Once in four, or six weeks; and then they come before their pupils with a highly elaborate and finished discourse – a banquet for the king, and not for the people. It is just the preaching to discourage an humble, and spoil an ambitious aspirant for the ministry. This will do occasionally; but it will never do as the habitual example for the imitation of the young. They will never be broken into the harness after this sort. Far better were it to fall back upon the old method of instruction by the pastors of the churches, than to have our young men subjected to the evils of such a purely scholastic training. Our theological teachers ought to be men who have known something of 'the burden and heat of the day', – men who have been in the field in sunshine and amid storms, in seed-time and in harvest; not literary men merely, not preachers to a selected few, with 'itching ears', but men who have come in contact with the common mind, and preached the Gospel to the common people.

There is another thought also which is worthy of some consideration. It has been before intimated, that when a student at law, or at medicine, has finished his course at the law or medical school, so far as my knowledge extends, he is put under the tuition of a practising lawyer or practising physician. Let the same thing be done with our students in theology. On completing their theological course, let their respective presbyteries *require* them to spend three, or six months, with some settled pastor. They will find still, that they have something to learn; they will receive

The Fitting Education for the Christian Ministry

important instruction, and at the same time will do good. We know little of them under the present arrangement; and I believe I speak the unanimous voice of the presbytery with which I am connected, that, but for the fact that they have employed three years in pursuing their theological course, and but for the recommendation of their professors, not a few of them would have been refused their licence to preach the Gospel. It is one thing to impart theological knowledge, and another to form ministers of Christ. The human heart is a most wicked and deceitful thing. It cannot be trusted with a purely scholastic training. Rigid orthodoxy, and well-defined symbols of faith, will not always bind men whose idol is a learned, rather than a spiritual and useful ministry; and whose love and pride of learning so ensnare them, that when hardly pressed, they will be too strongly tempted to seek the honour that cometh from men, rather than abide the consequences, in a literary age of which they themselves may be the brightest constellations, if witnessing a good confession. It is 'while men sleep, that the enemy sows tares'. American pastors and churches must be blind indeed, if they have not seen enough to convince them that the gradual incursions of error have crept upon them unawares, from the institutions of theological science. It is true they have crept in from the influence of men, who, in some instances, have been settled pastors before they became professors. But they were men who were once 'good men, and true', and who became corrupted after they left the pastoral office. 'If these things be done in the green tree, what shall be done in the dry?' Let us take heed lest we fall from our steadfastness. 'Hold fast that thou hast; let no man take thy crown!'

While, therefore, we would hesitate to go back to the old method of educating the Christian ministry, and would sustain and honour our theological seminaries, we would say, for Christ's and the church's sake, spare no effort to give them the best direction, and to throw into them the most sacred influence. Let the church perpetuate the work, which in former years she so nobly began, and in the behalf of her sons, call for teachers of sound and thorough literary attainments, disciplined by the toil and experience of the pastoral office. The safety and excellence of the seminaries in the Presbyterian Church is found thus far in this combined influence. Like the original apostolical college, so wisely established by the Saviour, age with youth, pastoral experience with scholastic learning, the ardour of literary enterprise with matured and chastened piety, bound together as in a 'covenant of salt', have, under God, made our seminaries what they are. Let us do our best endeavours, under the favour of a kind Providence, not simply to keep them what they are, but to make them better. The venerable men who in the vigour of their manhood, and at no small personal sacrifice, left the most important congregations in the land for the purpose of conducting these infant institutions, will soon sleep with their fathers. Thankful are we that they have lived so long, and have performed such essential service. Their hoary head is still a crown of glory to the institutions, so long moulded by their unwearied effort, faith, and prayer. There let them remain, and like the distinguished statesman who breathed his last in the American Capitol, breathe forth their last influence with their latest breath, in the halls of which they have so long been the adornment! Nor is there any one truth of its kind that ought to be more deeply felt, than that if the time should ever arrive, when the places they have so long occupied shall be occupied by men of no pastoral experience, the glory of these institutions will have departed.

Let not these remarks be either misunderstood, or wilfully perverted. The writer would be among the last to aid in introducing teachers to our theological seminaries, the vigour of whose days, like his own, has already been exhausted in the pastoral office. Those for such a service should be men, not in the decline, but in the strength of human effort; men whose meridian rays now cheer us, and whose light, when it begins to grow dim, shall be the tranquil, and clear, and prolonged twilight of the northern sky. Long may the light of these sacred institutions shine! The God of Zion grant that it may be the light of a high-born and heaven-sustained piety, and an accomplished erudition! We would look to them, not as the proud Greek looked toward the grove of Academus, or the mount where Apollo struck his lyre; but rather as the devout Hebrew was wont to look to the halls where Samuel taught, and David sang, and to the hallowed mountain where the Great Teacher spake, and employed whole nights in prayer. Let them be baptized with this Spirit! let the dews of heaven fall upon them! let them ever be imbued with the atmosphere of Zion!

21: *The Pecuniary Support of Ministers*

It falls in with the legitimate design of our remarks, to call the reader's attention to another topic that is somewhat delicate in its nature and still more so to be enlarged upon by a minister of the Gospel. It is a topic which it were more befitting and decent for someone to urge, who is not himself a party interested in such a discussion. I have not known it seriously undertaken and urged, save by one native layman. The late Jeremiah Evarts, a name that will not soon be forgotten by the American churches, the friend of missions and the able and fearless advocate of the red men of our own wilderness, once presented this subject in a strong light to the churches of New England. The topic is the *claims of the pulpit for a competent and honourable pecuniary maintenance.*

The writer has some advantages for presenting a subject like this to the consideration of the churches, above the great mass of his ministerial friends. For the most part, the maintenance of settled pastors in our large cities is highly creditable to the congregations whom they serve. Not only our wants, but our comforts are cared for: it becomes us to be grateful to God and to the generosity of our congregations that we are allowed to employ our time in the appropriate duties of our high calling, 'free from worldly cares and avocations'. Since, in this particular, we have nothing to ask for ourselves, we are the more bold to urge the claims of those who are less favoured, though equally deserving. But while we ask this indulgence, our best apology for presenting the subject is that it falls within the range of our instructions as contained in the Word of God.

If the importance of the subject does not at once strike the mind of the reader, he has but to give it a few moments' thought, and to recur to the distinguished men in other lands whose pen has been employed in discussing it. *Selden,* in his treatise *On Tithes; Bingham,* in his *Antiquities of the Christian Church; Prideaux, On Tithes; Hooker,* in his *Ecclesiastical Polity; Comber,* in his *Vindica-*

tion of the Divine Right of Tithes, against Selden; together with several more modern anonymous writers of great ability, in the *Quarterly*, and *Edinburgh Review*, in the *Monthly Magazine*, and in *Blackwood's Edinburgh Magazine*, have given the subject prominence, not only in the religious, but the literary and political world.

For the origin of *tithes* we must go farther back than the Mosaic Law. When Abraham returned from his victory over Chedorlaomer and his confederate kings, he 'gave tithes of all' to Melchizedec, the priest of the most High God. There is no reason to believe that he paid the tenth part of his annual income, but a tenth part of the spoil which he took from Chedorlaomer and the kings that were with him. The Apostle, in his Epistle to the Hebrews, speaks of this tithe as 'a tenth part of the *spoils*'. There are some commentators, and among the best, Bishop Patrick, who argue from this payment of a tenth of the spoil taken in war, that it must have been the custom to pay to the priests the tenth of all other things. When Jacob was at Bethel, 'he vowed a vow, saying, If God will be with me, and keep me in this way that I go, and will give me bread to eat, and raiment to put on, so that I come again to my father's house in peace; then shall the Lord be my God; and this stone which I have set for a pillar shall be God's house; and of all that thou shalt give me I will surely give the *tenth* unto thee.' We are not able to discover that the lights of reason and nature would have suggested this payment of tithes for religious purposes; and are strongly disposed to believe that it was of divine origin, and formed a part of the patriarchal dispensation.

However this may be, it was expressly commanded by God under the law of Moses. When the land of Canaan was divided among the tribes of Israel, no portion was allotted as an inheritance to the tribe of Levi. They were to be dispersed among all the other tribes; forty-eight cities were appointed for their residence; the family of Aaron, to which the priesthood belonged, was of this tribe; and instead of the portion of country, such as was allotted to each of the other tribes, each tribe was required to furnish provision for the priests and Levites who should dwell among them, and who constituted the settled ministry of Israel. This provision consisted of one-tenth part of the gross produce of the soil; the first born of the cattle to the priests, and one-tenth of the increase to the Levites.* Besides this, the Levites had a large quantity of land in the suburbs of the forty-eight cities allotted for their residence.

Not a few writers of high distinction have maintained, from these premises, that tithes, under the Christian dispensation, are due to the ministers of the Gospel by divine right. The argument is summarily this: that all those positive institutions under the Mosaic economy which are not expressly abolished, and for the continuance of which there are the same reasons under the Christian dispensation, ought to be regarded as permanent. Bingham, in his *Antiquities of the Christian Church*, shows this to have been the doctrine of *Origen, Jerome*, and *Augustine*. Augustine uses an argument of his own, of how much weight the reader must judge. 'The Pharisees paid tithes. Our Lord says, *"Except your righteousness exceed the righteousness of the Scribes and Pharisees, ye shall not enter into the kingdom of heaven."* But if he whose righteousness ye are to exceed gave tithes, and you give not a thousandth part, how can you be said to exceed him whom you do not so much as equal?' *Bingham*, indeed, asserts that 'it is generally agreed by learned men, that the ancients accounted tithes to be due of divine right'. *Spotswood*, in his *History of the Church of Scotland*, states the divine right of tithes to be indisputable; and says, 'He that will not wilfully shut his eyes against the truth, cannot but know it.' We certainly are no believers in this doctrine. The conclusion of Hooker is the sound conclusion, and he supports it by irrefragable argument: 'We are now free from the Law of Moses, and consequently not thereby bound to the payment of tithes.'

Evils of a most serious kind have been the result of the *jure divino* doctrine of tithes. 'The first converts to the Christian religion', says the Quarterly Review, 'gave a tenth part of the produce of their land, as a reasonable standard of a *voluntary* compensation to its ministers. When this religion acquired a surer footing, and converts became more numerous, the provision which had been previously received as the *spontaneous liberality* of its professors, began to be regarded as a *right* established by custom. In the course of the eighth century, the growing force of custom, aided by the

---

*From this example, the clergy of Christendom gave one-tenth of their tithes to the Pope, which, at the Reformation in England, was transferred to the crown.

operation and influence of the Canon Law, rendered the payment of tithes an *imperative obligation*.' The Emperor *Constantine* was the first prince who settled upon the clergy a standing allowance out of the public treasury. This allowance was taken away by his nephew, *Julian*; a third part of it was restored by his successor, *Jovian*; and was afterwards confirmed by the code of *Justinian*, in the year 533. But the clergy were not satisfied with this. Synods and Councils at length came in to enforce the obligation of *tithes*; the spiritual sword was wielded; and the anathemas of a terrific excommunication were thundered against all who refused to obey.* *Selden* allows that 'nothing was more common than decrees of councils, concerning this matter, all over Christendom'. In progress of time, these anathemas were disregarded; those there were who refused to pay their tithes; and the result was recourse to the civil authority to enforce the law of the church. A law to this effect was enacted by *Pepin*, the King of France, in the year 764: the same year, a similar law was introduced into *Bavaria*; in 779, *Charlemagne*, the son of *Pepin*, confirmed the law of his father; and in 789, having conquered the Saxons, and compelled them to adopt the Christian religion, he imposed the same law upon them, including the tithe of labour. In 794, at Frankfort, and in 804, at Saltzburg, he made a similar law for Germany. Having extended his dominions into Italy, A.D. 800, his laws extended thither also; and shortly afterwards, laws enforcing the payment of tithes were passed in Spain.

In all this, there was little else than the desire to conciliate the formidable power of the Church of Rome.† The State defended the Church, taking good care that the Church in return should defend the State. *Pepin* had usurped the crown of *Childeric*, and was willing to purchase at any price, the sanction of the Popes. *Charlemagne*, the great establisher of tithes in Christendom, was influenced by no purer motives than his father. He was a bad man; shamefully licentious, and if possible, more cruel. The Pope and

---

*A canon to this effect was made in the second Council of Mascon, in the diocese of Lyons, in 585.
A similar canon was made at a Council at Seville, in Spain, in 590.
In the Council of Friuli also, a canon to the same purpose was made for Italy in 791.
†This assertion is justified by facts. See Daniel's *History of France*; Gifford's *ditto*, Sismondi's *Histoire des François*; Belarius's *Lives of the Popes*; Card's *Life of Charlemagne*; Gibbon's *History of the Decline and Fall of the Roman Empire*; Mosheim's *Ecclesiastical History*.

The Pecuniary Support of Ministers

he swore everlasting friendship to each other over the tomb of St. Peter; and while he conferred upon the Pope immense estates and dukedoms, the Pope crowned him Emperor of the West, and thus placed him on the pinnacle of his ambition.

Tithes were introduced into England just as they were on the Continent, and not far from the same time. Long before the union of the seven kingdoms under *Egbert*, the Christian religion was established all over England; and, though not without difficulty, was brought to acknowledge the authority of the Roman Pontiff. A single Council had urged the payment of tithes from the authority of the Law of Moses; tithes were paid in the province of Canterbury as early as the middle of the eighth century; but they had not yet been enforced by the laws of the kingdom. In the latter part of this century, Offa, the most powerful of the Saxon kings, for his treacherous murder of *Ethelbert*, made a pilgrimage to Rome in order to obtain a pardon from the Pope. *Adrian* granted him a pardon on condition of bounty to the Church; and on his return, he passed a law giving her the tithes of all his kingdom. This law was confirmed by *Ethelwulf*, in a Parliament at Winchester, and a grant of tithes made to all the clergy of England. About thirty years after passing the grant of Ethelwulf, *Alfred* his son, published a body of laws for the better government of the kingdom, in which he strictly enjoined the payment of tithes to the clergy. This law was afterwards renewed by *Edward* the Elder; by *Athelstan*, the son of Edward; by *Edmund* the brother of Athelstan; by *Edgar* the son of Edmund; by *Ethelred*, by *Canute*, by *Edward the Confessor*; by *William the Conqueror*; by *Henry I*; by *Stephen*; by *Charles I*, *Charles II*, and *James II*. This law has been in existence for a period of nearly a thousand years; the lands of the kingdom are sold subject to this condition; and no present possessor of tithable land can say that his ancestors ever possessed it exempt from this ecclesiastical law.

Having their origin from the churches in Great Britain, the churches in this country, while they were far from believing that tithes were the original maintenance of ministers under the Gospel, were slow in adopting the doctrine that the ministry were not entitled to a support by the laws of the land. They regarded the Jewish law on this subject rather as something in the form of a *precedent*, than as an authoritative *law*. It was not the letter they cared for, but the spirit. The thought was often repeated in their public assemblies, 'Take heed that thou forsake not the Levite, as

[213]

long as thou livest upon the earth.' They eschewed the doctrine of tithes, as they abhorred Prelacy and Rome; but they adhered to the doctrine of a legal support for the ministers of the Gospel. In the New England States this legal provision existed until quite a late period in their history. Within the recollection of many persons now living, no man in the community was there exempted from an annual assessment for the support of the Gospel in that particular denomination of Christians to which he belonged. If he belonged to no denomination, or was a professed infidel, he was still constrained to bear his proportion of the burden in sustaining an institution from which he received so many indirect benefits, and which was so intimately inwoven with the best interests of the State.

Yet have we no hesitation in saying, that the voluntary principle is the true principle; not only is it more in keeping with the spirit of our free institutions, but with the spirit and genius of Christianity. The great Head of the church has thrown the support of his ministers upon the unconstrained liberality of those who attend on their ministrations; or rather upon their *rectitude and justice*; thus putting to the test their loyalty to him, and their own views of the value of a preached Gospel. It is the revealed law of his kingdom, that 'they who serve at the altar shall live by the altar'. (*1 Cor. 9.13*) This is indeed but a republication of that great law of nature, that 'the labourer is worthy of his hire'; yet is such a law, distinctly published, no unnecessary statute. If God did not see fit to leave the question of the temporal support of his ministers to the discretion of the people, by that very decision he expressed his own judgment of the dependence of his ministers, and of the duty of the people to furnish them a competent and generous supply. This is the *spirit* of the Jewish law. And nothing is more obvious than that the great principle of this statute is embodied in the teachings of the New Testament. When the Saviour sent forth the early teachers of Christianity, he directed them to 'provide neither gold, nor silver, nor brass in their purses; nor scrip, neither two coats, neither shoes, nor yet staves'. *They* were not to provide them, because they were to be provided by others. If they possessed them, they were not to provide them; they were to be provided by the people among whom they laboured. The express reason which he assigns for this injunction is the law to which we have referred, 'the workman is worthy of his hire'.

The Apostle Paul, in writing to the Corinthians, devotes a

paragraph to this subject. 'Who goeth a warfare at any time at his own charges? Who planteth a vineyard, and eateth not of the fruit thereof? Or who feedeth a flock, and eateth not of the milk of the flock? Say I these things as *a man*? or saith not the law the same also? For it is written in the law of Moses, Thou shalt not muzzle the mouth of the ox that treadeth out the corn. Doth God take care for oxen? Or saith he it altogether for *our sakes*? For our sakes, no doubt, this is written: that he that plougheth should plough in hope; and that he that thresheth in hope should be partaker of his hope. If we have sown unto you *spiritual* things, is it a great thing if we shall reap your *carnal things*? If others be partakers of this power over you, are not we rather? Nevertheless we have not used this power: but suffer all things, lest we should hinder the Gospel of Christ. Do ye not know that *they which minister about holy things live of the things of the temple*, and they which wait at the altar are partakers with the altar? Even so hath the Lord ORDAINED that they which *preach* the Gospel should *live* of the Gospel.'

It is no unnatural exposition to regard this passage as indicating the duty of the Church in respect of her temporal maintenance of the ministry. It is the *ordaining* of her great Head, that 'they which preach the Gospel should live of the Gospel'. It is certainly a fair question, too, What are we to understand by the phrase, 'shall *live* of the Gospel'? The answer to this question must be found in the kind and liberal spirit of Christianity, and in the bosoms of those in whom that spirit dwells. The amount of support to which every faithful minister is entitled, is one of those relative duties which falls within the comprehensive precept, 'Whatsoever ye would that men should do unto *you*, do ye so to *them*.' It is no extravagance to say, that it is the duty of the people to elevate their ministers above want; to enable them to be honest men, respectable men, charitable and public-spirited men. They ought to have the opportunity, not only of being employed in the appropriate duties of their office, but of discharging its functions advantageously. And is it too much to say, that they ought to be enabled to educate their children, and make some provision for old age; or, should they be cut off in the midst of their days, some provision for the widow and the fatherless when they themselves sleep in the dust? From the divine appointment in reference to the support of the Levitical priesthood, and from the nature of the case, it is quite obvious that the Christian law on this subject cannot be interpreted to mean any thing less than a *comfortable support for the situation in which the party is placed by the Divine Providence*. As great diversity exists in the location of the ministry, so this circumstance must give rise to diversity in the amount of their support. It is only some general rules that can be adopted in regard to it. And the general law, beyond controversy, is, that it should be sufficient to enable those who preach the Gospel to live 'of the Gospel'.

This is the *law* of God's house. It is a revealed precept which men have no more right to transgress than any other precept in the Bible. It has no specified penalty; it is one of those laws which the Great Lawgiver will enforce in his own way, and by penalties that are executed in the dispensations of his observing and searching Providence. He has put in his claim for such a portion of the property of his people, as shall furnish a comfortable support to his ministers; he claims this portion of their property, just as he does the Lord's Day, as his portion of their time. It does not belong to men; it is God's, just as truly as were the tithes under the Levitical Law. Ministers are his ambassadors; and the terms on which he employs them are, that they shall receive a competent support from the people to whom he sends them. They hold his draft upon them for this indefinite amount; and it is for them to honour, or dishonour, the draft of their redeeming King.

To what extent he is honoured in this claim, is an inquiry which will not endure the most rigid scrutiny. It is no uncommon thing for ministers to receive no *stated and stipulated* support whatever; but to depend exclusively upon the annual, or periodical *subscriptions* of those to whom they minister. This is too uncertain a dependence; it is fickle as the heart of man; nor ought any minister to be thus ensnared and tempted to shape his ministrations so as to please men, rather than save them, or to please any one part of his people, rather than another. The permanence of the pastoral relation has been not a little affected by such arrangements as these; nor were it any marvel if, where they prevail, no such permanent relation should ever be recognized.

It is no uncommon thing, too, for congregations who stipulate to furnish their minister a stated salary, to put his own delicacy to the test, by imposing the duty on him of begging it from the pulpit. Such arrangements are *degrading* to the ministry, and cannot fail to be injurious to the influence of the ministry.

There is also a most dishonourable failure on the part of many

The Pecuniary Support of Ministers

congregations to meet their engagements with their minister; they meet them as suits their convenience, or do not meet them at all. They treat their minister as they dare not treat a hired servant, and deny him his rights, because they know that he would be slow to enforce them by legal process.

Ministers, not a few, also there are, not in new and poor districts merely, but in those that are well cultivated and rich, who have not a decent maintenance; and who, without some unlooked for interposition of Providence, must in their advanced years become the beneficiaries of the public bounty. The consequence is that although their hearts may be set upon their work, their time and their hands are employed in secular concerns. It is in vain to think of their being diligent and devoted ministers: the thing is impossible; they must have bread. All this is wrong. It is 'robbing God'. It is refusing him his 'tithes and offerings', and taking the bread from his own house. Many a pastor who has loved his flock as his own soul, and would rejoice to serve them with unwearied diligence, is constrained to accuse them before God, for withholding what he gives to the fowls of the air.

We are not pleading for a *wealthy* ministry; we should be sorry to see ministers wealthy, unless they happen to become so by inheritance, or by unlooked-for domestic alliances. And even then, it requires more self-denial than the most of ministers possess, under such circumstances, to make full proof of their ministry. There is little doubt that the overgrown wealth of very many of the ministers, and more of the bishops of the Church of England, is a curse both to the ministers and people. Wealthy ministers are not the men who are most useful in the church. The evangelical Dissenters of England have accomplished far more for the interests of vital piety, than all its ecclesiastical aristocracy.

The ministers of the Gospel in North America are not much exposed to enter into the service of the church from the 'love of filthy lucre'. We do not solicit for them wealth; but we do solicit competence. We do not desire them to be independent of their people; but we do desire to see them raised above the dependence of paupers. They are a divinely appointed instrumentality for accomplishing the most important and glorious work which God is accomplishing in this apostate world; and their qualifications and their circumstances ought not to be a matter of indifference either to themselves or to others. Taking human nature as it is, the extremes of wealth and poverty are alike unfriendly to their influence. Anxious cares and bitter temptations are the growth of both, and they agitate the heart. Wealth perplexes; poverty discourages, and by it the spirit of a minister is depressed and broken. A minister may be pitied as a *poor man*; but so long as he is the object of compassion, he is not respected as a servant of the most High God.

I cannot help regarding this subject as one of great importance to the church of God. It is not easy to account for this reluctance to support the Gospel. If it were nothing more than a sense of *justice*, one would think this alone sufficient to rescue the ministry from this depression. Men are slow to admit that they are *indebted* to their religious teachers. They acknowledge other claims: they do not hesitate to allow a fair and full recompense to their legal, or medical adivsers; yet feel little compunction in withholding a suitable recompense from their spiritual guides. There are narrow views on this subject. Men there are who live in the enjoyment of every convenience, who grudge their minister what they do not refuse to the operatives in their manufactories, or the labourers in their fields.

The radical difficulty would seem to be, that there are so many in the community who regard the Gospel as of little value, and the instructions of the pulpit of little importance, either to themselves, to their children, or to their fellow-men. Yet if the Bible and universal experience may be relied on, there is nothing which can be less safely dispensed with than the stated ministrations of God's sanctuary. As 'godliness is *profitable*, having the promise of the life that now is, as well as that which is to come'; so is a preached Gospel. Without it a well-governed community becomes lawless; a peaceful community is involved in broils; an intelligent community becomes ignorant; a rich community is vicious and ruined; a community that is poor becomes more impoverished. The vices which the Sabbath and the sanctuary would restrain and suppress cost tenfold more than a preached Gospel. Upon the mere principles of a wise and rigid economy, no people, be they ever so poor, can afford to live without a Christian minister. If cities and towns and villages would not bring down upon themselves a burden of pauperism which is too heavy to be borne, and multiply their almshouses and their prisons to an extent that shall fill them with alarm, they must do more to check the evil at the fountain head, by supplying the poor with a laborious and faithful ministry.

No philanthropy can augment the physical resources of a people that is regardless of its moral resources. It is but for a community to outgrow the means for its religious instruction, and it has outgrown the means for its prosperity. There is nothing that tells so effectively on the well-being of the great mass of society, as the instructions of the Christian pulpit.

If from this glance at 'the life that now is', we turn to 'that which is to come', what shall we say? I make no apology here for using the language of the great Dr. Owen, from a discourse preached before the English Parliament in the year 1646. Among all the modern appeals for the extension of the Gospel, I find nothing so earnest, or so stimulating. 'No men in the world', says this eminent writer, 'want help like them who want the Gospel. Of all distresses, want of the Gospel cries the loudest for relief. A man may want liberty, and yet be happy, as Joseph was; a man may want peace, and yet be happy, as David was; a man may want plenty, and yet be full of comfort as Micaiah was; but he that wants the Gospel, wants every thing that should do him good. A throne without the Gospel is but the Devil's dungeon; wealth without the Gospel is fuel for hell; advancement without the Gospel, is but going high to have the greater fall. What do men need that want the Gospel? They want Jesus Christ, for he is revealed only by the Gospel. He is all and in all, and where he is wanting, there can be no good. Hunger cannot truly be satisfied without manna, the bread of life, which is Jesus Christ; and what shall a hungry man do that hath no bread? Thirst cannot be quenched without a living spring, which is Jesus Christ; and what shall a thirsty soul do without water? A captive, as we all are, cannot be delivered without redemption, which is Jesus Christ; and what shall the prisoner do without his ransom? Fools, as we all are, cannot be instructed without wisdom, which is Jesus Christ; without him we perish in our folly. All building without him is on the sand, and will surely fall. All working without him is in the fire, where it will be consumed. All riches without him have wings, and will fly away.

'A dungeon with Christ is a throne, and a throne without Christ is hell. Nothing so ill, but Christ will compensate. All mercies without Christ are bitter, and every cup is sweet that is seasoned with but a drop of his blood; he is truly the love and delight of the sons of men. He is the Way; men without him are Cains, wanderers, vagabonds. He is the Truth; men without him are liars, like the devil who was so of old. He is the Life; men without him are dead, dead in trespasses and sins. He is the Light; men without him are in darkness, and go they know not whither. He is the Vine; those that are not grafted in him are withered branches, prepared for the fire. He is the Rock; men not built on him are carried away with a flood. He is Alpha and Omega, the First and the Last, the Author and the Ender, the founder and the finisher of our salvation; he that hath not him, hath neither beginning of good, nor shall have an end of misery. O blessed Jesus, how much better were it not to be, than to be without thee; never to be born, than not to die in thee. A thousand hells come short of this, eternally to want Jesus Christ, as men do who want the Gospel. They want all holy communion with God, wherein the only happiness of the soul doth consist. Without him, the soul in the body is a dead soul in a living sepulchre. They want all the ordinances of God, the joy of our hearts, and the comfort of our souls. O the sweetness of a Sabbath! the heavenly raptures of prayer! O the glorious communion of saints, which such men are deprived of! If they knew the value of the hidden pearl, and these things were to be purchased, what would such poor souls not part with for them? They will at last want heaven and salvation. They shall never come into the presence of God in glory; never inhabit a glorious mansion. They shall never behold Jesus Christ, but when they shall call for rocks and mountains to fall on them, and to hide them from his presence. They shall want light in utter darkness; want life under the second death; want refreshment in the midst of flames; want healing under the gnawing of conscience; want grace, continuing to blaspheme; want glory, in full misery; and which is the sum of all, they shall want an end of all this: for "their worm dieth not, and their fire is not quenched."'

Such thoughts as these have not often been addressed to the English Parliament. It is a tremendous inquiry, *What do men need, that lack the Gospel?* 'If our Gospel be hid, it is hid to them that are *lost.*' Men who are destitute of it are destitute of the only appointed means of salvation; for there is salvation in no other. There are no other means of fitting men for heaven; no other instrument of turning them from darkness to light, and from the power of Satan unto God; nor is it possible that it should have a saving effect upon those who do not enjoy it. A community without the preached Gospel! There is nothing worth living for in such a community. It may be rich in rivers, in ore, and luxuriant in soil; it may be well watered as the plains of Sodom, and as accursed as they. I would not educate a family of children in such a community, for all the prairies between the Alleghany and the Rocky Mountains. Of what value are lands, and rivers, and forests, if the pearl of great price is not there?

We are driven to the conclusion, that the deficiency in the support of ministers is to be attributed to a defective estimate of this hidden pearl.

22: *Prayer for Ministers*

Such is the importance of the Christian ministry, that we are constrained to solicit for it one particular favour. It is a request in which we feel a deep personal concern. *Pray for us.* 'Pray for us', says Paul; pray for us is the hearty response from every Christian pulpit in the land, and in the wide world. If the prayers of good men were solicited by such a man as Paul; and if, with his giant intellect, his eminent spirituality, and his intimate communion with God and things unseen, this holy man needed this encouragement and impulse in his work, who will not say 'Brethren, pray for us, that the word of the Lord may have free course and be glorified!'

It is a delightful thought to a young man entering upon the ministry of reconciliation that, unworthy as he is, the prayers of thousands of God's people are continually going up, on his behalf, to his Father and their Father, to his God and their God. He seems to hear the church of God saying to him, We cannot go to this sacred work, but we will follow you with our prayers! He seems to hear many a Christian parent say to him, We have no son to send to this hallowed vocation; but go *you* to it, and you shall not lack an interest in our prayers! Not a few of the churches of this land have enjoyed the high privilege of sending forth into the spiritual harvest no inconsiderable number of beloved youth from their own more immediate family. And it has been the usage of such churches, to an extent that is gratefully remembered, to assemble for the more special service of commending their young brethren to the care and faithfulness of a covenant-keeping God. How fitting, in every way, is such a service! how full of encouragement to the heart that trembles under a view of the responsibilities of the sacred office! how delightful this spiritual impetus to a mind almost ready to sink under its own conscious infirmities! And how unspeakably precious the thought to all who labour in this great work, whether in youthful, or riper years, that they are thus habitually remembered in the prayers of the churches! Let the thought sink deep into the heart of every church, that their minister will be very much such a minister as their prayers may make him. If nothing short of Omnipotent grace can make a Christian, nothing less than this can make a faithful and successful minister of the Gospel.

We entreat the churches to regard with a more deliberate and devout mind the great work itself to which their ministers are devoted. To explain the doctrines and enforce the duties of genuine Christianity; to defend the truth against all the subtlety and versatility of error; to sustain within their own minds that sense of God's presence, and of those moral sanctions which are revealed in his Word, and that deep and tender impression of the things that are unseen and eternal, that are necessary to give earnestness, and that consistent life and deportment that are necessary to give effect to their preaching; to do this in a way that shall adapt itself to times, places, occasions and characters, and without being disheartened by difficulties, appalled by enemies, and weary of the yoke which they have taken upon them, is no ordinary work If a people are looking for rich discourses from their minister, their prayers must supply him with matter; if for faithful discourses, their prayers must urge him, by a full and uncompromising manifestation of the truth, to commend himself to every man's conscience in the sight of God; if for powerful and successful discourses, their prayers must make him a blessing to the souls of men. Would they have him come to them in the fulness of the blessings of the Gospel of peace, with a heaving bosom, a kindled eye, and a glowing tongue, and with discourses bathed in tears and elaborate with prayer? their prayers must urge him to pray, and their tears inspire his thrilling heart with the strong yearnings of Christian affection. It is in their own closets that the people of God most effectually charge upon the soul of their beloved ministers, to take heed to the ministry they have received of the Lord Jesus.

And who and what are ministers themselves? Frail men, fallible, sinning men, exposed to every snare, to temptation in every form; and, from the very post of observation they occupy, the fairer mark for the fiery darts of the foe. They are no mean victims the great Adversary is seeking, when he would wound and cripple Christ's ministers. One such victim is worth more to the kingdom of darkness than a score of common men; and on this very account, their temptations are probably more subtle and severe than those encountered by ordinary Christians. If this subtle Deceiver fails to destroy them, he artfully aims at neutralizing their influence by quenching the fervour of their piety, lulling them into negligence, and doing all in his power to render their work irksome. How perilous the condition of that minister then, whose heart is not encouraged, whose hands are not strengthened, and who is not upheld by the prayers of his people! It is not in his own closet and on his own knees alone, that he finds security and comfort, and ennobling, humbling, and purifying thoughts and joys; but it is when they also seek them in his behalf, that he becomes a better and happier man, and a more useful minister of the everlasting Gospel.

Nothing gives a people so much interest in their minister, and interest of the best kind, as to pray for him. They love him the more, they respect him the more, they attend more cheerfully and profitably on his ministrations, the more they commend him to God in their prayers. They feel a deeper interest in his work the more they pray for him; and their children feel a deeper interest both in him and in his preaching, when they habitually listen to supplications that affectionately commend him to the throne of the heavenly grace.

The results of a preached Gospel are associated with the most interesting realities in the universe. Nay, they form no small part of these affecting realities themselves. There are no such bright and refulgent exhibitions of the ever-blessed and adorable Godhead, as are made where a preached Gospel has free course and is glorified. That wondrous exhibition of the Divine nature, that progressive development which is in itself so desirable, and in its consequences so endeared to every holy mind, never shines forth with such impressive distinctness and subduing lustre, as when the hearers of his truth and grace, proclaimed from lips of clay, indicate that appearing of his great glory. Had the people of God on the earth minds as pure as the seraph intellect around the throne, with what deep concern, solicitude and prayer, would they watch the course and follow the labours of the humble and faithful ambassadors of the cross, as they proclaim this glorious Gospel, and as the effects of their preaching discover new and perpetual exhibitions of the manifested Deity! The effects of their preaching upon the souls of men are nothing less than the savour of life unto life in them that are saved, and in them that perish of death unto death. The same light and motives that are the means of fitting some for heaven, abused and perverted, only fit others for hell.

O it is at a fearful expense that ministers are ever allowed to enter the pulpit without being preceded, accompanied, and followed by the earnest prayers of the churches. It is no marvel that the pulpit is so powerless, and ministers so often disheartened when there are so few to hold up their hands. The consequence of neglecting this duty is seen and felt in the spiritual declension of the churches, and it will be seen and felt in the everlasting perdition of men; while the consequence of regarding it would be the ingathering of multitudes into the kingdom of God, and new glories to the Lamb that was slain.

On his own behalf therefore, and on the behalf of his beloved and respected brethren in the ministry, the writer would crave an interest in the prayers of all who love the Saviour and the souls of men. We are the dispensers of God's truth and at best fall far below our mighty theme. The duties of our calling return upon us with every returning week and day. They often come upon us with many and conflicting demands. They sometimes put all our thoughts in requisition, and at the very time when we have lost the power of thinking; and all the ardour and strength of our affections, when we are the least susceptible of them. There is associated with these demands that pressing solicitude, and corroding anxiety, which exhausts our vigour, prostrates our courage, and drinks up our spirits. And then there are so many disappointments in our work, that we need the sympathy of prayer.

Our spirit is sometimes stirred within us, and we go forth to our people flushed with the hope of rescuing them from everlasting burnings; and in some hapless hour of self-sufficiency, we vainly imagine the work and triumph are our own. We are instant in season, and out of season; we make a business of preparing for the conflict, sometimes polishing our arrows and sometimes leaving them rough and barbed. We put on our armour, and enter the field with the determination to lay out all our strength, and with the confident assurance that we must do execution. But what a lesson of self-abasement! We cannot convert a single soul. 'We have piped unto them, and they have not danced; we have mourned unto them, and they have not lamented.' We urge the Divine commands, and they trample upon his authority; we urge his threatenings, and they despise his justice; we speak of his promises, they heed not his faithfulness; of his Son, and they tread him under their feet; of his patience and long-suffering, but their impenitence and obduracy are proof against them all. We reason and expostulate with them, until the obstacles to their conversion seem to us to rise the higher by every effort to surmount them; until we sink in despondency, and cry out, What mighty power can break these adamantine hearts? what omnipotent grasp can rescue these perishing men from everlasting burnings? O ye blood-bought churches, your ministers need your prayers, for the exceeding greatness of that power which God wrought in Christ when he raised him from the dead.

We have a concert of prayer for the heathen, another for Sabbath schools, and another for the blessing of God upon the distribution of religious tracts. Why should we overlook the great means of God's own appointment for the salvation of men? May there not be something in the form of a concert of prayer for the ministers of the Gospel? If nothing better can be suggested, why may there not be a general understanding among Christian men, and Christian families, to set apart the morning of every Lord's Day, for this great and special object? This was the usage in the family of my venerable father, and it has long been my own. And it is a most precious privilege. The time is a fitting one; and such a service would not fail to exert a delightful influence on the privileges of the sanctuary. 'Before they call I will answer; and while they are yet speaking I will hear.' Should God give to the churches the spirit of prayer for their ministers, it would be with the purpose of answering it. 'He will regard the prayer of the destitute, and not despise their prayer.' It is written, that 'on every dwelling-place of Mount Zion, he will create a fire and smoke'; nor will the altar be profaned, nor the incense less fragrant, if those words of hope are more often upon the lips of those who offer it, 'Clothe thy priests with salvation, that thy saints may shout with joyfulness!' Nor is this all. Let the ministers of the Gospel have an *habitual* remembrance at the domestic altar. 'It is no small thing', says a modern writer of our own city, 'for any congregation to have daily cries for God's blessing ascending from a hundred firesides. What a spring of refreshment to a pastor! The family devotions of praying Kidderminster, no doubt, made Baxter a better minister, and a happier man; and it is possible we are reaping the fruits of them in his *'Saints' Rest,'* and *'Dying Thoughts.'**

Ye then, that make mention of the Lord, keep not silence, and give him no rest. When the churches cease to pray for ministers, ministers will no longer be a blessing to the churches. Brethren, *pray for us,* that we may be kept from sin; that we may walk circumspectly, not as fools, but as wise, redeeming the time; that our hearts may be more devoted to God, and our lives a more impressive exemplification of the Gospel we preach; that we may be more completely girded for our work and our conflicts, and put on the whole armour of God; that we may be more faithful and more wise to win souls, and that we may keep under our body, and bring it into subjection, lest after having preached to others, we ourselves be cast away. When we turn our thoughts toward barren ordinances and a fruitless ministry, our hearts sink within us, and we would fain throw ourselves at the feet of the churches and implore a remembrance in their prayers. If you ever enter into the 'secret place' of the Most High, and get near the heart of him your souls love, plead earnestly that his own power may attend the stated ministrations of his Gospel. If ever you lie on Jesus' bosom, remember *us.* Open your desires; tell your Immanuel of his costly sacrifice and wonderful love; tell him of his power and our weakness; speak to him of the unutterable glory, and the interminable anguish beyond the grave. With tears of solicitude urge your suit, and tell him that he has committed the treasure to earthen vessels, that the excellency of the power may be all of God.

**Thoughts on Family Worship*, by James W. Alexander, D.D. No family should lack this most valuable, seasonable, and beautiful volume.

23: *The Consideration Due to the Christian Ministry*

In adverting to the duties of the people, growing out of the relation which exists between them and the ministers of the Gospel, we are constrained to go a step farther. If we have given a just view of the importance of the pulpit, *then has the Christian ministry strong claims on the kind and respectful consideration of their fellow-men.*

We speak not of that consideration which they deserve as *men*; in this respect they ask no more than the law of courtesy demands, and than they, in common with others, are entitled to, from the varied degrees of personal merit. A man of enlightened and enlarged views, of honourable feeling and correct deportment, of enterprising spirit and unobtrusive and courteous habits, most certainly does not lose his claim to the public confidence, because he happens to be a minister of the Gospel. Yet is there a large class of men by whom such a man is regarded almost as having *lost caste*, from the mere fact that he cheerfully takes up his cross and follows his divine Lord! A man from the middle, or even the lower orders of society, who in other and purely secular vocations has successfully contended with obstacles and discouragements by which so many others have been disheartened, and made his way to competency and usefulness, is respected and honoured for the honest, bold, and persevering traits of character which have procured him advancement. Yet how many such men are found in the Christian ministry with few tokens of public regard! Through difficulty and trial they travel on; through evil report and good report, through conflict and temptation, they hold on their way, and sink almost unnoticed to their grave. With few exceptions, the educated and regular clergy of the American churches are men of unexceptionable character; where they are not so, not only have they little claim on the public consideration as *men*, but still less as ministers of the Gospel. Even an incautious, discourteous and rude minister has no cause for complaint, if he pays the forfeit of his own folly in the loss of public esteem and confidence.

But the consideration of which we speak has respect more especially to *the office*, than to the person of the preacher. The tendency of the age is to depreciate the office of the Christian ministry. It is a melancholy tendency. 'Public opinion is the queen of the world.' Ministers of the Gospel are greatly dependent on the esteem and confidence of their fellow-men. Yet may it not be denied that they have not that strong hold upon the respect and confidence of the community which they enjoyed in the earlier periods of our national history. With some exceptions, they have not that influence they once exerted in their own churches; they are not looked up to by the young, nor affectionately greeted by the old. They have not that place in benevolent and religious institutions which was once assigned to them; and where they occupy them, it is rather for the secondary purpose of augmenting the pecuniary resources of these institutions, than of mingling with their more serious and important counsels. And what is much more to be lamented, their influence is scarcely felt, out of the pulpit, in the education of the young, and is being rapidly excluded from the colleges of the land. Few portions of the country, unless it be New England, are looking to their clergy to mould the character of their youth, and preside over their more distinguished seminaries of learning. The public mind has taken the alarm lest the power of the pulpit, without which no important literary institution can be well governed, should exert too controlling an influence in the intellectual and moral discipline of those youth who are the hope of the church, and the pride of their country. Even in New England, the barrier has been broken over; and in other States so frequently, that there is not a little danger lest it be broken down.

There are some obvious, and probably some latent causes for this state of things. The genius and spirit of our political institutions, is exceedingly sensitive to every thing in the form of clerical influence; in some respects it is wisely so; but it is not impossible that this apprehension may be carried to an injurious excess. The civil disabilities to which the Christian ministry, of every name, are subjected by the States of New York and Virginia, and more especially as they affect the influence of the clergy on the great subject of education, is just the blow which gives to such a man as Thomas Jefferson, and other enemies of Christianity, their long-sought triumph. Whether these States, on this system of educating their youth, will be the gainers by it, time will show. The loose notions on the subject of the divine warrant and authority of Christian ministers to preach the Gospel and dispense its ordinances, exclusive of every other class of men, so heedlessly assailed by portions of the daily press, and so eagerly received by many of their readers, inflict a deeper wound than was ever designed by their authors. The system of Sabbath schools, desirable as is its influence upon the ignorant and untaught, extended as it is to the children of our churches, necessarily severs the rising generation from that pastoral care of the young which belongs to their ministers.

Nor are ministers themselves guiltless in this matter. Ever since the spurious religious excitement which, a few years since, burst upon so many parts of the land, the ministerial character has been losing its influence. Christian men, and intelligent men of the world, who were wont to reverence the office of the ministers of the Gospel, could not respect men who did not respect themselves. There have been, also, exciting questions, before the public mind, in which ministers, have manifested a zeal and a recklessness which have had little tendency to sustain the honour and dignity of the ministerial character. The too prevalent impression, that candidates for the office are to be sought for, and found exclusively among the poorer, if not the lower orders of society, and the consequent multiplication of ministers, many of whom are not fitted for their office, the loungers about our large cities, of men of too large expectations, or ministers for public charity in every part of the land, which accomplish little more than the defraying the expenses of the applicants, some of which are undertaken for this sole object; together with the whole system of *secularizing* the pulpit, by making those who occupy it quite as much the solicitors for money as they are the preachers of the Gospel, are things that are not a little degrading to the ministerial character. A strange minister scarcely comes among us, but the people at once suspect him to be a beggar.

There are portions of the land too, where the bond which unites pastor and people is scarcely stronger than that which binds the people to their schoolmaster; nor did this evil originate with the people, but from the love of change in ministers. But, 'though last, not least', the *unhallowed divisions* among ministers themselves have exerted no small influence in producing impressions un-

The Consideration Due to the Christian Ministry

favourable to the ministerial character. How can ministers hope for the confidence and love of the churches, when they have so little confidence and love toward one another? How can the world, or the church, respect a divided and wrangling ministry? Who shall speak well of ministers, if they *speak ill of one another*? Ah, it is this divisive spirit, engendering so much of rivalry both in ministers and churches, and terminating in chilling alienation, unwarrantable suspicions, and so effectually barring all hearty and prayerful co-operation, that has weakened our strength in the way. We have but to survey large portions of the church, and compare the influence of ministers with what it was in former days, in order to be convinced that, from some, or all of these causes, the ministry are the losers.

Whatever the causes may be, the fact is a lamentable one. By how much the ministers of the Gospel are depreciated in any community, by so much is their great end and object depreciated; and by so much are that community the sufferers. Ministers, for the most part, are not obtrusive men. They do not seek spheres of responsibility and influence beyond their own appropriate charges. It is well if they can be prevailed on to occupy such spheres when solicited. They have enough to do at home, and they know well how to labour cheerfully and alone. There is no class of men who more promptly obey the first intimations of public opinion that bid them toil in retirement. But the inquiry forces itself upon us, Is this right? Is it the course of true wisdom, or sound policy? Does the ministerial office deserve this neglect? Is any thing gained by thus obscuring its lustre? Is it for the benefit of mankind thus to cripple the power of the pulpit? Does not every blow at this institution of heavenly wisdom, recoil with redoubled force upon the community?

On a topic of such practical concernment, it were well to listen to the voice of experience. What is that voice in this land, and in all lands illumined by the progress of the Protestant Reformation? What is it in Switzerland, in Holland, in England? What is it in that favoured land where Scottish learning and philanthropy have so long been measured by the influence of the pulpit; and where God's ministers, without any of the arrogance of the Papal priesthood, have stood foremost in every literary and benevolent enterprise, and in maintaining the dignity and influence of their office, have only yielded to the wishes of the people? What was it in

New England, for almost two centuries? Who founded her colleges? The ministers of the Gospel. Who originated her Missionary, Bible, Tract, Temperance, and Education Socities? The ministers of the Gospel. Who made the little State of New Jersey what it is; gave it her literature, and sanctified her bar, and identified her religion and learning? Who but the ministers of the Gospel!

This growing severance in the land of the best interests of the community from the pulpit, is an unnatural severance; it is putting asunder what God has joined together. It can hardly be supposed that a class of men, appointed to be the teachers of mankind on the all-important subject of religion, should occupy a sphere that is purely religious; because, unless interdicted by public opinion, it is impossible, in the nature of the case, that their influence should not extend beyond it. If the pulpit exerts a salutary influence, public opinion ought to be in its favour. Bad men can hardly be supposed to be its patrons; but it is passing strange that there should be good men who so thoughtlessly unite in this popular crusade against the ministers of Christ. We say in all honesty and frankness to such men, that the pulpit needs their favour, in order to accomplish, in the best manner, the objects which are as dear to them as to Christ's ministers.

In every age of the world, those persons have been the enemies of true religion, and of the best interests of mankind, who have been the opposers of Christ's ministers. A wicked ministry deserves no favour; a devout and devoted one has claims upon esteem and confidence that cannot wisely be disregarded. Sir Matthew Hale, who is pronounced by Lord Ellenborough to have been 'one of the greatest Judges that ever sat in Westminster Hall', in a letter to his children, among other excellent counsels, gives them the following advice in regard to their treatment of the ministers of the Gospel. 'Reverence your minister; he is a wise and good man, and one that loves you, and hath a tender care and respect for you. Do not grieve him, either by neglect or disrespect. Assure yourselves, if there be any person that sets any of you against him, or provokes, or encourages any of you to despise, or neglect him, that person, whoever he be, loves not you, nor the office he bears. As the Divine Providence hath placed him to have a care of your souls, so I must tell you, I do expect you should reverence and honour him for his own, and for your, and for his office' sake.'

The Consideration Due to the Christian Ministry

A statesman and jurist, second to none in this land, in his argument before the Supreme Court of the United States, in the case of Stephen Girard's Will, expresses the following thoughts: 'I take it upon myself to say, that in no country in the world, upon either continent, can there be found a body of ministers of the Gospel who perform so much service to man, in such a full spirit of self-denial, under so little encouragement from Government of any kind, and under circumstances, always much straitened and often distressed, as the ministers of the Gospel in the United States, of all denominations! They form no part of any established order of religion; they constitute no hierarchy; they enjoy no peculiar privileges – in some of the States they are even shut out from all participation in the political rights and privileges enjoyed by their fellow-citizens; they enjoy no tithes, no public provision of any kind. And this body of clergymen has shown, to the honour of their own country, and to the astonishment of the hierarchies of the old world, that it is practicable in free governments to raise and sustain a body of clergymen, which for devotedness to their sacred calling, for purity of life and character, for learning, intelligence, piety, and that wisdom which cometh from above, is inferior to none, and superior to most others. I hope that our learned men have done something for the honour of our literature abroad. I hope that the courts of justice and members of the bar of this country have done something to elevate the character of the profession of the law; I hope that the discussions in Congress have done something to meliorate the condition of the human race, to secure and extend the great charter of human rights, and to strengthen and advance the great principles of human liberty. But I contend that no literary efforts, no adjudications, no constitutional discussions, nothing that has been done or said in favour of the great interests of universal man, has done this country more credit at home and abroad, than the establishment of our body of clergymen, and the general excellence of their character, their piety, and learning.'

Moses, the great Hebrew Legislator, and the divinely appointed leader of God's ancient Israel, in blessing that people just before he went up to the top of Nebo, to 'die there in the mount', pronounced the following benediction upon *the house of Levi*. 'And of Levi he said, Let thy Urim and thy Thummim be with thy holy one! for they have observed thy word and kept thy covenant. They shall teach Jacob thy judgments and Israel thy law; they shall put incense before thee, and whole burnt offering upon thine altar. *Bless, Lord, his substance, and accept the work of his hands! Smite through the loins of them that rise against him and of them that hate him, that they rise not again!*' How many have felt the withering influence of this early imprecation!

When the Saviour sent forth the early preachers of his Gospel, he appended to their commission this protecting clause: 'He that heareth you, heareth me; he that despiseth you, despiseth me; and he that despiseth me despiseth him that sent me.'

The Apostle Paul, notwithstanding all his characteristic delicacy, could not suppress the injunction, 'Obey them that have the rule over you; for they watch for your souls as they that must give account, that they may do it with joy and not with grief; for that is *unprofitable for you!*' He repeats the injunction in his counsels to Timothy, when he says, 'Let the presbyters that rule well be accounted worthy of double honour; especially those who labour in word and doctrine!'

It is of but little consequence to the writer, whether these suggestions be heeded or unheeded. The time is short during which they may affect *him*. These lips will soon be silent; dust will be upon them. 'To-day,' says the Oriental proverb, 'we visit the tombs of our friends; to-morrow, they visit ours.' Compared with the past, his days of labour must be few, his steps faltering and slow, his pilgrimage confined within narrow bounds. But the sacred ministry will live when he dies; and it is his earnest desire and prayer that it may be a useful and honoured ministry. The fruit is ripening which will afford a rich harvest; happy and honoured be the men whose privilege it shall be to gather and garner it! The ministry of reconciliation was instituted for the purpose of exerting an important agency in the work of man's salvation; we ask for it only that consideration which its importance demands.

24: *The Responsibility of Enjoying the Christian Ministry*

It is not easy to estimate the debt of gratitude which those portions of the earth owe to the distinguishing goodness of God, who enjoy the stated ministrations of his word. The Christian ministry is among the selectest blessings which can be enjoyed by men, one of the most important elements of individual, social, and national prosperity. It is the institution which, above all others, makes Christian lands what they are, girds them with a zone of light, and sheds upon them the balmy influences of heavenly mercy.

'What nation', said Moses to ancient Israel, 'is there so *great*, that hath *statutes and judgments so righteous*, as all this law which I set before you this day?' This was the pre-eminence of the Hebrew state; they were a better instructed and better governed people, a holier and happier people, than any of the surrounding nations. The God of Abraham was a 'glory in the midst of them, and a wall of fire round about them'. There he set his 'tabernacle for a shadow in the daytime from the heat, and for a place of refuge, and for a covert from storm and from rain'. Speaking of the restoration of that backsliding and chastised people, after days of darkness and rebuke, God himself says to them, 'Turn, O backsliding Israel, for I am married unto you; and I will take you one of a city and two of a family, and I will bring you unto Zion. And I will give you' – what is the gift that this greatest of all givers will give to his restored and re-espoused people? 'I will give you *Pastors* according to mine heart, which shall feed you with knowledge and understanding.' The Psalmist, in speaking of them, says, 'Blessed are the people who know the joyful sound; they shall walk, O Lord, in the light of thy countenance.' If this pre-eminence was enjoyed by the Jewish people, under a comparatively dark and shadowy dispensation, with how much stronger propriety does it belong to Christian lands, enjoying, as they do, so much clearer light, and that 'better covenant, founded upon better promises'?

This is not a subject on which the Scriptures speak in doubtful or unemphatic language. They tell us of the *gifts* of God to men; above all others do they magnify his 'unspeakable gift', the gift of his only and well-beloved Son. They speak too of gifts which his Son bestows, as the rewarded and rewarding Mediator; gifts which he purchased by his death, and of which he is the honoured dispenser. When he ascended up on high, 'he gave gifts to men', worthy of his royal bounty, and such as he himself selected as the most fitting and striking expressions of his munificence on his first accession to his mediatorial throne. 'He gave – some, apostles; and some, prophets; and some, evangelists; and some pastors and teachers; for the perfecting of the saints, for the work of the ministry.'

These are the gifts he bestows *on us*. The 'lines have fallen to us in pleasant places, and we have a goodly heritage'. We may glory in the vastness of our territory, and in the rapid growth of an enterprising population; we may survey with high and honest exultation the blessings of that civil and religious liberty which we have received from our fathers; but, if we are not recreant to the trust committed to us, and feel as they felt, we shall prize the Christian ministry. Amid all the beautiful and varied scenery which delights our eye as we look over this broad land, we shall not overlook her ten thousand churches; and amid all our delighted exultation, we shall remember that it is written, 'How beautiful upon the mountains are the feet of him that bringeth good tidings, that publisheth peace; that bringeth good tidings of good, that saith unto Zion, Thy God reigneth!'

Privilege and obligation are but correlative terms. The greater the privilege, the greater the duty, and the greater the sin of leaving it unperformed. We ask more for the pulpit than that it be provided with a pious and well-educated ministry; and we ask more for the ministry, than that it should receive an adequate pecuniary support, and be respected, and encouraged. We claim for it a practical regard of the truths it inculcates, and the duties it enforces. We ask for it that character, those hopes, and those efforts which it was instituted to attain and advance.

The first great duty which the pulpit urges, is 'repentance toward God, and faith in our Lord Jesus Christ'. It holds up the simplicity of the method of salvation by a crucified Redeemer; the simplicity of a spiritual faith in Jesus Christ, in opposition to that righteousness which is by the deeds of the law; the simplicity of Christian worship, in opposition to the tedious and complicated observances of all false religions. The just expression and proof of its power is found, when those who enjoy its dispensations cordially receive this system of truth and grace, and confide in that Saviour through whom they are delivered from the curse of the law; whose blood answers every charge, covers every sin, enforces every plea, and itself pleads with irresistible power. Here lies the first and great responsibility of those who are favoured with the Christian ministry. Men do not truly meet any one of its claims until this duty is performed. Their obedience to the Divine authority begins here; it is vain for them to think of any thing like conformity to his will, so long as they reject him whom God has sent, and refuse his instructions who comes to them with so many attestations of his divine mission. We call upon men, therefore, everywhere, to renounce their pretensions to self-righteousness, to feel their sin and condemnation, to be sensible of their inability to save themselves, to be conscious that they have no claims, no merit, and to throw themselves upon him who is the Author and Finisher of this great salvation. We call upon them to feel that for any good purpose they have nothing, and need all things; to bow at his footstool, who is so holy that the heavens are not clean in his sight; and there, where archangels bow, and devils tremble, to smite upon their breasts, and say, 'God be merciful to me a sinner!'

Whence is it that men listen to the message brought to them by the Christian ministry, with not half the interest and eagerness with which they listen to a lecture on themes of mere secular interest? A lecture on astronomy, or history, or some important department in the arts; a mere play at the theatre, or song at the opera, or a paragraph from the press, telling of battles lost or won, and treaties ratified or rejected, holds them in silent thought and admiration. But the lessons of God's redeeming love, the song that was first rehearsed by angels on the plains of Bethlehem, the treaty of peace between heaven and earth, signed with the name of the ever-blessed and adorable Trinity, and sealed with the blood of the Lamb – whose eye sparkles, whose bosom glows at messages like these? and where are the voices that repeat these glad tidings? Bold operations in business interest them; the aged gather up their wandering and rouse their torpid thoughts, and the young take fire at the doubtful enterprise; but tell them of durable riches and righteousness, of heavenly gems and diadems brighter than Gabriel wears, and they make light of it; it is tame. To listen to it is a task.

What miserable, what guilty delusion is this! I look around me, and see men following their different secular pursuits with all the ardour and zeal they are capable of exercising. Difficulty and dangers do not discourage them, but rather give energy to their efforts; they are not phantoms and trifles that they are pursuing, but realities. But there is one thing about them all which they have forgotten, and that is, their *uncertainty*. They 'know not what shall be on the morrow'. They are eagerly grasping the 'greatest, the most slippery *uncertainties*'. This is a remarkable fact in the history of man. There is but one *certain event* in all his future course. Be he high or low, rich or poor, learned or unlearned, happy or miserable, young or old, the friend of God, or his enemy; there is not one among all the millions of our race, who can, with certainty, anticipate any other event in his future history, save the single one, that he *must die*. But shut out this message of God's redeeming mercy, and what a fearful certainty is death! Peradventure his course may be serene and cheerful up to that hour of sadness; but there darkness overshadows him – terror agitates him – deep and heavy clouds settle over the gates of death. All beyond, what is it? Yet is there a 'clearing' even through this dark valley; a bright opening; a vista of the heavenly world. O there is every thing in death to make us dread its approach, apart from those principles and hopes, which rise like the star of promise on the soul!

'Go and teach all nations, baptizing them in the name of the Father, and of the Son, and of the Holy Ghost.' The Ancient of Days, the Son of man, the Spirit of truth and grace in all their undivided love authorize this mission, and stand pledged to confirm the message which it bears. The words of men may be counsels of wisdom; the words of God have the force of law. The words of men are of doubtful verity; the words of God are truth. The words of men may be unaccomplished words; God's counsel shall stand, and he will do all his pleasure. The heavens and the earth shall pass away, but his words shall never pass away. Wonderful as these truths are, gracious as they are, and tremendously fearful as they are, they are as unchangeable as the Deity; they are settled in heaven, and established for ever. There is all the sincerity about them which belongs to the essence of truth and goodness; all the authority belongs to them which belongs to Infinite rectitude and Omnipotent justice. They are fixed and permanent as this throne; they will never be retracted, never altered; nor are they revealed in such a way as to stifle our hopes, or excite one needless fear. There is nothing wavering, nothing uncertain in relation to any one feature of this Gospel; come what will, it will stand in all its forms and colours, in all its promises, and in all its threatenings. Whether men receive, or reject it, it shall pursue its steady course, impelled by an unseen, but Omnipotent hand, and bring everlasting glory to its Divine Author.

How constraining the motive, then, to listen and obey when God thus addresses us! How solemn the admonition, 'See that ye refuse not *him that speaketh*; for if they escaped not who refused him that spake on earth; how much more shall not we escape, if we refuse him that speaketh from heaven!' There was binding authority in the message of the ancient dispensation; God was its Author. Yet was it preparatory only to the one that 'cannot be moved'. God 'who at sundry times, and in divers manners spake unto the fathers by the prophets, hath in these last days spoken unto us by his Son'. Were an angel from heaven to visit our world, we should crowd around him, and should be anxious to know the errand on which he came. Angels *have* descended in times far gone by, and men listened to their errand with astonishment. But their message was a very subordinate one to that brought by the Son of God. 'For if the word spoken by angels was steadfast, and every transgression and disobedience received a just recompense of reward, how shall they escape who neglect so great salvation, which at the first began to be spoken by the Lord, and was confirmed unto us by them that heard him.' We have the same testimony. Men disregarded the voice of God's prophets; they stoned some, killed some; 'yet having one Son, he sent *him*, saying, They will reverence my Son!' It is the Saviour's voice by whom this message is uttered. He bows his heavens and comes down. He walks amidst the golden candlesticks. When his ministers speak in his name, he is with them; when his people meet together, he is there. He will be sanctified in them that come nigh him, and before all the people will he be glorified.

It is a solemn thought, too, that to those who reject this divine message, *it is as though no real message had been revealed*. We have spoken of the power of the pulpit, of the constituent elements of that power, and of the correlative obligations of its ministry; but what is all this to the man who disregards the message it brings? It is as though the pulpit had no power; nay, it is as though there were not a Christian pulpit in the world. It is as though there were no Sanctuary, no Sabbath, and no Gospel, and all the light of these precious hopes were blotted out in the darkness of Paganism, and in the gloom of the grave. Shall it be thus? Shall the voice of nature demand these instructions, and shall that affecting cry for help be suppressed? Shall the pulpit win its ten thousand triumphs, through darkness, through trial, through enemies, through the faggot and the gibbet; and shall there be obduracy, more powerful than they all, that leaves the dwellers in Christian lands bound in chains to the ignominious car of sin and death? We have spoken of what the pulpit has done. Time would fail to tell of the millions whom it has made holy and happy. They have lived in peace, and when death came, have lifted their eyes to the eternal hills whence cometh their help. Over a world strewed with the ruins of a thousand generations, this message of heavenly mercy has passed with a life-giving power, quickening them who were dead in sin, and raising them up to sit together in heavenly places in Christ Jesus.

O the blessedness of this sweet hope in Christ! Just conceive of a man in the state of William Howard, so distressed by a view of his sins and danger, that he says, 'So great was the anguish of my soul, that I lamented God had spared Noah and his family. O that they had been swept away by the Deluge; then I had never been!' And after he had become reconciled to God through Jesus Christ, speaking of his joy, he says, 'My tongue, or pen can faintly describe it. All the bliss that I had ever enjoyed was no more like it than midnight darkness is like the meridian sun. It was heaven indeed; something of the real nature of heaven I then enjoyed. My soul was wrapt in the embraces of the adorable Jesus, and I was so overpowered with holy love that I was lost to everything else.' It is related of the Countess of Huntingdon, that she was brought to the knowledge of the truth as it is in Jesus, through the instrumentality of the single remark of the Lady Margaret Hastings, that 'since she had known and believed in the Lord Jesus Christ, she had been as *happy as an angel*'. When the Sun of righteousness beams on the soul, sometimes rising like the faint light of the morning, and sometimes bursting upon the benighted mind in meridian splendour, joys visit it that are alternately serene and rapturous, now tranquil, and now unspeakable and full of glory.

The brightest earthly career has its trials, and they are trials which find no relief and no alleviation but from the Divine presence and favour. Here alone is the febrifuge for the burning heart; the pillow for the aching head.

> How soft to lean on Heaven!
> To lean on Him on whom archangels lean.

This world forsakes us on the approach of the winter's storm; before the chill blasts of adversity it retires. Not so the religion of the Gospel. Misery in all its forms has peculiar attractions for this message of heavenly mercy. The spirit of the world and the spirit which is of God often meet at the door of human wretchedness; but the former leaves it because the sources of its joy are dried up; the latter enters because there are sources of bitterness, and tears to be wiped away. Such love and pity are found in the Gospel of Christ, and only there, for misery and poverty like ours. Not until this celestial messenger is made welcome, can men be holy or happy. The voice of reason, the voice of conscience, the voice of God, every cross and disappointment and trial repeats the call, 'My son, give me thy heart!' And O that, from that insatiable thirst for happiness so deeply implanted in the soul of man, every one of my readers may respond, My heart, blessed Lord, will I give!

But there is another alternative. 'He that is not with me', says the Lord Jesus, 'is against me.' *Those who reject this message of the Christian ministry do so on their own responsibility, and at their own peril.* 'If thou be wise, thou shalt be wise for thyself; but if thou scornest, thou alone shalt bear it.' Men who have been distinguished for the success which crowned their labours, have also been distinguished for making hard hearts harder, and blind eyes blinder. There is a reason for this in the nature of their message; for the very truths which are most fitted to interest and impress, when long and perseveringly rejected, only leave the mind more obdurate. This is the way men become ripe for destruction; it is in the midst of scenes of mercy, where they wander as in a desert and parched land, and whence they go at last, where there is not a drop of water to cool their tongue. This is the direful catastrophe. *This will be the end of disregarding and rejecting the message of the Christian ministry.* As God liveth, this will be the mournful end of rejecting these messages of heavenly mercy. It is no common responsibility that such men incur. If the smallest talent must be accounted for, what account must they render who all their lifetime have been favoured with a preached Gospel, and who have only heard and rejected this gracious message? How bitter the reflections of such a man, as he sees the last hours of human life passing away, and the lamentation is extorted from his bosom, 'The harvest is past, the summer is ended, and I am not saved!' What a fearful transition will that be from the Christian sanctuary to the bar of God! There will be mourning then, when 'many shall come from the east and from the west, and from the north and from the south, and sit down with Abraham and Isaac and Jacob in the kingdom of God, and they themselves are cast out'. Ah, they know not what they do, to whom God has given a faithful ministry, and who reject the great salvation. They are not the atheist, and the infidel, and the immoral only who perish. Large and free as it is, the love of God is no refuge even for the moral and the orthodox, who treat the message of his ministers as they treat their Master, and tread it under their feet. It is the last message. Infinite love makes its greatest effort here. It cannot do more. 'There remaineth no more sacrifice for sin.'

When the rich man in the parable lifted up his eyes in hell, and saw Abraham afar off, and Lazarus in his bosom, he cried and said, 'Father Abraham, have mercy on me, and send Lazarus, that he may dip the tip of his finger in water, and cool my tongue; for I am tormented in this flame!' The time will come when the despisers of our message will cry for mercy, whether they ever did before or not. They will cry long and loud; they will lift up their voice in awful distress; but there shall be none to answer. Nor will it be long before that day of calamity shall come. It may be forty years; it may be twenty; it may be ten; it may be five; it may be two; it may not be one. Eternity is nearer than they think of, and that place of torment is as near as eternity. We know not what a day may bring forth. Yesterday is fled upon the eagle wings of time; to-morrow belongs to God and not to man. These golden Sabbaths will soon have passed away, and the voice of the living ministry will soon be silent among the silent dead. Could those who die in their sins

The Responsibility of Enjoying the Christian Ministry

come back again and live, its message would not be so urgent. But they come not. You call, and they answer not again. You look for them in the visions of the night; but it is all a dream. They appear not to mortal eyes; they speak not to mortal ears. They are not in heaven, but are shut up in hell. Would that the man who rejects the salvation of God could be transported to eternity for an hour, if it were but to witness the agony of those who once occupied a place in God's sanctuary, and whom nothing could induce to fall in with the redemption that is in Christ Jesus! O dreadful doom! not to be described by mortal tongue; yet to be endured by every mortal man that refuses this offered mercy!

If the writer dwells a moment longer on thoughts like these, it is because they are affecting thoughts to his own mind, as a preacher of the everlasting Gospel. The Christian ministry is God's selected instrumentality in accomplishing his purposes of grace. It is set for the defence of the Gospel, and for the vindication of the Divine government over this fallen world. Eternity alone can disclose the responsiblity of preaching this Gospel; eternity alone can disclose the responsibility of rejecting it. Think of a man sitting for ten, or twenty, or forty, or sixty years under the varied influences of an instructive pulpit. To what a vast amount of truth has he listened! How much toil and ingenuity have been expended in order to frame arguments to convince his understanding, to construct appeals that should rouse his conscience, to furnish illustrations that might interest him, and to urge motives that might persuade him to become reconciled to God! How often has he trembled at the rebuke, and wept under the affecting persuasions that would fain have constrained him to become a Christian! Who can measure the responsibility of such a man, even though he may have listened to the meanest pulpit in the land! *That pulpit*, what will be the testimony, and what his recollections of *that pulpit*, when the Saviour there made known shall judge the world in righteousness! What a stream of light has poured from it upon many a benighted mind, which, if it had enlightened Sodom and Tyre, they would have repented long ago in sackcloth and ashes!

Men who enjoy a faithful Christian ministry know too much of God and his Christ to consent to go away into everlasting burnings. Better for them to have died from the womb, or as an hidden, untimely birth that had not been, as infants which never saw the light, than to have been dwellers in this world of mercy, and at last make their bed in that lake of fire.

Behold, ye despisers, and wonder and perish! Adore, ye lovers of God and the Gospel of his Son, that by the foolishness of preaching he is pleased to save them that believe!

OTHER SOLID GROUND TITLES

We recently celebrated our eighth anniversary of uncovering buried treasure to the glory of God. During these eight years we have produced over 225 volumes. A sample is listed below:

Biblical & Theological Studies: *Addresses to Commemorate the 100th Anniversary of Princeton Theological Seminary in 1912* by Allis, Machen, Wilson, Vos, Warfield and many more.
Notes on Galatians by J. Gresham Machen
The Origin of Paul's Religion by J. Gresham Machen
A Scientific Investigation of the Old Testament by R.D. Wilson
Theology on Fire: *Sermons from Joseph A. Alexander*
Evangelical Truth: *Sermons for the Family* by Archibald Alexander
A Shepherd's Heart: *Pastoral Sermons of James W. Alexander*
Grace & Glory: *Sermons from Princeton Chapel* by Geerhardus Vos
The Lord of Glory by Benjamin B. Warfield
The Person & Work of the Holy Spirit by Benjamin B. Warfield
The Power of God unto Salvation by Benjamin B. Warfield
Calvin Memorial Addresses by Warfield, Johnson, Orr, Webb…
The Five Points of Calvinism by Robert Lewis Dabney
Annals of the American Presbyterian Pulpit by W.B. Sprague
The Word & Prayer: *Classic Devotions from the Pen of John Calvin*
A Body of Divinity: *Sum and Substance of Christian Doctrine* by Ussher
The Complete Works of Thomas Manton (in 22 volumes)
A Puritan New Testament Commentary by John Trapp
Exposition of the Epistle to the Hebrews by William Gouge
Exposition of the Epistle of Jude by William Jenkyn
Lectures on the Book of Esther by Thomas M'Crie
Lectures on the Book of Acts by John Dick

To order any of our titles please contact us in one of three ways:

Call us at **1-866-789-7423**
Email us at **sgcb@charter.net**
Visit our website at **www.solid-ground-books.com**

www.ingramcontent.com/pod-product-compliance
Lightning Source LLC
Chambersburg PA
CBHW031139160426
43193CB00008B/188